MILITANT ISLAM REACHES AMERICA

Daniel Pipes

W. W. NORTON & COMPANY

NEW YORK   LONDON

For information about permission to reproduce selections from this book, write to
Permissions, W. W. Norton & Company, Inc., 500 Fifth Avenue, New York, NY 10110

The text of this book is composed in Goudy with the display set in Friz Quadrata
Composition by Sue Carlson
Manufacturing by The Haddon Craftsmen, Inc.
Book design by Mary A. Wirth
Production manager: Andrew Marasia

LIBRARY OF CONGRESS CATALOGING-IN-PUBLICATION DATA
Pipes, Daniel, 1949–
Militant Islam reaches America / by Daniel Pipes.—1st ed.
p. cm.
Includes bibliographical references and index.
ISBN 0-393-05204-4 (hardcover)
1. Islamic fundamentalism—United States. 2. Muslims—United States—Political activity.
3. Islam and politics—United States. 4. United States—Politics and government. I. Title.

BP67 .U6 P57 2002
320.5'5—dc21   2002006482

W. W. Norton & Company, Inc., 500 Fifth Avenue, New York, N.Y. 10110
www.wwnorton.com

W. W. Norton & Company Ltd., Castle House, 75/76 Wells Street, London W1T 3QT

1 2 3 4 5 6 7 8 9 0

MILITANT
ISLAM
REACHES
AMERICA

BY THE AUTHOR

Slave Soldiers and Islam: The Genesis of a Military System (1981)

In the Path of God: Islam and Political Power (1983)

An Arabist's Guide to Egyptian Colloquial (1983)

The Long Shadow: Culture and Politics in the Middle East (1989)

Greater Syria: The History of an Ambition (1990)

The Rushdie Affair: The Novel, the Ayatollah, and the West (1990)

Friendly Tyrants: An American Dilemma (co-editor, 1991)

Damascus Courts the West: Syrian Politics, 1989–91 (1991)

Sandstorm: Middle East Conflicts and America (editor, 1993)

Syria Beyond the Peace Process (1996)

The Hidden Hand: Middle East Fears of Conspiracy (1996)

Conspiracy: How the Paranoid Style Flourishes, and Where It Comes From (1997)

Just six days after September 11, 2001, President George W. Bush took time to visit the Islamic Center in Washington, D.C., where he met with American Muslim leaders, who, ironically, had apologized in the past for militant Islam. (ERIC DRAPER)

To Anna Pipes,
Artistic Spirit

CONTENTS

INTRODUCTION

Ayatollah Khomeini came to power in Iran in 1979 with "Death to America" as his slogan, and hundreds of Americans lost their lives to militant Islam over the subsequent two decades. It was not, however, until the shock of September 11, 2001, that Americans finally focused attention on this foe. Of the many questions prompted by the four suicide hijackings, perhaps the most profound and disturbing, not to say confusing, were those touching on the motives of the perpetrators and the broader question of the enemy's nature and goals.

Public statements did not answer the many questions. There was Osama bin Laden proclaiming a violent *jihad* on the United States and here was President George W. Bush declaring that Islam "teaches peace."[1] Which spokesman was one to listen to? Or what was one to make of Laura Bush denouncing the brutal treatment of women by the Taliban in Afghanistan and describing this as "a central goal of the terrorists," while going on to absolve Islam of any role in the tragedy ("The severe repression and brutality against women in Afghanistan is not a matter of legitimate religious practice. Muslims around the world

xi

have condemned the brutal degradation of women and children by the Taliban regime")?[2] Why would terrorists oppress women if this did not have something to do with their Islamic outlook?

There are many other questions, too, starting with the most basic ones. What is the connection between Islam and the acts of violence carried out in its name? Is it useful to distinguish between Islam and the extreme version of the religion known variously as militant Islam, radical Islam, fundamentalist Islam, or Islamism? Is it further useful to distinguish between the violent and the political variants of militant Islam? Can Al-Qaeda be ascribed to a cult rather than to Islam? Does militant Islam result from poverty? Are Islamists medieval? Do American Muslims suffer from entrenched bias? The figure for the number of Muslims living in the United States was said by some to reach 6–7 million and by others 1 million; what is it? Do American Muslims intend to integrate or do they wish to remake the country in their own image? Does African-American Islam connect back to the slaves forcibly brought to the United States? Is the Nation of Islam truly Islamic?

These issues have been at the center of my work for over thirty years. I began my studies with the Arabic language, Muslim history, and related subjects in college. I then spent three years at university-level institutions in Cairo, traveled through much of the Muslim world, received a Ph.D. in Middle Eastern history at Harvard University, taught this subject at the University of Chicago and at Harvard, worked on it in the State and Defense Departments, and wrote three prior books on it.

As a non-Muslim, I write primarily for fellow non-Muslims, helping them understand what is often a remote subject. My role is primarily one of explanation and interpretation, though I also try to help formulate correct policies. Not being a Muslim, I by definition do not believe in the mission of the Prophet Muhammad, but I have enormous respect for the faith of those who do. I note how deeply rewarding Muslims find Islam as well as the extraordinary inner strength it imbues them with. Having studied the history and civilization of the classical period, I am vividly aware of the great Muslim cultural achievements of roughly a millennium ago.

I approach the religion of Islam in a neutral fashion, neither praising it nor attacking it but in a spirit of inquiry. Neither apologist nor booster, neither spokesman nor critic, I consider myself a student of this subject. I ask such questions as: What is the nature of Islam's principles, customs, and implications? How does Islamic law affect Muslim societies? Are there elements common to Muslim life from West Africa to Southeast Asia, yet absent elsewhere?

Though neutral on Islam, I take a strong stand on militant Islam, which I see as very different, and which forms a central subject of this book. I see militant Islam as a global affliction whose victims count peoples of all religions. Non-Muslims are losing their lives to it in such countries as Nigeria, Sudan, Egypt, and the Philippines. Muslims are the main casualties in Algeria, Turkey, Iran, and Afghanistan. Islamism is perhaps the most vibrant and coherent ideological movement in the world today; it threatens us all. Moderate Muslims and non-Muslims must cooperate to battle this scourge.

The essays here divide into two parts, on the phenomenon of militant Islam and the Muslim presence in the United States.

Part I begins with "Is Islam a Threat?," a general introduction to the phenomenon of militant Islam. I reply to the question in the negative but then argue that militant Islam is indeed a threat. This essay sets forth my basic outlook on the topic of militant Islam: how it emerged from the trauma of modern Muslim history, its key features, its differences from traditional Islam, and the characteristic woes it imposes on Muslims and non-Muslims alike.

The collapse of the Soviet Union in 1991 prompted loose talk about Islam replacing Marxism-Leninism as the West's necessary enemy. In symbolic terms, it was said that green (Islam's color) had replaced red (communism's color) in the West's rogues' gallery. I dispute this in "The Imaginary Green Peril," examining military confrontation and mass immigration issues, the two elements of this thesis, and conclude that in both respects the fear is exaggerated. A decade after the Soviet Union's demise, I still agree with dismissing the military threat; but the issue of immigration now concerns me more than it did in 1990, when I first wrote this piece.

Almost simultaneous with that analysis, Bernard Lewis argued that militant Islam is engaged in no less than a "clash of civilizations" with the West,[3] coining a phrase that three years later Samuel Huntington would make famous as the title of an article (and later a book). In his work, Huntington interprets current strife in civilizational terms rather than ideological ones. I disagree, holding instead that what confronts us now is a battle for the soul of Islam (chapter 3). We hear disproportionately from militant Islam, but there exists a credible, moderate Islam, which must play a critical role if Muslims are ever wholeheartedly to join the modern world. The leading light, the brightest hope of this contingent, is the Republic of Turkey, but its representatives can be found everywhere (and notably, chaffing under the rule of the mullahs in the Islamic Republic of Iran).

"Do Moderate Islamists Exist?" replies to the argument, made by many academics and also by the U.S. government, that one can divide between good and bad Islamists, the former relying on political means and the latter on violent ones. Instead, I hold that this creates a false dichotomy because all Islamists are part of the same enterprise and their differences are relatively superficial. I conclude that there is no basis for finding the seemingly less violent of them acceptable. I offer specific guidelines for American policy based on the premise that all Islamists are a problem, making this one of only two chapters in the book with policy recommendations.

A widespread consensus, both Muslim and Western, holds that the surge in militant Islam results from economic stress. In "Does Poverty Cause Militant Islam?" I argue otherwise by showing the absence of a meaningful correlation between the two phenomena. Neither standard of living nor economic growth can predict whether a person or society will turn to militant Islam. Indeed, if one looks closely at the backgrounds of September 11's nineteen suicide hijackers, "money, education and privilege," as one wit notes, would seem to be the root causes of their radicalism and violence. I do not, however, offer an alternate mechanism in this chapter for predicting militant Islam, finding this to be too large and complex a phenomenon to try to tie to any single variable. Instead, I see it arising from frustration and a deeply bruised sense of identity.

The English translation of an Arabic book arguing for an Islamic form of economics offers an opportunity to look in more detail at one aspect of Islamist thinking. The prolific Lebanese writer Samih 'atef El-Zein premises his work on the idea that "No problem can occur or

event take place for which there is not an explanation in Islamic law."
"The Glory of Islamic Economics" summarizes his thinking, then
pokes holes in El-Zein's analysis before coming to the serious conclusion that no matter how lacking his argument, it needs to be taken
seriously; the past century has shown that dumb minds can do extraordinary damage.

"The Western Mind of Militant Islam" was provoked in May 1994,
when I took part in a panel discussion in Washington, D.C., about militant Islam and a person in the audience responded to my argument
with, "I work for a think tank, an Islamically oriented one. I listen to
Mozart; I read Shakespeare; I watch the Comedy Channel; and I also
believe in the implementation of Shari'a.[4] The unlikely combination
of the Comedy Channel and the Shari'a mystified me, prompting this
article. Interestingly, this is one of my few analyses that has met with
the approval of some Islamists.

That same May 1994 panel discussion spurred me in another way,
too. The panel was introduced by former Senator George McGovern.
I took advantage of his presence to ask him about his views on militant Islam and quickly realized that he approached this new threat to
the United States much as he had the previous threat of Marxism-
Leninism. A little introspection made it apparent to me that, while
coming from the other side of the political spectrum, I did the same. In
"Echoes of the Cold War Debate," I argue that the liberal-conservative
divide that defined views toward communism and the Soviet Union
still holds, defining both one's basic outlook toward militant Islam and
the attendant policy prescriptions. Then as now, "Liberals say co-opt
the radicals. Conservatives say confront them. As usual, the conservatives are right."

The gist of "The U.S. Government: Patron of Islam?," co-authored
with Mimi Stillman, came as a surprise. It was one thing to hear individual statements by high government officials stretching back a
decade and another to collect them, sort them, and ponder them. This
latter task suggested a more cohesive and powerful message than had
been evident from occasional remarks: "By dismissing any connection
between Islam and terrorism, complaining about media distortions,
and claiming that America needs Islam," we concluded, official
spokesmen "have turned the U.S. government into a discreet mission-

ary for the faith." Assuming that this is not their intention, the message of this essay is that government officials should be much more careful when they speak about Islam.

The four-volume *Oxford Encyclopedia of the Modern Islamic World* provides an opportunity to review the best that current scholarship has to offer on the subject of Islam. As the title "A Monument of Apologetics" suggests, I found that, in an age when objective knowledge has faded as a goal, scholarship readily turns into partisanship and that this plague reaches even into a major reference work published by a prestigious press.

Part II, on Islam in the United States, opens with an essay written well before September 11 but unpublishable until the events of that day opened Americans' imaginations to the threat of militant Islam. "We Are Going to Conquer America" reviews declarations by Islamists, some public and others not, about their agenda for the United States. They do have an ambitious program. Bizarre as it may seem, they seek nothing less than to bring the Shari'a to bear in the land of the free. The main argument between Islamists is not about the desirability of this outcome, on which they all agree, but about the best method to achieve it. Some Islamists advocate violence and others prefer legal means (conversion, political action). In this article, as in much of Part II, I rely to a great extent on the information made available by militant Islamic individuals and groups.

It is a sad to see how many American converts to Islam—whether black or white, rich or poor, members of Nation of Islam or normative Islam[5]—hate their own country. Perhaps the two most prominent symbols of this pattern are Jamil Al-Amin, known previously as H. Rap Brown, and John Walker Lindh. Al-Amin, a middle-aged black nationalist with a long career of criminality, has been convicted of the murder of a police officer. Lindh, the young son of privilege who joined the Taliban in Afghanistan, was charged with providing material support and resources to a foreign terrorist organization. "Conversion and Anti-Americanism" documents the pattern they exemplify and finds two main reasons why converts go this route: personal temperament and the immigrant Muslim milieu. Converts to Islam in the United States are generally alienated from the society in which they live; and then they are influenced by the immigrant Muslims' generally low regard for the United States—an often potent combination.

"Fighting Militant Islam, Without Bias" takes up the arch-delicate question of policy toward Islamists who live in the West. Americans having woken up to the fact that militant Islam is their enemy, how should they look at and deal with the adherents of this ideology who are their neighbors? By way of an answer, I offer a series of policy recommendations on ways to combat militant Islam.

"Catching Some Sleepers" raises the problem of the unseen enemy; to a very great extent, militant Islam's war on the United States depends on placing "sleepers" (hidden agents, activated only to engage in an operation) inside the country. For the country intelligently to protect itself requires guidelines about the sort of profile a sleeper might have. Although sleepers go to considerable efforts to hide themselves, shedding their militant Islamic characteristics and even engaging in activities antithetical to Islam, they do still retain a number of potentially identifying characteristics; I provide a long but necessarily incomplete list of these.

The self-appointed guardians of American Muslim interests— organizations such as the American Muslim Council, the Council on American-Islamic Relations, and the Muslim Public Affairs Council— all tell a sad—and convincing—tale about discrimination being "part of daily life for American Muslims." One might think that this community lags socioeconomically, endures the outrages of prejudice, and suffers harsh media assaults. Given these beliefs, I examined publications of the above three organizations, as well as other sources, and found none of this to be the case. In "Are American Muslims the Victims of Bias?" I show that Muslims are flourishing in the United States and are the beneficiaries of much goodwill and even protectiveness, as indicated by an array of governmental policies, media reports, corporate actions, and court decisions.

It was not so long ago that Westerners could converse freely about Muhammad, Islam, Muslims, and militant Islam, just as they still can about parallel Christian subjects. No longer. "How Dare You Defame Islam" surveys the ways in which violence and intimidation have shut down the frank discussion of these issues. It has reached the strange point that, in a secular, Christian-majority country like the United States, a biographer of Jesus has freedom to engage in outrageous blasphemies while his counterpart working on Muhammad feels constrained to accept the pious Muslim version of the Prophet's life. I present this silencing as something significant in itself and a potential first step toward the imposition of Islamic law.

This is followed by a specific instance of such intimidation. In May 1994, the Palestinian leader Yasir Arafat was secretly taped referring to the Oslo accords as "no more than the agreement signed between our Prophet Muhammad and the Quraysh in Mecca." To figure out just what Arafat might have intended by this coded statement, a number of American political analysts dusted off their books on early Islamic history. Their conclusion—that Arafat was signaling his intention to break his agreements with Israel when he grew sufficiently strong to do so with impunity—displeased some American Muslim groups, which did their best, with considerable success, to close down any discussion of the matter. "Lessons from the Prophet Muhammad's Diplomacy" both explains the complex historical context of this debate and reviews the militant Islamic attempts to close down a frank discussion.

An eighty-five-page federal affidavit issued in July 2000 provided the information base for "Charlotte's Web: Hizbullah's Career in the Deep South." By restructuring the affidavit and turning its legalese into English, then adding some other sources, I put together the story of a gang of Hizbullah supporters who engaged in a wide range of scams to raise money for their favorite charity, Lebanon's leading militant Islamic group. The nerve and disdain of their operation was almost as appalling as the blundering inabilities of the many government agencies supposed to protect the country from their likes. In all, this episode offers an unusually complete and compelling account of militant Islam's operational activities in the United States.

"Christian anti-Semitism is yesterday's problem; Muslim anti-Semitism is tomorrow's." So I concluded on reviewing Muslim attitudes toward Jews. In words and deeds, the rage and hostility of militant Islam is something Jews have not yet comprehended, much less begun making preparations to combat. "America's Muslims vs. America's Jews" stands as my warning that militant Islam threatens to bring to an end the golden age of American Jewry.

The next three chapters focus on African-American Islam. America's first Muslims were neither immigrants nor converts but slaves brought in shackles from Africa. Oddly, this lost saga began receiving attention only in recent years. "Muslim Slaves in American History" reports on the most literary and ambitious effort to discern their lives and their legacy, Sylviane Diouf's *Servants of Allah: African Muslims Enslaved in the Americas*.

Muslim history stretches back fourteen centuries, but not until 1913 did a variant form of Islam spontaneously appear in a distant country and grow into a significant movement that would become the Moorish Science Temple of America, founded in Newark, New Jersey. This institution led American blacks in the 1930s to the Nation of Islam and that in turn in the 1960s led them to normative Islam. Focusing on the central figure of Elijah Muhammad, the man who dominated the Nation of Islam for over forty years, "The Rise of Elijah Muhammad" provides an overview this movement's changes, and specifically its progression from odd cult to normative Islam.

"The Curious Case of Jamil Al-Amin" recalls the long, undistinguished, but highly public career of the former H. Rap Brown. Called "the violent left's least-thoughtful firebrand" in the 1960s, he was in the docket at the time of writing, accused of having murdered an Atlanta policeman in March 2000. His case holds interest in itself but all the more so because Al-Amin had become a leading figure in American Muslim life. As a result, almost all the national Muslim organizations have flocked to his side; I note that their solidarity was with a man who was twice on the FBI's most-wanted list, not with the orphans of the deceased police officer, and argue that this shows the extremist nature of these organizations.

The conclusion, "Who Is the Enemy?," offers a way to win the war on terrorism by taking two steps: weakening militant Islam in dozens of countries around the world, including the United States, and then helping moderate Muslims to get their message out. Although the moderates appear—and in fact are—weak, they have a crucial role to play, for they alone can reconcile Islam with modernity and help Muslims return to the success they need and deserve. In closing, I offer a way to go beyond the problems and horrors of the present. To do so, however, requires a recognition by the U.S. government that the enemy is not a featureless "terrorism" but militant Islam.

PART I

MILITANT ISLAM

❖❖❖

The Makkah Hilton in Mecca, Saudi Arabia, carries the American flag into the heart of Islam. Located just meters from the Holy Haram (the flat, white-roofed building to the right), the hotel's 598 rooms tower over the holiest site in all Islam. And while the hotel is part of an American chain, travelers are warned that "this hotel is only accessible to visitors of Muslim Religion." The hotel boasts a fully air-conditioned prayer hall accommodating twenty thousand worshipers, making it probably the largest hotel chapel in the world.   (HILTON HOTELS)

1

IS ISLAM A THREAT?

Does Islam threaten the West? No, it does not. But militant Islam does threaten it in many and profound ways. There is, indeed, no comparable danger in the world today.

One cannot emphasize too much this distinction between Islam—plain Islam—and its militant Islamic version. Islam is the religion of about 1 billion people and has been the host of one of the world's great civilizations. It is a fast-growing faith, particularly in Africa, but also around the world. In contrast, militant Islam is a utopian ideology, initiated in the twentieth century, that attracts only a portion of Muslims (perhaps 10 to 15 percent), seeks to capture control of governments, and is nakedly aggressive toward all those who stand in its way, no matter what their faith.

To understand how this distinction arose and what is its significance requires a review of the Muslim historical experience.

Islam's Fortunate History . . .

The adherents of Islam find their faith immensely appealing, for Islam has an inner strength that is quite extraordinary. Muslims are confident that they have the best religion. As a leading figure in the Islamic Republic of Iran explains, "Any Westerner who really understands Islam will envy the lives of Muslims."[1] Or as two scholars put it, "the world of men in their families" goes far to explain the appeal of Islam."[2] Far from being embarrassed about Islam being temporally the last of the three major Middle Eastern monotheisms, Muslims believe that their faith not only preceded Judaism and Christianity but also improves on both. They see Judaism and Christianity as but defective variants of Islam, God's final, perfected religion. This inner sense of confidence helped imbue Muslims with an unparalleled loyalty to their religion.

Added to this internal confidence was the fact that Muslims enjoyed outstanding success during their first six or so centuries. To be a Muslim meant to belong to a winning civilization. This pattern of success started right at the beginning: in A.D. 622, Muhammad fled Mecca as a refugee, then returned there in 630 as its ruler. By the year 715, Muslim conquerors had assembled an empire that reached Spain in the west and India in the east. Muslims boasted some of the most powerful armies, the highest standards of living, the best health, the most impressive rates of literacy, and the most impressive scientific and technical advances. In the words of Martin Kramer, a historian, "Had there been Nobel Prizes in 1000, they would have gone almost exclusively to Moslems."[3]

Muslims, not surprisingly, came to see a correlation between their faith and this mundane success, to assume that it had a message for them; they believed themselves the favored of God, both spiritually and in the world. This connection remains strong even at present. 'Ali Hoseyni Khamene'i, Ayatollah Khomeini's successor as leader of Iran, makes this point when he declares that "The path of Islam is the path of prosperity."[4] More broadly, the analyst Reuel Marc Gerecht adds, centuries of experience meant that for many Muslims, "battlefield victories, aircraft carriers, and ICBMs [became] the most convincing proof that God has chosen your side."[5]

. . . and Troubled Present

In modern times, however, those battlefield victories have been notably lacking, as have prosperity and scientific breakthroughs. The origins of this Muslim decline began in the thirteenth century, the point at which Muslim atrophy and Christendom's advances became discernible. Nonetheless, for some five hundred years hence, Muslims remained largely oblivious to the extraordinary developments taking place in Europe. Typical of this phenomenon was Ibn Khaldun, the leading Muslim intellectual, who, from his perch in North Africa, wrote about nearby Europe around 1400, "I hear that many developments are taking place in the land of the Rum, but God only knows what happens there!" Blinded by a self-confidence characteristic of his world, he just had no interest in the Christians to his north.

This ignorance rendered Muslims very vulnerable when the time came that they no longer could ignore the facts around them. Perhaps the most dramatic alert came in July 1798, when Napoleon Bonaparte landed in Egypt, at the very center of the Muslim world, and with stunning ease conquered Egypt. He showed the reluctant Muslims just how far they had fallen from their medieval splendors and he did so in a manner that could not be gainsaid. Other assaults on Muslims followed, so that a century later most of them had been incorporated within one or other European empire. As this collapse unfolded, a sense of incomprehension spread among Muslims. What went wrong? they asked themselves. They wondered whether God had abandoned them and how they could reverse this awful trajectory. In this—the huge contrast between medieval success and more recent tribulations—lies the trauma of modern Islam.[6]

Muslim society has a hard time explaining what caused the loss of power and prominence. Nor has the passage of time made matters easier, for while individual Muslims have flourished, their societies and countries have remained well behind the West. Whatever index one looks at, Muslims can be found clustering toward the bottom, whether in terms of military prowess, political stability, economic development, corruption, lack of human rights, health, longevity, or literacy. Anwar Ibrahim, the former deputy prime minister of Malaysia, estimates that whereas Muslims make up just one fifth of the world's total population, they constitute more than half of the 1.2 billion people living in abject poverty.[7] Muslims also lag when one looks at Nobel Prize winners, Olympic medallists, or any other easily gauged international standard. There is a pervasive sense of debilitation, encroachment, and things having gone seriously wrong. As a Muslim religious leader in Jerusalem put it, "Before, we were masters of the world and now we're not even masters of our own mosques."[8]

Searching for answers to escape this dilemma, Muslims have developed three major responses: secularism; reformism; and fundamentalism. Secularism holds that Muslims can only advance by emulating the West. Yes, Islam is a valuable and esteemed legacy, but its public dimensions must be put aside so that it becomes a private faith. In particular, the sacred law of Islam (the Shari'a), which governs such matters as the judicial system, the manner in which the state goes to war, and the nature of social interactions between men and women, should be discarded in its entirety. The leading secular country is Turkey, where Kemal Atatürk in the period 1923–38 imposed extraordinary changes on an overwhelmingly Muslim population. Although many of his reforms eroded over the decades, Turkey does remain mainly secular. Overall, secularism is a minority position among Muslims, with very few instances other than Turkey, and even there it is under attack.

Reformism, which offers a murky middle, is very popular. Whereas secularism forthrightly calls for learning from the West, reformism sneakily appropriates from it. The reformist says something like, "Look, Islam is basically compatible with Western ways. It's just that we lost track of our own achievements, which the West exploited. We must now go back to our own ways by adopting those of the West." To permit this to happen, reformers reread the Islamic scriptures in a Western light. For example, the Qur'an permits a man to take up to four wives—but only on condition that he treats them equitably. Traditionally, Muslims understood this verse as permission for a man to take four wives. But because in the West a man is allowed only one, the reformists chose to interpret the scripture in a new way: the Qur'an, they say, requires a man to treat his wives equitably, which is clearly something no man can do, so Islam in fact prohibits more than a single wife.

Reformists applied this sort of reasoning across the board. With regard to science, they said that Muslims should have no problem, for science is in fact Muslim. They recalled that the word *algebra* comes from the Arabic, *al-jabr*. Algebra being the essence of mathematics and mathematics being the essence of science, all of modern science and technology stems from work done by Muslims. So there is no reason to resist Western science; it is just a matter of reintegrating what the West took (or stole) in the first place. In case after case, reformists appropriate Western ways under guise of drawing on their own heritage. The reformists' goal is to imitate the West without acknowledging as much. Though intellectually bankrupt, this is politically very useful and explains why reformism is very widespread.

Militant Islam's Main Features

The third response to the modern trauma is fundamentalism, also known as Islamism or militant Islam. It has three main features: a devotion to the sacred law, a rejection of Western influences, and a turning of faith into ideology.

Militant Islam holds that Muslims are lagging today because they're not good Muslims; to regain the old glory means a return to old ways, and that is mainly achieved by living fully in accord with the Shari'a. Were Muslims to do so, they would regain their successes of a millennium ago. This, however, is no easy task, for the sacred law contains a vast body of regulations touching every aspect of life, many of them contrary to modern practices. (The Shari'a somewhat resembles Jewish law, but nothing comparable exists in Christianity.) For example, the law forbids usury or any taking of interest, which impedes finances. It calls for the cutting off of hands of thieves, which runs contrary to all modern sensibilities, as does the covering of women and more broadly, the separation of the sexes. Militant Islam not only calls for the application of these laws as of old, but for their far more rigorous application than ever before was the case. Before 1800, the interpreters of the law softened it to get around the difficult parts; for instance, they figured out a way to avoid the ban on interest. The Islamists reject such modifications, demanding instead that Muslims apply the Shari'a in its totality, without exception.

In their effort to build a way of life based purely on the Shar'i laws, Islamists strain to reject all aspects of Western influence—customs, philosophy, political institutions and values. Despite these efforts, they absorb vast amounts from the West. For one, they need modern technology, especially its military and medical applications. For another, they themselves tend to be modern individuals, and so are far more imbued by Western ways than they wish to be or acknowledge. In endless ways, small and large, Islamists import assumptions and customs from the West. Friday in Islam is not a day of rest but a day of congregation; they see it as the Muslim equivalent of the Sabbath. The laws of Islam do not apply to everyone living within a geographical territory, only to Muslims; but for Islamists, the laws are territorial in nature, as an Italian priest living in Sudan found out not long ago, when he was flogged for possessing alcohol. Even Ayatollah Khomeini, who was more traditional than most Islamists, failed in his effort to found a government purely on the principles of Shi'i Islam. He ended up with a *republic* based on a *constitution* that represents the *nation* via the decisions of a *parliament* which is chosen through popular *elections*—every one of these Western concepts. Militant Islam stealthily appropriates from the West while denying that it is doing so.[9]

Perhaps the most important of these borrowings, and our third point, is the Islamist learning from the West about all-encompassing ideologies. Militant Islam turns the traditional religion of Islam into a twentieth-century-style ideology. The word *Islamism* is a useful and accurate one, for it indicates that this phenomenon is an "-ism" comparable to other "-isms" of the twentieth century—a belief system about ordering power and wealth. Islamism represents an Islamic variant of the radical utopian ideas of our time; following fascism and Marxism-Leninism comes Islamism. Like earlier visions with a radical utopian content, it seeks to build the just society by regimenting people according to a preconceived plan, only this time with an Islamic orientation.

This Islamic-style totalitarianism holds that if Muslims only live in strict accord with the sacred law of Islam, they will also regain the wealth and strength they had in the glorious medieval period. In the process, it infuses a vast array of Western political and economic ideas within the religion of Islam. Whereas a traditional Muslim would say something like, "We are neither Jews nor Christians, but Muslims," a member of the Muslim Brethren from Egypt says that "We are neither socialist nor capitalist, but Muslims."[10] Such vaunting of Islam as the best ideology, not the best religion, neatly exposes the Islamists' focus on power.

Further, Islamists see their adherence to Islam primarily as a form of political allegiance; though usually pious Muslims, they need not be. Plenty of Islamists seem to be rather impious. The mastermind of the 1993 World Trade Center bombing in New York, Ramzi Yusuf, had a girlfriend while living in the Philippines and was "gallivanting around Manila's bars, strip-joints and karaoke clubs, flirting with women." From this and other suggestions of loose living, his biographer finds "scant evidence to support any description of Yousef as a religious warrior." The FBI agent in charge of investigating Yusuf concluded that "He hid behind a cloak of Islam."[11] The same pattern applies to several of the September 11 suicide hijackers: in Massachusetts they hired escorts from Day and Night Encounters; in Florida they hired lap dancers at the Pink Pony strip club; in New Jersey they patronized Nardone's Go-Go Bar; and in Nevada at least six of them partied on the Las Vegas Strip.[12]

On a societal level, Ayatollah Khomeini hinted at the irrelevance of faith in early 1989, in a letter he wrote to Mikhail Gorbachev as the Soviet Union was rapidly failing. The Iranian offered his own government as a model:

> I strongly urge that in breaking down the walls of Marxist fantasies you do not fall into the prison of the West and the Great Satan. . . . I call upon you seriously to study and conduct research into Islam. . . . I openly announce that the Islamic Republic of Iran, as the greatest and most powerful base of the Islamic world, can easily help fill up the ideological vacuum of your system.[13]

Khomeini here seems to suggest that the Soviets should turn to the militant Islamic ideology; converting to Islam would almost seem to be an afterthought. A leading Iranian official confirmed this point when he said that this letter was "intended to put an end to . . . views that we are only speaking about the world of Islam. We are speaking for the world."[14] It may even be the case—Khomeini only hints at this—that Islam for him had become so disembodied from faith, he foresaw a non-Muslim like Gorbachev adopting Islamic ways without becoming a Muslim. If so, the transformation of Islam from faith to political construct is then complete.

Contrary to its reputation, militant Islam is not a way backward; as a modern-style ideology, it offers not a means to return to some old-fashioned way of life but a way to steer the shoals of modernization. With few exceptions, notably the Taliban in Afghanistan, Islamists are city dwellers who have to cope with the problems of modern urban life—not people in the countryside. For example, the challenges facing career women figure prominently in militant Islamic discussions; they worry what a woman who must travel by very crowded public transportation can do to insulate herself from being groped. The Islamists have a ready reply: she should cover herself, body and face, and signal through the wearing of Islamic clothes that she is not approachable. More broadly, they offer an inclusive and alternative way of life for modern people, one that rejects the whole complex of popular culture, consumerism, and individualism in favor of a closed Islamically based order.

Militant Islam's Contrast with Traditional Islam

Although militant Islam is often seen as a form of traditional Islam, it is something profoundly different—and far more dangerous. Traditional Islam seeks to teach human beings how to live in accord with God's will; militant Islam aspires to create a new order. The first is self-confident, the second deeply defensive. The one emphasizes individuals, the other communities. The one is a personal credo, the other a political ideology.

Much else distinguishes militant Islam from Islam as it was traditionally practiced, including this emphasis on public life (rather than faith and personal piety); its leadership by schoolteachers and engineers (not religious scholars); and its Westernized quality (seeing Friday as a Sabbath, thereby imitating the Jewish Saturday and Christian Sunday).

The differences are starkest when one looks at the two sets of leaders. Traditionalists go through a static and lengthy course of study in which they study a huge corpus of information and learn the Islamic verities much as their ancestors did centuries earlier. Their faith reflects a millennium and more of debate among scholars, jurists, and theologians. Militant Islamic leaders tend to be well educated in the sciences, not in Islam; when in their twenties or so, they discover problems that their modern learning cannot cope with, so they belatedly turn to Islam. They ignore nearly the entire corpus of Islamic learning and read the Qur'an on their own and interpret it however they see fit. As autodidacts, they dismiss the traditions and apply their own (modern) sensibilities to the ancient texts, leading to an oddly Protestantized version of Islam.

The modern world stymies traditional figures who, educated in old-fashioned subjects, have not studied European languages, spent time in the West, nor mastered its secrets. For example, the traditional religious figures rarely know how to exploit the radio, television, or Internet to spread their message. In contrast, militant Islamic leaders usually know Western languages, often have lived abroad, and tend to be very well versed in technology. Symbolically, the Internet has hundreds of militant Islamic sites but few traditionally pious ones. François Burgat and William Dowell note this contrast in their study of North Africa:

> The village elder, who is close to the religious establishment and knows little of Western culture (from which he refuses technology a priori) cannot be confused with the young science student who is more than able to deliver a criticism of Western values, with which he is familiar and from which he is able to appropriate certain dimensions. The traditionalist will reject television, afraid of the devastating modernism that it will bring; the Islamist calls for increasing the number of sets . . . once he has gained control of the broadcasts.[15]

In brief, militant Islam represents a thoroughly modern effort to come to terms with the challenges of modernization.

Traditionalists fear the West, but Islamists are eager to challenge it. The late mufti of Saudi Arabia, 'Abd al-'Aziz bin Baz, represented the scared old guard. In the summer of 1995, he warned Saudi youth not to travel to the West for vacation because "There is a deadly poison in traveling to the land of the infidels and there are schemes by the enemies of Islam to lure Muslims away from their religion, to create doubts about their beliefs, and to spread sedition among them." He urged the young to spend their summers in the "safety" of the summer resorts in their own country.[16]

Islamists are not completely impervious to the fear of these schemes and lures, but they have ambitions to tame the West, something they do not shy from announcing for the world to hear. They have different strategies. The most crude simply want to kill Westerners. In a remarkable statement, a Tunisian convicted of setting off bombs in France in 1985–86 which killed thirteen people told the judge handling his case: "I do not renounce my fight against the West which assassinated the Prophet Muhammad. . . . We Muslims should kill every last one of you [Westerners]."[17] Others plan to expand Islam to Europe and America, using violence if necessary. An Amsterdam-based imam declared on a Turkish television program: "You must kill those who oppose Islam, the order of Islam or Allah, and His Prophet; hang or slaughter them after tying their hands and feet crosswise . . . as prescribed by the Shari'a."[18] An Algerian terrorist group, the GIA, issued a communiqué in 1995 that bristled with threats and showed the Eiffel Tower exploding: "We are continuing with all our strength our steps of jihad and military attacks, and this time in the heart of France and its largest cities. . . . It's a pledge that they [the French] will have no more sleep and no more leisure and Islam will enter France whether they like it or not."[19] Sheikh Omar Abdel Rahman of the 1993 World Trade Center bombing fame spoke the same way about the United States.

This contrast not only implies that militant Islam threatens in a way that the traditional faith does not; it also implies that traditional Muslims, who are often the first victims of militant Islam, hate this ideology. The great majority of Muslims disagree with the premises of militant Islam, and a small number do so vocally. A few, like Salman Rushdie and Taslima Nasrin, have acquired global reputations, but most toil more obscurely. Among the better known opponents of militant Islam is Naguib Mahfouz, Egypt's Nobel Prize winner for literature in 1988, who commented after being stabbed in the neck by an Islamist at the age of eighty-three: "I pray to God to make the police victorious over terrorism and to purify Egypt from this evil, in defense of people, freedom, and Islam."[20] Tujan Faysal, a female member of the Jordanian parliament, calls militant Islam "one of the greatest dangers facing our society" and compares it to "a cancer" that "has to be surgically removed."[21] Çevik Bir, one of the key figures in dispatching Turkey's militant Islamic government in 1997, flatly states that in his country, "Muslim fundamentalism remains public enemy number one."[22]

If Muslims feel this way, so may non-Muslims; being anti-militant Islam in no way implies being anti-Islam. As an ideology, militant Islam can claim none of the sanctity that Islam the religion enjoys. While remaining respectful of the Islamic faith, outsiders can in good conscience criticize and combat militant Islam.

Militant Islam in Practice

Like other radical ideologues, Islamists look to the state as the main vehicle for promoting their program, if necessary through coercive ways. Indeed, given the nature of their quite impractical scheme, state enforcement is critical to the realization of their ideology. Toward this end, Islamists often lead the opposition—as in Egypt, Turkey, Saudi Arabia—or have gained significant power—as in Lebanon, Pakistan, Malaysia. Their tactics are often murderous; in Algeria, a militant Islamic insurgency has led to the deaths of some 100,000 persons since 1992.

And when Islamists do take power, as in Iran, Sudan, and Afghanistan, the result is invariably a disaster, both for the subjects of those regimes and for the outside world. Economic decline begins immediately; Iran is the best example, where for two decades and more the standard of living has almost relentlessly gone down. Personal rights are disregarded, as spectacularly shown by the reestablishment of chattel slavery in Sudan. Repression of women is an absolute require-ment; this was seen most dramatically under the Taliban in Afghanistan, where women were excluded from schools and jobs.

A militant Islamic state is almost by definition a rogue state, not playing by any rules except those of expediency and power, a ruthless institution that causes misery at home and abroad. Islamists in charge means that conflicts proliferate, society is militarized, arsenals grow, and terrorism becomes an instrument of state. It is no accident that Iran was engaged in the longest conventional war of the twentieth century (eight years long, 1980–88, against Iraq) and that both Sudan and Afghanistan have been in the throes of decades-long civil wars. Islamists repress moderate Muslims and treat non-Muslims as inferior specimens.

Militant Islam since the mid-1970s has been on the ascendant for a full quarter century and more, becoming a powerful force over this period. Its many successes should not be understood, however, as wide-spread support for militant Islam. Instead, the power that Islamists wield reflects their being a highly dedicated, capable, and well-orga-nized minority. A little like cadres of the Communist Party, they make up for numbers with activism and purpose.

Cannot Be Laughed Off

Islamists espouse deep antagonism to non-Muslims in general, Jews and Christians in particular. They hate the West both because it is a traditional opponent—the old rival Christendom in a new guise—and because of its huge cultural influence. Some of them have learned to moderate their views so as not to upset Western audiences, but this is a thin sugarcoating that should take no one in. Militant Islam is an aggressive global force that explicitly seeks global hegemony just as its fascist and Marxist-Leninist precursors did. In the words of one elected Turkish official, "We want the whole world to become Muslim, because Islam is the solution to all problems."[23] Prominent Islamic writers, such as Murad Wilfried Hoffmann, a German convert, have predicted that Islam's ascension to being the dominant world religion is inevitable in this century.

These Islamists cannot merely be laughed off. They must be taken seriously and shown that they cannot impose their totalitarian ways.

2

THE IMAGINARY
GREEN PERIL

Richard Condon, author of *The Manchurian Candidate*, declared in 1990: "Now that the Communists have been put to sleep, we are going to have to invent another terrible threat."[1] This is, of course, complete nonsense. Communists have hardly been "put to sleep," but have plenty of punch left in them, especially in the Third World. Further, Americans did not invent the Soviet threat—tanks, ICBMs, and a global ideology made it real enough. And far from needing "another terrible threat" to replace the Soviet Union, we should look to perfecting liberty and free markets here at home. If that's too heady, we ought to be quite happy to go back to watching baseball games or saving money for the next vacation.

Still, let us grant that communism is dead and that the West should beware a fallback villain; who shall it be? There aren't many obvious candidates. Drug traffickers and apartheidists can do in a pinch; but both of these are minor actors, limited in time as well as space—and reactionary South Africans are not even hostile to the West. Some Americans looked to Japan or the Common Market after

1992 as the coming menace; but really, democratic countries cannot fill this role. A real enemy must inspire more visceral feelings than do exchange rates and trade imbalances.

And so it is that increasing numbers of Americans and Europeans are turning to a very traditional boogeyman—the Muslim. This profound and ancient fear is far from imaginary. The Arab conflict with Israel could escalate to nuclear warfare, as could Pakistan's dispute with India. Iranian terrorism against the West severely wounded two American presidents. Iraqi invasions into Iran and Kuwait represented a plausible effort to grab over half the world's oil reserves.

Nor is the idea of the Muslims as the outstanding threat to Western civilization entirely new. As early as 1984, Leon Uris explained that his purpose in writing *The Haj*, a novel, "was to warn the West and Western democracies that you can't keep your head in the sand about this situation any longer, that we have an enraged bull of a billion people on our planet, and tilted the wrong way they could open the second road to Armageddon."[2] It was not until 1989, however, that Muslim-phobia took off, a by-product of the orgy of speculation that accompanied Mikhail Gorbachev's reforms and the liberation of Central Europe.

Speculations about a Muslim threat divide into two distinct types. Some observers point to hostile states and the military forces bent on *jihad* (Islamic righteous war). Others focus on migrants to the West and fear a subversion of Western civilization from within. For the latter, the mischief of a Saddam Husayn or Mu'ammar al-Qadhdhafi poses fewer dangers than that of their followers living in our midst.

Jihad

The last time Muslims physically threatened Christendom (a term increasingly coming back into vogue) was in 1683, when Ottoman soldiers camped outside the walls of Vienna. The memory of this event has been revived in more recent years. Thus, William S. Lind, who once served as an adviser to Gary Hart, worried in 1989 that "the implication of a Soviet collapse, of the disintegration of the traditional Russian empire, might be that Moslem armies would again be besieging the gates of Vienna."[3]

Peter Jenkins, a leading British commentator, concurs. He sees

today's problem in light of a conflict going back six and a half centuries: "keeping Islam at bay was Europe's preoccupation from 1354,
when Gallipoli fell, until the last occasion on which the Turks stood at
the gates of Vienna in 1683. It is once more a preoccupation in the
face of the Islamic Revolution."[4] Leonard Horwin, a former mayor of
Beverly Hills, neatly doubled the time span in a 1990 letter to *The Wall
Street Journal*: "The real confrontation is between Judeo-Christian civilization . . . and militant Islam. . . . One thousand three hundred years
of militant Islam verify that it cannot tolerate the sovereign presence
of the *dhimmi* ("inferior") people, whether Christian (e.g. Lebanon) or
Jewish (Israel)—save so long as the dhimmis can defend themselves."[5]
Looking to the future, editorial writers at London's *Sunday Times* found
that the concept of containment still held: "Almost every month the
threat from the Warsaw Pact diminishes; but every year, for the rest of
this decade and beyond, the threat from fundamentalist Islam will
grow. It is different in kind and degree from the cold war threat. But
the West will have to learn how to contain it, just as it once had to
learn how to contain Soviet communism."[6] Ideological enthusiasms
like Marxism-Leninism will wax and wane, these writers were saying,
but the Muslim adversary remains permanently in place.

Far from representing the eccentric thoughts of a few commentators, such fears appear to touch a nerve deep in the Western psyche. To
cite one piece of survey research, a poll conducted in mid-1989 asked
French citizens "Which of the following countries appear to you today
to be the most threatening to France?" In response, 25 percent
answered Iran, 21 percent the USSR, and 14 percent the Arab countries in general. More than half the respondents—57 percent to be
exact—believed that one or more of the Muslim states are most threatening to France.[7] Similar opinions can be found in the other countries
of Western Europe.

Some Muslims, the Islamists, encourage these fears. For one, they
declare that the great conflict of this age is not that between the
United States and the former Soviet Union, or between capitalism and
communism, but between the West and Islam. They see Russia as part
of the West. A member of Hamas, the militant Islamic Palestinian
group, holds that "it is a battle of civilizations, and the Russians are
part of it."[8] Some Muslims, like the president of Iran, go further and
declare that "East and West have joined forces" against Islam.[9]

Islamists boast they will win this battle of titans. Editorialists at *Jomhuri-ye Islami*, a Tehran daily, put it baldly in early 1990: "Western-ers have correctly understood that the world movement of Islam is the biggest threat to the 'corrupt Western empire.' " The newspaper argued that Muslims must prove how "the world movement of Islam" can defeat the West.[10] 'Ali Akbar Mohtashemi, a leading Iranian hard-liner, has even greater aspirations: "The world in the future will have several powerful blocs. The Islamic power will play a decisive role in this. . . . Ultimately Islam will become the supreme power."[11] From Morocco to Indonesia, Muslims of a militant Islamic disposition share this outlook.

Answering *Jihad*

All of which brings us to the question of how the West should respond. While the question is too new to have received much attention, the main lines of a response can be discerned. For some, the key step lies in building cooperation between Western states. On the mundane level, industrial democracies should band together and preserve the liberal traditions of freedom of speech, freedom of religion, and the like; and they should cooperate against terrorism and other acts of vio-lence. The North Atlantic Treaty Organization (NATO) should be extended outside the European theater. The Strategic Defense Initia-tive should be developed for use against Iraqi or Libyan missiles.

More imaginative are those notions which would reach out to the former Soviet Union—or, more accurately, the Christian portions of the Soviet empire—as an ally against the Muslims. As the three Slavic republics, the three Baltic republics, Moldavia, Georgia, and Armenia, return to their historic allegiances, they can extend the population and geography of Europe. The most provocative notion has to do with building a military alliance with these peoples, and especially the Rus-sians. *The Sunday Times* calls on the West and Russia jointly to "pre-pare for the prospect of an enormous and fundamentalist Islamic wedge," stretching from Morocco to China."[12] In one of the most orig-inal geopolitical assessments of recent years, William Lind has sug-gested that "Russia's role as part of the West takes on special importance in the light of a potential Islamic revival. . . . The Soviet Union holds the West's vital right flank, stretching from the Black Sea to Vladivostok."[13] Walter McDougall, the Pulitzer Prize–winning historian, sees Russia as an ally in the clash of civilizations. He worries that

> Should the Russian empire in Central Asia threaten to collapse, a full-scale religious war fought with nuclear, chemical, and biological weapons is not impossible. The Iraqis and Iranis have already proven themselves capable of it, and the desperate and frustrated Russians certainly possess the means. Even more than Israel/Palestine, the old caravan routes of Central Asia may contain the site of the next Sarajevo. Which side would "the others, who call themselves Christians" support?[14]

These ideas prompt several responses. To begin with, they are a great improvement over the supine policies that many Western states, especially European ones, have adopted in recent years. It is better to exaggerate the danger of Iraqi thuggery than to lick Saddam Husayn's boots—as too many Westerners have done since the oil boom of 1973–74.

Further, the fear of Islam has some basis in reality. From the battle of Ajnadain in 634 until the Suez crisis of 1956, military hostility has always defined the crux of the Christian-Muslim relationship. Muslims served as the enemy par excellence from the *Chanson de Roland* to the Rolando trilogy, from *El Cid* to *Don Quixote*. In real life, Arabs or Turks represent the national villains throughout Southern Europe. Europeans repeatedly won their statehood by expelling Muslim overlords, from the Spanish *Reconquista* beginning in the early eleventh century to the Albanian war of independence ending in 1912.

Today, many Muslim governments dispose of large arsenals; the Iraqi military, for example, has more tanks than does the German and deploys the sort of missiles banned from Europe by the Intermediate Nuclear Force Treaty. Middle East states have turned terrorism into a tool of statecraft. About a dozen Muslim states have chemical and biological war capabilities. Impressive capabilities to manufacture a wide range of materiel have been established in Egypt, Iraq, Iran, Pakistan, and Indonesia. Were it not for the Israeli strike of 1981, Saddam Husayn would by now have his finger on a nuclear trigger.

To make matters worse, Muslims have gone through a terrible

trauma during the last two hundred years—the tribulation of God's people who unaccountably found themselves near the bottom of the economic heap. The strains of this prolonged failure have been enormous and the results terrible; Muslim countries host the most terrorists and the fewest democracies in the world. Specifically, only Turkey and Pakistan are fully democratic, and in those two countries the system is frail. Everywhere else, the head of government reached power through force—his own or someone else's. As in the rest of the world, autocracy invites leaders to pursue their own interests. The result is endemic instability plus a great deal of aggression.

But none of this justifies seeing Muslims as the paramount enemy.

For one thing, not all Muslims hate the West. Muslims who most hate the West—the Islamists—constitute a small minority in most places. Survey research and elections suggest that dyed-in-the-wool Islamists most places constitute no more than 15 percent of the Muslim population. Muslims are not fanatical by nature, but are frustrated by their current predicament. Most of them wish less to destroy the West than to enjoy its benefits.

For another, Muslims are not now politically unified and never will be so. The Iraqi invasion of Kuwait made this obvious for the whole world to see, but many other examples come to mind. Lebanon and Syria are in the throes of working out conflicting nationalist claims, Syria and Iraq have divergent ideological programs, Iraq and Iran claim overlapping territories, while Iran and Saudi Arabia espouse contrasting religious visions. Arab unity seems always to fail, as do the other schemes to bind Muslims politically together.

The violence of the Middle East symptomizes these disagreements. The Iraq-Iran War, a purely Muslim conflict, lasted a horrifying eight years and consumed in its peak days as many lives as the Arab-Israeli conflict has over four decades. Today, Muslims confront each other in Iraq and Saudi Arabia. Others of the faithful are clashing with each other in the Western Sahara, Chad, Lebanon, Afghanistan, and Central Asia. Indeed, the record suggests that wars between Muslims are two or three times more common than those waged against infidels. Even if Muhammad's people were once again to plan a siege of Vienna, then, their internal disputes would make their effort about as ineffective as their war on Israel.

Then, too, there is the fact that more Muslim governments cooperate with the West than threaten it. Turkey is a member of NATO. The rulers of Morocco, Tunisia, Egypt, Pakistan, and Indonesia have cast their lot with their Western allies. Saudi Arabia and the other oil-rich states have invested so heavily in the West, their interests are directly tied up with it. The picture is hardly one of uniform hostility.

For all these reasons, while *jihad* may not be utterly impossible, it exists outside the realm of serious discussion about American policy.

Muslim Immigration

Ironically, the other worry results from precisely the fact that so many Muslims are attracted to the West. They like it so much they want to be part of it. As David Pryce-Jones notes, millions of Muslims "ask little better for themselves than to abandon their own societies for a European one."[15] The growing Muslim immigration to the West raises a host of disturbing issues—cultural this time, not military—especially in Western Europe.

All immigrants bring exotic customs and attitudes, but Muslim customs are more troublesome than most. Also, they appear most resistant to assimilation. Elements among the Pakistanis in Britain, Algerians in France, and Turks in Germany seek to turn the host country into a Islamic society by compelling it to adapt to their way of life.

On a small scale, they demand that factories keep to the Islamic calendar, with its distinctive holidays and special rhythms; or that public schools be segregated by sex and teach the principles of Islam. A significant body of Muslims, especially followers of Ayatollah Khomeini, appear to hope they can remake Europe and America in their own image. And they are not shy to say so. The editor of a Bengali-language newspaper in England, Harunur Rashid Tipu, explained that the leaders of the Young Muslim Organisation seek ultimately "to build an Islamic society here."[16] In the Rushdie affair, the Muslim diaspora in the West and the regime in Tehran created a cultural and political crisis that struck at the heart of Western values of free speech and secularism, confirming the worst fears of many in the West.

Of course, to build an Islamic society means taking political power. And while this is remote, it is just foreseeable. A French woman of North African origins told a reporter, "Tomorrow I will be mayor, the day after president of the republic."[17] In West Germany, one hears it said by politicians that "In the year 2000 we will have a federal chancellor of Turkish origins."[18] In perhaps the most extreme manifestation of this concern, Jean Raspail, the French intellectual, wrote a novel, *The Camp of the Saints*, depicting a Muslim takeover of Europe by an uncontrolled influx of Bangladeshis.[19]

Middle East leaders, such as the Wahhabis of Saudi Arabia and Mu'ammar al-Qadhdhafi of Libya, overtly encourage such aspirations. But it is the Iranian government that most aggressively advocates Muslim interests, even to the point of encouraging defiance of the authorities. In one statement, a hard-line Iranian newspaper declared that "the ever-increasing influence of Islam in the contemporary world is undeniable, whether the Western world likes it or not."[20] On another occasion, Tehran warned that Muslims living in the United Kingdom may be forced "to seek ways outside the law to guard their rights."[21]

Understandably, such bellicosity spurs anxiety among Westerners, even fears that Muslims will succeed in subverting the liberal tradition. In London, Peregrine Worsthorne expressed a widespread British sentiment in *The Sunday Telegraph*:

> Islamic fundamentalism is rapidly growing into a much bigger threat of violence and intolerance than anything emanating from, say, the [extreme right] National Front; and a threat, moreover, infinitely more difficult to contain since it is virtually impossible to monitor, let alone stamp out, the bloodthirsty anti-Jewish and anti-Christian language being preached from the pulpits of many British mosques. . . . Britain has landed itself with a primitive religious problem that we had every reason to suppose had been solved in the Middle Ages.[22]

Similar concerns can be heard in Russia too, where there is less concern about the former Soviet Union's 55 million Muslims gaining independence than that Muslims intend to move north and take over Moscow itself.

These concerns have political potency. Jean-Marie Le Pen, leader of the French movement to oust immigrants, characterizes Islam as "a religion of intolerance" and openly fears "an invasion of Europe by a Muslim immigration."[23] He heads a political party, the Popular Front, which explicitly advocates expelling immigrants from France. The

Republicans in West Germany and xenophobic groups in other countries share Le Pen's outlook and program.

The far right looms large to the Muslim immigrants, insecure and
largely disenfranchised as they are. Crude remarks and jokes, especially
among Germans ("What is the difference between a Jew and a Turk?"
"The Jew already got what he deserves, the Turk has yet to get it"), lead
some Muslims to worry about a Holocaust lying ahead. Kalim Siddiqui,
director of London's Muslim Institute, spoke of "Hitler-style gas chambers for Muslims";[24] Shabbir Akhtar, a member of the Bradford Council of Mosques, wrote that "the next time there are gas chambers in
Europe, there is no doubt concerning who'll be inside them."[25] However exaggerated, these statements reflect a genuine apprehension.

Demography

Demographic facts underlie Western fears both of *jihad* and of immigration. Population growth permeates the Muslim consciousness with
confidence about the future and imbues Westerners with a sense of
foreboding.

Muslims number nearly 1 billion individuals. They constitute
more than 85 percent of the population in some thirty-two countries;
they make up between 25 and 85 percent of the population in eleven
countries; and significant numbers but less than 25 percent in another
forty-seven countries.

In contrast to Westerners, who are not able even to maintain their
present numbers (recently, only Poland, Ireland, Malta, and Israel
have naturally growing populations), Muslims revel in some of the
most robust birth rates in the world. According to a 1988 study by John
R. Weeks, a California-based demographer, countries with large numbers of Muslims have a crude birth rate of 42 per 1,000; by contrast, the
developed countries have a crude birth rate of just 13 per 1,000. Translated into the total fertility rate, this means 6 children per Muslim
woman, 1.7 per woman in the developed countries. The average rate
of natural increase in the Muslim countries is 2.8 percent annually; in
the developed world, it is a mere 0.3 percent.[26]

These higher rates apply in almost every Muslim country from
North Africa to Southeast Asia, as well as within the confines of a sin-

gle country. Take the former Soviet Union: Muslims there sustained a birth rate fully five times that of the non-Muslims. While Muslims constituted only 16 percent of the Soviet population, they accounted for 49 percent of the population increase between 1979 and 1989.[27]

Some see in this demographic imbalance the single greatest challenge to Western civilization. Patrick Buchanan has summed up these fears with his customary panache: "For a millennium, the struggle for mankind's destiny was between Christianity and Islam; in the 21st century, it may be so again. . . . We may find in the coming century that . . . cultural conservative T. S. Eliot was right, when the old Christian gentleman wrote in 'The Hollow Men,' that the West would end, 'Not with a bang but a whimper'—perhaps the whimper of a Moslem child in its cradle."[28]

High Muslim birth rates already drive politics in the two non-Muslim states of the Middle East. Christians lost control of Lebanon after Muslims became a majority there. The challenge of maintaining a Jewish majority lies near the heart of the Israeli political debate; the local Muslim population keeps up a fertility rate of no less than 6.6 children per woman (1981 estimate).[29] Comparable political tensions have arisen on the fringes of the Middle East—in Ethiopia, Cyprus, Armenia, and Serbia—as the minority Muslim population climbs toward either political power or majority status.

Of course, the situation is very different in the West, but there too Muslim populations are growing. Muslims total 2–3 million in the United States and about 11 million in West Europe. Over 3 million Muslims live in France, about 2 million in West Germany, 1 million in the United Kingdom, and almost 1 million in Italy. Half a million Muslims live in Belgium. Five centuries after the fall of Granada, Spain now hosts 200,000 Muslims. Muslims outnumber Jews and have become the second largest religious community in most West European countries. In France, Muslims outnumber all non-Catholics combined, including both Protestants and Jews. In the United States, Muslims already number as many as Episcopalians; they could become the second largest religious community in about ten years.

Further, the Muslim birth rate far exceeds that of native Europeans and Americans, so that one fifth of all children born in France have a father from North Africa and Muhammad is one of the most common given names in the United Kingdom. Estimates pointed to the Muslim population of West Europe reaching 20 to 25 million by the year 2000.[30]

Muslim densities are particularly notable in some cities. London is home to 500,000 Muslims and West Berlin to some 300,000. They make up 10 percent of the population in Birmingham, the second largest city of Great Britain; in Bradford, where protests against Salman Rushdie's *Satanic Verses* gathered intensity, they constitute 14 percent of the population. They make up one quarter of the population in Brussels, Saint-Denis (a suburb of Paris), and Dearborn, Michigan.

Responding to Immigration

Fears of a Muslim influx have more substance than the worry about *jihad*. West European societies are unprepared or unwilling to deal with the massive immigration of brown-skinned peoples whom they perceive as cooking strange foods and not exactly maintaining Germanic standards of hygiene. Muslim immigrants bring with them a chauvinism that augurs badly for their integration into the mainstream of the European societies. The signs all point to continued clashes between the two sides. Put differently, Iranian zealots threaten more within the gates of Vienna than outside them.

Still, none of this amounts to Richard Condon's notion of "another terrible threat" in any way resembling the Soviet danger. Muslim immigrants will probably not change the face of European life: pubs will not close down, secularist principles will not wither, freedom of speech is not likely to be abrogated. The movement of Muslims to Western Europe creates a great number of painful but finite challenges; there is no reason, however, to see this event leading to a cataclysmic battle between two civilizations. If handled properly, the immigrants can even bring much of value, including new energy, to their host societies.

The United States faces less of a problem, as a result of a long tradition of immigration and the healthy attitudes that go with it. Being an American depends far less on ancestry than on shared values, and this encourages enfranchisement. Meritocratic ethics and an open educational system do much to integrate the next generation. Should Islamists move to the United States and choose to remain outside the mainstream culture, that too can be accommodated, as made clear by the Amish Mennonites in Pennsylvania or the Hasidic Jews in New York City.

There is a final point. The prediction that Communists will be replaced by Muslims as the main threat suggests that ideological divisions will give way to communitarian ones. And this conforms to Francis Fukuyama's thesis about the end of history—where the "end of history" means not that time when literally nothing happens, but (as befits a term coined by the philosopher Hegel) a time of no further advancement in the understanding of the human condition; that is, the moment when no new ideologies can be devised. If history in this sense should end, what one thinks will lose importance; who one is becomes key.

But Fukuyama's prediction seems most improbable. A great and bloody argument over the human condition has been the driving force of history for two centuries, from the French Revolution to the Nicaraguan civil war. It seems too far-fetched to think that this deeply divisive intellectual dispute will entirely burn itself out, to be replaced by the atavistic hostilities prevailing before 1789.

Returning to the issue of Muslims and the West, my skepticism about the end of ideology leads me to the following conclusion: Future relations between Muslims and Westerners depend less on crude numbers or place of residence and much more on beliefs, skills, and institutions. The critical question is whether Muslims will modernize or not. And the answer lies not in the Qur'an or in the Islamic religion, but in the attitudes and actions of nearly a billion individuals.

Should Muslims fail to modernize, their stubborn record of illiteracy, poverty, intolerance, and autocracy will continue, and perhaps worsen. The sort of military crisis that Saddam Husayn provoked might well become yet more acute. But if Muslims do modernize, there is a reason to hope. In this case, they will have a good chance to become literate, affluent, and politically stable. They will no longer need to train terrorists or target missiles against the West; to emigrate to Europe and America; or to resist integration within Western societies.

3

BATTLING FOR THE
SOUL OF ISLAM

A battle is now taking place for the soul of Islam. On one side
stand the moderates, those Muslims eager to accept Western
ways, confident to learn from outsiders, oriented toward democracy,
and ready to integrate in the world. On the other stand the Islamists—
fearful, seeking strong rule, hoping to push the outside world away.

Which group will prevail, the moderates or the Islamists, has great
importance. A militant Islamic victory could turn the Middle East into
the world's most violent region. If Islamists win, repression, weapons of
mass destruction, and warfare are likely to proliferate. They will close
down the peace process with Israel and restart the fighting. Regional
commerce will decline and foreign investment will dry up, impover-
ishing the region. Westerners will suffer from an increase in terrorism,
from higher-priced oil, and from uncontrolled immigration out of the
region.

Whether this vision will come to pass depends in large part on two
countries: Turkey, which represents the moderate trend; and Iran,
which carries the militant Islamic banner. These two countries are

roughly evenly matched in population and resources. The trouble is, however, that the Turks don't quite realize yet that they are engaged in this battle. The West can help wake them up to the danger and also help them confront the Islamists.

The Militant Islamic Threat

Islam took on a new role in public life in February 1979, when Ayatollah Khomeini established the Islamic Republic of Iran. Never before had Islam provided a government with an ideological outlook; nor had a regime come to power in modern times so determined to impose its militant Islamic vision (meaning, above all, an intent to apply the sacred law of Islam, the Shari'a) in its own domain and to spread it throughout the Muslim world.

Khomeini and his associates achieved considerable success. By imposing radically new institutions and customs on Iranians, they managed in just fifteen years to alter the basic texture of daily life in Iran. For example, a parliament came into being and disposed of real powers, yet only those who accepted the Islamic revolution's basic tenet (that men of religion must run the country) could hold office. And another example, small but indicative: the regime banned traditional wedding songs, requiring that marriages be celebrated with political chants like "Salute to the martyrs," "Death to the opponents of the supreme jurist," and other dreary slogans.[1]

Abroad, the mullahs (Iranian men of religion) are not shy about their plans to spread the revolution. Ayatollah 'Ali Meshkini, a leading regime figure, explains that "the Islamic Republic of Iran was the start of the story. An Islamic and divine government, much like that of Iran and better, will be created in . . . Egypt, Algeria, Morocco, Iraq, Lebanon, and Pakistan. They will all come together and will be the Islamic republics."[2] In short, the Khomeinists hope to replicate the Islamic Republic of Iran throughout the Muslim world.

The mullahs have partially succeeded in this effort. Their allies already rule in the Sudan, and others may win power in Tajikistan, Afghanistan, Lebanon, Egypt, and Algeria. Further, Tehran has acquired significant influence over developments in Iraq, Bahrain, the United Arab Emirates, and Bosnia.

The Khomeinists achieve so much less through money—mismanagement and war have left the country poorer than in the shah's time, with a discontented citizenry demanding improvements in its standard of living—than through an extraordinary act of will. This will takes two forms. First, the mullahs promote Ayatollah Khomeini's vision of society through an ambitious media campaign in Iran and abroad, in many languages and in many countries, utilizing every instrument from short-wave radio to scholarly books. Their efforts have established Khomeinism as a live option throughout the Muslim world. Second, they intimidate those who offer alternatives to the Khomeinist scheme—moderate Muslims, Western educators in the Middle East, Iranian dissidents in exile—by threatening these ideological foes, killing them, and generally forcing them to keep quiet.

The hush now descending over Muslim intellectual life testifies to the success of this double-pronged offensive. Islamists nearly destroyed the venerable American University of Beirut. They forced Salman Rushdie to lead a fugitive's life, while injuring or killing his publishers or their translators in Japan, Italy, and Norway. They forced Taslima Nasrin to flee for her life from Bangladesh, angry at her "blasphemy." They knifed Naguib Mahfouz in the neck and assassinated the prominent Egyptian secularist Farag Fodah. In Algeria, they launched a systematic campaign of assassination against the country's leading intellectuals, journalists, and artists.

These are just the conspicuous examples; the full extent of the intimidation reaches throughout the region's cultural life. Political leaders run scared, intellectuals keep their mouths shut, and artists engage in self-censorship. As militant Islamic ideas infiltrate the schools, children no longer have access to a modern outlook. In brief, the silencing of moderate Muslims means that the moderate strain of thought is disappearing in Muslim cultures in favor of obscurantist doctrines.

The Battle

Where this trend will lead is quite clear. Many Islamists and Westerners predict a confrontation between Islam and the West. In the first category, Kalim Siddiqui declares that "The struggle between the emergent civilization of Islam and the decadent civilization of the West will occupy the centrestage of history for most of the 21st century."[3] In the second, Samuel Huntington speculated in a much noted 1993 article and his subsequent book that the centuries-old military interaction between these two civilizations "could become more violent" in the future.[4]

But a showdown between whole civilizations is unlikely. To be sure, the occasional attack on a Western target does take place—such as the strikes on the World Trade Center in New York and the Pentagon in Washington, D.C., the attack on the Jewish center in Buenos Aires of 1992, or the explosion at the USS *Cole* in 2000—but this is a mere fraction of the militant Islamic violence against fellow Muslims. The killings in Algeria make this point: yes, some eighty foreigners were killed, but their number pales besides the tens of thousands of Muslims who lost their lives in the conflict.

The real battle, this suggests, is taking place among Muslims themselves, between the Islamists and the moderates. Islamists seek not to convince Westerners of the validity of their vision, but their coreligionists, most of whom reject it. Non-Muslims are mostly bystanders to the great ideological battle of the post–Cold War era.

The standoff between moderate Muslims and Islamists will be long and difficult. The moderates face a daunting challenge, which is to stand up to the intimidation and terrorism of the Islamists. The exiled Iranian journalist Amir Taheri has rightly argued that this behavior needs "to be faced and fought, and must eventually be defeated by forces of life in the Muslim world."[5]

Will the "forces of life" rise to the occasion? The answer depends in great part on the citizens of a country not often thought about in this connection: the Republic of Turkey.

Turkey's Threat to Iran

In the final analysis, the battle between moderate and militant Muslims will be determined by the decisions of peoples in two countries, Turkey and Iran. Just as Iran has become the Islamists' homeland, Turkey represents their ultimate enemy.

This position reflects, first, the Republic of Turkey's status as the great success story of the Muslim world. Whether one looks at political stability, economic growth, or cultural achievement, Turkey has no

Muslim match. Personal freedoms and human rights are greater than anywhere else. (However unhappy the fate of Kurds in Turkey may be, they flee from Iraq into Turkey, and not the other way around.) One can validly criticize this or that about Turkey, but its twentieth-century development represents the main alternative to the instability, violence, and repression that characterize so many Muslim countries.

Second, Turkey threatens Islamists because it has a uniquely well formulated and widely accepted philosophy of secularism. The Kemalist doctrine of laicism has been tested in elections over fifty years and enjoys a proven support among the Turkish population. No other Muslim country has anything remotely like it, a fact that becomes evident when politicians in Egypt, Tunisia, and Algeria crack down on militant Islamic violence. Lacking secularist ideas with which to combat Islamists on the level of ideology, they treat visionaries as common criminals. Thus, a leading figure of Egyptian Islam, Grand Imam of Al-Azhar Jadd al-Haqq 'Ali Jadd al-Haqq, pronounced that those who engage in violence in the name of Islam "are not Islamists and do not represent Islam. They are criminals who must be punished."[6] This crude approach invariably alienates Islamists without countering their appeal.

Third, Turkey's membership in NATO worries the Iranians. It suggests that the Turks' loyalties lie ultimately with Turkey's fellow democracies, not its fellow Muslims. Khomeini apparently feared Turkish territory would be made available to NATO forces to launch an attack on the Islamic Republic of Iran.

Finally, Turkey worries the Islamists because it has the only population willing to stand up and be counted in the fight against extremism. Egyptians mounted no public demonstration to protest the killing of Farag Fodah; but Turks responded to the murder of the prominent anti-Islamist journalist Uğur Mumcu by turning out on the streets in the tens of thousands, chanting: "Turkey will not become another Iran . . . Let those who want the Shari'a go to Iran . . . Death to Islamic terrorism."

Islamists must feel insecure so long as Turkey remains a secularist society with a democratic government, a free market, civil liberties, and a membership in NATO. Just as the Western model ultimately undermined the Soviet experiment, the Turkish model threatens to undermine the Khomeinist experiment. For militant Islam to survive, the mullahs need democracy in Turkey extinguished, the market restricted, civil liberties curtailed, the Shari'a applied, and the country out of NATO—in effect, an Islamic Republic of Turkey.

Iran's Threat to Turkey

While not yet prepared to take Turkey on frontally, the Iranians do already engage in a wide range of actions against Ankara, including internal sabotage and external aggression. Even before he attained power in Iran, Ayatollah Khomeini was already justifying interference in Turkey, saying that "Demands for an Islamic state are now being heard in Turkey . . . partly as a result of what is happening in Iran."[7] The Iranian regime, along with Saudi elements, too, actively provides clandestine aid to groups—like the Süleymancıs and Milli Görüş— which share their vision of overthrowing the government and replacing it with a militant Islamic order.

The Iranian leadership sometimes chooses baldly to interject itself in Turkish affairs. In 1989, for example, when the Turkish courts prohibited female university students from wearing a modesty headscarf over their hair, the Khomeini government intruded itself into this controversy. Iranian newspaper editorials attacked Ankara and small radio transmitters reaching eastern Anatolia rallied protests action against the court's decision. The Iranians threatened to reduce trade with Turkey from $1 billion a year to $400 million, or less. Manuchehr Motaki, the Iranian ambassador to Ankara, warned that "Turkey must respect the requirements of our Islamic Revolution,"[8] and both sides withdrew their ambassadors.

Those who resist their message face violent retribution. In January 1993, Iranian-sponsored assassins killed Uğur Mumcu. A month later, Iran's supreme leader, 'Ali Hoseyni Khamene'i, warned a Turkish writer and publisher not to translate *The Satanic Verses*: if they did, he warned, "the sons of Islam in Turkey will know what their duty is."[9] Not long after, Islamists burned down a hotel in Sivas where leftists intellectuals were staying, killing thirty-seven.

Just as Turkey represents a challenge to the militant Islamic vision, Iran poses one of the most formidable threats to Turkey's security.

Turkey's Burden

To stave off the militant Islamic threat, Turks need to call on a full range of economic, military, and diplomatic measures. But ideology is probably the most important weapon of all, for (as in the case of the U.S.-Soviet face-off) ultimately the two sides offer rival visions of life. Turks will need to emulate the mullahs and disseminate their own ideas to the Muslim world. They will find a ready audience, including students hungry for alternatives, politicians facing down Islamists, and intellectuals in need of moral support.

For Turks, exporting ideas has several implications, few of them welcome. It means:

- Paying more attention to the Middle East, a troubled region Turks have happily ignored for decades and are still generally reluctant to engage with.
- Translating works of the Kemalist legacy into Persian and Arabic, toning down their Turkish-oriented quality to render them more suitable to a non-Turkish audience, and adding up-to-date introductions to make them suitable to the twenty-first century.
- Extending the domestic institutions for spreading the laic ideas of Kemalism to the outside world and subsidizing them heavily. Embassies should make these materials widely available, either free or at minimal cost. Radio should broadcast them, conferences study them. Other initiatives (sponsoring writers with a Kemalist outlook, establishing film competitions) would further spread their impact.
- Accepting the sacrifices in both treasury and blood that standing up to the Islamists will involve. The Islamists observe few rules, so their opponents should be prepared for vicious responses. Turkish reluctance to confront this radical movement is understandable—no one wants to butt heads with fanatics.

As the only country that can provide a convincing alternative to the militant Islamic vision, Turkey carries a heavy burden. This said, resisting the Islamists does not increase Turkey's risks: it only brings them forward by a few years. The Islamists already intend to eliminate the Kemalist tradition and turn Turkey into an Islamic Republic; standing up to them doesn't change their course of action, only speeds up their schedule, perhaps compelling them to do combat with Turkey before they are ready for it. If Islamists are not dealt with now, they will become even more dangerous in the future.

The Islamists' great strength lies in their energy and determination; their weakness lies in the ugliness of their sentiments and the hopelessness of their approach. In the end, they are bound to lose the cultural battle, but (again, as in the case of Marxism-Leninism) the process could take decades and cause much damage.

Turks seem not yet to realize what the mullahs know: that militant Islam will rise or fall depending on what Turks do, and that Iran and Turkey are therefore engaged in a mortal combat. Much hinges on whether or not Turks wake up in time to hold their own.

Which Will Survive?

To make this conflict more complicated, both Iran and Turkey are vulnerable to the other's ideology. In Iran, rule by the Islamic Republic since 1979 has left much of the population thoroughly disillusioned and some observers of Iran speculate that the imposition of Islamic strictures for all these years could lead to a radical rejection of the faith in the future. Laurent Lamote (the pseudonym of a French scholar) wrote in 1994 that "Islam is not longer seen as a subversive force but as the official ideology. . . . As domestic problems have worsened, more and more religious officials have realized that, were the government to fall, it would pull the clergy down with it. Islam would thus be endangered in Iran. The pragmatists in power are, therefore, trying to gradually laicize at least the administration."[10]

Writing under a pseudonym (note the proliferation of false names; honest analysts of Iran worry for their safety), Reuel Gerecht noted that "The excesses of marrying religious principle to power have exhausted and impoverished the nation [of Iran]. Political clerics and Islamic militancy must both start to retreat." Gerecht goes further, discerning in the detritus of the Islamic republic the victory of its arch enemy: "By depicting the Islamic revival as a rejection of Western culture, the leaders of Islamic militancy have set themselves up for an awful fall. They may have quite unintentionally helped trigger a post-militant Islamic tidal wave of American culture throughout the Middle East."[11]

To prevent this dire outcome, some lower-ranking mullahs are abandoning the government, even turning against it, a development that obviously carries potentially major implications for regime stability. (It is vaguely reminiscent of the workers' turn against the workers' paradise in Poland over a decade earlier.)

If Iran is moving away from militant Islam, Turkey is rushing in that very direction, led by Necmettin Erbakan—Turkey's leading politician and former prime minister—his associates, and their variously named political parties. Their success results from a splintered political scene and their persuasive answers to the country's problems. The most successful of these militant Islamic parties, *Refah Partisi* (Welfare Party), did so very well in the March 1994 municipal elections; it not only won the mayoral positions in Istanbul, Ankara, and twenty-two provinces but emerged as the single most popular political party in Turkey.

Turkish Islamists have great ambitions; indeed, they hope to pick up where the Iranian revolution left off. Refah's secretary general, Oğuzhan Asıltürk, talked of an "excitement that will spread around the Islamic world when Refah comes to power in Turkey. Refah will be the support, the fulcrum around which the other Muslim countries will gather and reorganize."[12] Others agreed. Abdurahman Alamoudi of the American Muslim Council in Washington, D.C., said that a Turkey with Refah in power would set an example to all Muslim countries.[13]

The Islamic revolution had a further effect in Turkey, creating a division between the old-style, within-the-system Islamists who worked with the state and the new, more radical ones who reject the state. This difference came to be symbolized by a willingness to attend mosque services on Fridays: the former did, the latter did not (and so came to be known as *cumasızlar*, the "anti-Friday ones"). In more recent years, while the two groups have found common ground (Refah moved in the radicals' direction) and Iranian influence faded somewhat, Iran remains a powerful force in Turkey, a country where the Islamists "have adopted Iran as their model for imposing social and political reform on the Turkish state."[14]

In a sense, the question is, which state will outlast the other:

whether Turkey turns to militant Islam faster or slower than Iran leaves it. The survivor can expect to have great influence over the future course of the Muslim world. Unfortunately, Western states are not making it easy for Turkey to win this contest.

The West's Role

In the end, the great ideological battle of the post–Cold War era will be decided by Muslims, not by outsiders. The militant Islamic challenge will succeed or fail depending on what its adherents and its opponents do. Still, the West is an important bystander that can significantly affect the outcome of the confrontation between Iran and Turkey.

Western European states should dwell less on Turkey's problems, its human rights abuses in particular, and more on its successes. This does not mean abandoning concern about torture in Turkey, the burnings of villages, or other barbarisms; those must always be condemned and worked against. But such efforts must be taken in context; it does no good to work against the Turkish republic so that it falls and is replaced by something far more vicious. Turkey has the best government in the Muslim world. So, even as one criticizes Ankara, let the state also be celebrated as a success story and as a model which the Muslim world would do well to emulate.

Finally, the European Union (EU) should brush aside the petty Greek maneuvering and German nativism to accept Turkey not only in a customs union but as a full-fledged member of the club. To do so has not just practical but also symbolic meaning. Even the most Western-oriented Turks despair at being shunned by the EU, seeing this as confirmation of their second-class status. As one Turkish commentator bitterly noted in 1995: "When communism ceased to be a threat, the changing balances in the [Atlantic] alliance brought about a return to the system that existed prior to communism. Christian enemies made brotherly peace; they forgave each other and again recalled their common enemy, Islam. Actually, this memory had never been forgotten; it had merely been shelved for a while."[15] Letting Turkey into the EU will cut down on these unpleasant suspicions.

As for the United States, to understand its interest in the Turkish-Iranian confrontation means appreciating Turkey's importance. Formally allied to Washington and proud of its Western face, striving to be modern, democratic, and capitalist, Turkey is a model the West hopes other Muslim countries will emulate. The trouble is, Americans tend not to appreciate Turkey. As a country neither wholly European nor wholly Middle Eastern, it confuses. As a state not prone to war, it attracts unduly little attention. As the historic enemy of Christendom ("the present terror of the world" was how Richard Knolles described the Ottoman Empire in 1604 in his *Generall Historie of the Turkes*),[16] Turkey suffers from a bad name, one which its current adversaries, the Greeks and the Armenians, do everything to perpetuate. In the process, whether intentional or not, they are aiding the mullahs.

The U.S. government should use its moral weight, military might, economic strength, and its diplomacy to encourage the Turks to stand strong. Washington can pressure the European Union to accept Turkey as a full-fledged member; signal Moscow how seriously it takes Ankara's concerns in the Balkans, Caucasus, and Central Asia; coordinate Iraq policy more closely with the Turks; and, of course, let the Turks know, again and again, that we stand by them in their travails with Tehran.

It is obviously in the American interest to do all possible to ensure that Islamists not destabilize Turkey. But beyond interest, that is also a responsibility. After standing loyally with the West through four decades of the Cold War, Turkish leaders have become psychologically dependent on American backing. As in Western Europe, the protracted conflict left Turkey quite unprepared for autonomous decision making; the leaders look to Washington for signals and prompts. U.S. officials would be remiss not to provide these.

In an era when immigration and militant Islam spur some of the greatest tensions in Western Europe, it will no doubt be hard to find much enthusiasm in France to increase links to Turkey. In the 1990s, during an era of American quasi-isolationism, it was hard to find much spirit in the United States for increasing links to Turkey. But in both cases the stakes are high. Much also hinges on whether or not the West wakes up in time. In the end, "The West needs to make a preference which line it wants to see [succeed]," says Turkey's former prime minister Tansu Çiller, "the Turkish model or the Iranian one."[17] The choice is there; and it is stark and unavoidable.

4

DO MODERATE
ISLAMISTS EXIST?

I n early February 1995, newspapers around the world featured a photograph taken in Cairo which showed, for the first time ever, the prime minister of Israel standing side by side with the king of Jordan, the chairman of the Palestine Liberation Organization, and the president of Egypt.

These gentlemen ostensibly met to discuss the faltering peace process between the Arabs and Israel. Yet this unprecedented event of an Israeli leader in conclave with Arab colleagues sent another signal too: Four leaders who shared a common problem—militant Islam—were ready to work together to deal with it. According to one account of the meeting, Yitzhak Rabin said that Israelis were the target of the militant Islamic attacks. Arafat jumped in and said, "Me too. They have threatened my life." At that point, Mubarak and Husayn both nodded their heads and said they too had personally been threatened by the radicals.[1]

The photograph neatly symbolized a great shift taking place in Middle Eastern politics. Arab-Israeli issues remain formally the main item on the agenda, but militant Islamic violence has become the greatest worry of nearly every government in the region. This shift marks a deep transformation for the Middle East. Through six decades, a politician's stance on the Arab-Israeli conflict defined more than anything else his standing in Middle East politics. No longer. In 1995, his position on militant Islam, the single greatest threat to the region, primarily determined his allies and his enemies.

This raises several issues: Why Middle Eastern leaders feel so threatened by militant Islamic movements; the possibility that they are exaggerating the threat; and what stance the U.S. government has adopted to deal with it.

A Variety of Threats

Though anchored in religious creed, militant Islam is a radical utopian movement closer in spirit to other such movements such as communism and fascism than to traditional religion. By nature antidemocratic and aggressive, anti-Semitic and anti-Western, it has great plans. Indeed, spokesmen for militant Islam see their movement standing in direct competition to Western civilization and challenging it for global supremacy. Let's look at each of these elements in more detail.

Radical utopian schema. Outside their own movement, Islamists see every existing political system in the Muslim world as deeply compromised, corrupt, and mendacious. As one of their spokesmen put it as long ago as 1951, "there is no one town in the whole world where Islam is observed as enjoined by Allah, whether in politics, economics or social matters."[2] Implied here is that Muslims true to God's message must reject the status quo and build wholly new institutions.

To build a new Muslim society, Islamists proclaim their intent to do whatever they must; they openly flaunt an extremist sensibility. "There are no such terms as compromise and surrender in the Islamic cultural lexicon," a spokesman for Hamas declares.[3] If that means destruction and death for the enemies of true Islam, so be it. Hizbullah's spiritual leader, Muhammad Husayn Fadlallah, concurs: "As Islamists," he says, "we seek to revive the Islamic inclination by all means possible."[4]

Totalitarian. Seeing Islam as the basis of a political system touching every aspect of life, Islamists are totalitarian. Whatever the problem, "Islam is the solution." In their hands, Islam is transformed from a personal faith into a ruling system that knows no constraints. They scrutinize the Qur'an and other texts for hints about Islamic medicine, Islamic economics, and Islamic statecraft, all with an eye to creating a total system for adherents and corresponding total power for leaders. Islamists are revolutionary in outlook, extremist in behavior, totalitarian in ambition.

Militant Islam differs in the details from other utopian ideologies but it closely resembles them in scope and ambition. Like communism and fascism, it offers a vanguard ideology; a complete program to improve man and create a new society; complete control over that society; and cadres ready, even eager, to spill blood.

Antidemocratic. In the spirit of Hitler and Allende, who exploited the democratic process to reach power, the Islamists are actively taking part in elections; like the earlier figures, too, they have done dismayingly well. Islamists swept municipal elections in Algeria in 1991 and won the mayoralties of Istanbul and Ankara in 1994. They have also had success in the Lebanese and Jordanian elections.

Once in power, the question arises whether they would remain democrats. There is not a lot of hard evidence on this point, Iran being the only case at hand where Islamists in power have made promises about democracy. (In all other militant Islamic regimes—Pakistan, Afghanistan, the Sudan—military leaders have dominated.) Ayatollah Khomeini promised real democracy (an assembly "based on the votes of the people")[5] as he took power. Once in charge, he partially fulfilled this pledge: Iran's elections are hotly disputed and parliament does have real authority. But there's an important catch: parliamentarians must subscribe to the principles of the Islamic revolution. Only candidates (including non-Muslims) who subscribe to the official ideology may run for office. The regime in Tehran thus fails the key test of democracy, for it cannot be voted out of power.

Judging by their statements, other Islamists are likely to offer even less democracy than the Iranians. Indeed, statements by militant Islamic spokesmen from widely dispersed countries suggest an open disdain for popular sovereignty.[6] Ahmad Nawfal, a Jordanian leader of the Muslim Brethren—the oldest, largest, most consequential militant Islamic group—said that "If we have a choice between democracy and dictatorship, we choose democracy. But if it's between Islam and democracy, we choose Islam."[7] Hadi Hawang of PAS in Malaysia made the same point more bluntly: "I am not interested in democracy, Islam is not democracy, Islam is Islam."[8] Or, in the famous (if not completely verified) words of 'Ali Belhadj, a leader of Algeria's Islamic Salvation Front (FIS), "When we are in power, there will be no more elections because God will be ruling."[9] Apologists for militant Islam like to portray it as a force for democracy, but this ignores the key pattern that, as Martin Kramer points out, "Islamists are more likely to reach less militant positions because of their exclusion from power. . . . Weakness moderates Islamists."[10]

Antimoderate. Militant Islam is also aggressive. Like other revolutionaries, very soon after taking power Islamists try to expand at the expense of neighbors. The Khomeinists almost immediately sought to overthrow moderate (meaning here non-Islamist) Muslim regimes in Bahrain and Egypt. For six years (1982–88) after Saddam Husayn wanted to quit, they kept the war going against Iraq; and they occupied three small but strategic islands in the Persian Gulf near the Straits of Hormuz. The Iranian terrorist campaign has reached from the Philippines to Argentina. The mullahs are building an arsenal that includes missiles, submarines, and the infrastructure for unconventional weaponry. In like spirit, Afghan Islamists have invaded Tajikistan. Their Sudanese counterparts reignited the civil war against Christians and animists in the south and, for good measure, stirred up trouble at Halayib, a disputed territory on Sudan's border with Egypt.

So aggressive are Islamists that they attack neighbors even before taking power. In early February 1995, as Algeria's FIS was fighting to survive, some of its members assaulted a police outpost along the Tunisian border, killing six officers and seizing their weapons.

Anti-Semitic. Consistent with Hannah Arendt's observation about totalitarian movements necessarily being anti-Semitic, Islamists bristle with hostility toward Jews. They accept virtually every Christian myth about Jews seeking control of the world, then add their own twist about Jews destroying Islam. The Hamas charter sees Jews as the ultimate enemy: they "have used their wealth to gain control of the world media, news agencies, the press, broadcasting stations, etc. . . . They were behind the French revolution and the Communist revolution. . . . They instigated World War I. . . . They caused World War II. . . . It was they who gave the instructions to establish the United

Nations and the Security Council to replace the League of Nations, in order to rule over the world through them."[11] Islamists discuss Jews with the most violent and crude metaphors. Khalil Kuka, a founder of Hamas, said that "God brought the Jews together in Palestine not to benefit from a homeland but to dig their grave there and save the world from their pollution."[12] Tehran's ambassador to Turkey said that "the Zionists are like the germs of cholera that will affect every person in contact with them."[13] Such venom is common coin in Islamist discourse.

Nor is violence confined to words. Especially since the September 1993 White House signing of the Israel-PLO Declaration of Principles, Hamas and Islamic Jihad have repeatedly targeted Israelis and other Jews, killing hundreds of Israelis.

Anti-Western. Long unnoticed by most Westerners, war was unilaterally declared on Europe and the United States by Ayatollah Khomeini in 1979. Islamists are responding to \ what they see as a centuries-long conspiracy by the West to destroy Islam, inspired by what they perceive as a Crusader-style hatred of Islam and an imperialist greed for Muslim resources. The West in turn has for centuries tried to neuter Islam. It has done so by luring Muslims away from Islam through both its vulgar culture—blue jeans, hamburgers, television shows, rock music—and its higher culture—fashion clothes, French cuisine, universities, classical music. In this spirit, a Pakistani militant Islamic group in 1995 deemed Michael Jackson and Madonna "cultural terrorists" and called for the two Americans to be brought to trial in Pakistan.[14] As Bernard Lewis notes, "It is the Tempter, not the Adversary, that Khomeini feared in America, the seduction and enticement of the American way of life rather than the hostility of American power."[15] Or, in Khomeini's own words: "We are not afraid of economic sanctions or military intervention. What we are afraid of is Western universities."[16]

Fearful of Western culture's hold over their own people, Islamists respond with vitriolic attacks denigrating Western civilization. It is crassly materialist, says 'Adil Husayn, a leading Egyptian writer, to see man "as nothing but an animal whose major concern is to fill his belly."[17] To dissuade Muslims from Westernizing, they portray the West's way of life as a form of disease. Kalim Siddiqui, the Iranian polemicist in Great Britain, deems Western civilization "not a civilization but a sickness." And not just any sickness, but "a plague and a pestilence."[18] Belhadj of Algeria's FIS ridicules Western civilization as "syphilization."[19]

Capitalizing on this hatred, militant Islamic groups have since 1983 resorted to anti-Western violence. Americans have been targeted in two bombings of the U.S. Embassy in Beirut, the Marine barracks in Beirut, the embassy in Kuwait, the World Trade Center in 1993, and the Pentagon and World Trade Center towers in 2001. Lesser incidents included the killing of American passengers on several airliners, many hostages seized in Lebanon, and several fatal incidents on U.S. territory. We can only guess how many incidents (like the plan to go after the Holland tunnel and other New York landmarks) were foiled; or how many lie yet in store.

Not willing to co-exist. Hatred against the West inspires a struggle with it for cultural supremacy. Islamists see the rivalry as cultural, not military. "It is a struggle of cultures," a Muslim Brethren leader explains, "not one between strong countries and weak countries. We are sure that the Islamic culture will triumph."[20] This victory will be achieved not by producing better music or coming up with a cure for cancer. Siddiqui vividly makes clear that Islam will triumph, rather, through will and steel: "American GIs clutching photos of their girl friends would be no match for the soldiers of Islam clutching copies of the Qur'an and seeking *shahadah* [martyrdom]."[21]

Islamists do not restrict their sights to the Muslim portion of the world's population but aspire to universal dominance. Siddiqui announces this goal somewhat obliquely: "Deep down in its historical consciousness the West also knows that the Islamic civilization will ultimately replace it as the world's dominant civilization."[22] Men of action share the same ambition. The gang that bombed the World Trade Center in 1993 had great plans. Omar Abdel Rahman, the blind Egyptian sheikh who guided them, was convicted of seditious conspiracy, that is, trying to overthrow the government of the United States. However bizarre this sounds, it makes sense from Abdel Rahman's perspective. As he sees it, the *mujahidin* in Afghanistan brought down the Soviet Union; so, one down and one to go. Not understanding the robustness of a mature democracy, Abdel Rahman apparently thought a campaign of terrorist incidents would so unsettle Americans that he and his group could take over. A Tehran newspaper hinted at how the scenario would unfold when it portrayed the February 1993 explosion at the World Trade Center as proof that the U.S. economy was "exceptionally vulnerable." More than that, the bombing would "have an adverse effect on Clinton's plans to rein in the economy."[23] Some Islamists, as we have since seen, really do think they can take on the United States.

U.S. Policy: The Record

Troublemaking by Islamists on U.S. territory pales, however, in comparison to the danger they pose in the Middle East; their seizure of power in just a few cantons there would likely create a new political order in the region, with disastrous consequences. Israel would probably face a return to its unhappy condition of days past, beleaguered by terrorism and surrounded by enemy states. Civil unrest in oil-producing regions could lead to a dramatic run-up in the cost of energy. Rogue states, already numerous in the Middle East (Iran, Iraq, Syria, Sudan, Libya), would multiply, leading to arms races, more international terrorism, and wars, lots of wars. Massive refugee outflows to Europe could well prompt a reactionary political turn that would greatly increase the already worrying appeal of neofascists such as Jean-Marie Le Pen, who won 18 percent of the vote in a French presidential election.

What steps did the Clinton administration take to protect Americans from such prospects? On the plus side, it made efforts to isolate and weaken Iran; unfortunately, no other industrial power agreed to commit itself in like fashion, virtually negating the impact of U.S. sanctions. Washington also focused world attention on atrocities committed by the Sudanese regime.

But if the Clinton administration was sound on Islamists already in power, it had terribly misguided ideas about Islamists in opposition. Rather than oppose them, it initiated dialogue with the Palestinian, Egyptian, and Algerian movements, and perhaps others. There was no reason to meet with these groups. But as former President Clinton, R. James Woolsey, Peter Tarnoff, Martin Indyk, and others explained, American policy opposed terrorism, not militant Islam. Most Islamists were seen as decent people, serious individuals espousing (in the words of Robert Pelletreau, Jr., then assistant secretary of state for the Middle East) "a renewed emphasis on traditional values."[24] So long as a group had no connections to violent activities, Washington encouraged it to pursue the political process.

The conflict, said these officials, was only with Islamists who resorted to violence. They didn't even accept that these violent elements were good Muslims, but portrayed them as criminals exploiting faith for their own malign purposes. "Islamic extremism uses religion to cover its ambitions," said national security adviser Anthony Lake.[25] In other words, those who use violence in the name of Islam are not just marginal to the militant Islamic movement; they are frauds whose activities go against its praiseworthy aims.

This distinction between good and bad Islamists leads to an important policy implication: that the U.S. government should work with the former and against the latter. Even as Islamists accused the United States and Israel of the most horrible crimes and announced their hatred of all things Western, the American government decided that these were people with whom it can do business. Hence the political relations with Hamas, Egypt's Muslim Brethren, and FIS.

Bad Advice

It would seem that the U.S. government received some bad advice. In part, the blame for the misguided U.S. policy had to fall on the shoulders of the usual suspects—academic specialists. While in the usual course of events the executive branch prefers not to rely on advice from outsiders, when it lacks expertise it does turn to specialists for help. Islam is one such issue. Since the Iranian revolution of 1978–79, U.S. diplomats have leaned on scholars of Islam to help them develop policy.

With almost a single voice, these specialists advised the government not to worry. Some in the mid-1990s said the militant Islamic challenge had faded. The usually sensible Fouad Ajami reported that "the pan-Islamic millennium has run its course; the Islamic decade is over."[26] Likewise, Olivier Roy, the influential French specialist, announced in 1992 that "the Islamic revolution is behind us."[27] Other analysts went further and said it never posed any danger in the first place. John Esposito, probably the most important of the academic advisers, published a book in 1992 dispelling the notion of an "Islamic threat."[28] Leon Hadar, an Israeli associated with the Cato Institute, dubbed the whole topic of militant Islam a "contrived threat."[29]

During the Clinton era, specialists posited at least two benefits to be gained from American dialogue with the Islamists. First, they assumed Islamists are bound to reach power (an assumption no less dubious than like predictions a generation ago about the inevitability of a socialist triumph) and counseled establishing early and friendly relations with them. Second, the specialists presented militant Islam as a democratic force that can help stabilize politics in the region, and so they deserve U.S. support. Graham Fuller, formerly of the Central Intelligence Agency and now at RAND, made the case for militant Islam as a healthy development: it "is politically tamable . . . [and] represents ultimate political progress toward greater democracy and popular government."[30] The Egyptian scholar Saad Eddin Ibrahim actually went so far as to suggest that Islamists "may evolve into something akin to the Christian Democrats in the West.[31]

The trouble with all this is that the notion of good and bad Islamists has no basis in fact. Yes, militant Islamic groups, ideologies, and tactics differ from each other in many ways—Sunni and Shi'i, working through the system and not, using violence and not—but every one of them is inherently extremist. Militant Islamic groups have evolved a division of labor, with some seeking power through politics and others through intimidation. In Turkey, for example, the Nurcus and the Necmettin Erbakan's Refah Partisi accept the democratic process, while the Süleymancıs and the Milli Görüş do not. In Algeria, much evidence points to seemingly more moderate FIS coordinating with the murderous Armed Islamic Group (GIA).

Non-Islamists understand that, by aspiring to create a new man and a new society, all Islamists in the end must work to overthrow the existing order. Non-Islamist Muslims know this because they have seen the gleam in the eyes of Islamists, heard their rhetoric, fended off their depredations, endured their murders. Deemed traitors, non-Islamists like Salman Rushdie or Taslima Nasrin are first in the line of fire, even ahead of Jews or Christians. They have tirelessly tried to educate Westerners on the subject of militant Islam, with dismayingly little response. As the militant Algeria secularist Saïd Sadi explains: "A moderate Islamist is someone who does not have the means of acting ruthlessly to seize power immediately."[32] The anti-Islamist president of Tunisia pointed out that the "final aim" of all Islamists is the same: "the construction of a totalitarian, theocratic state."[33] Osmane Bencherif, the then Algerian ambassador to Washington, echoed this sentiment: "It is misguided policy to distinguish between moderate and extremist Islamists. The goal of all is the same: to construct a pure Islamic state, which is bound to be a theocracy and totalitarian."[34] Perhaps the strongest statement comes from Mohammad Mohaddessin, director of international relations for the People's Mojahedin of Iran, a leading opposition force: "Moderate fundamentalists do not exist. . . . It's like talking about a moderate Nazi."[35]

Approaches to Militant Islam

If moderate Islamists do not exist, then the U.S. government needs a new policy toward militant Islamic opposition groups. But before proposing specific steps, four premises must be aired: The justification for having a policy in the first place; the need to draw a distinction between Islam and militant Islam; the burden on Americans to prove themselves; and the reason to work with the left against the right.

Justifying a policy toward militant Islam. At first glance, militant Islam appears to present a challenge unprecedented in the U.S. experience. The U.S. government—a determinedly secular entity—cannot formulate a policy toward a religion. But a closer look at militant Islam reveals the solution. Yes, Islam is indeed a faith, but its militant variant is a form of political ideology. Formulating a policy toward it is akin to a policy toward fascism or Marxism-Leninism.

Militant Islam is not Islam. It is necessary once again to distinguish between Islam and militant Islam. Islam is an ancient faith and capacious civilization; militant Islam a narrow, aggressive twentieth-century ideological movement. Distinguishing between Islam and militant Islam has two important benefits. First, it permits the U.S. government to adopt a sensible attitude toward both. A secular government cannot have an opinion on a religion, especially when it is practiced by significant numbers of its own citizens. But it most assuredly can have an opinion on an ideological movement that is hostile to its interests and values. Second, this distinction makes it possible to ally with non-Islamists. Many of them, including those quoted here, are fearless speakers of truth. Their insights guide those of us out-side the Islamic faith; their courage inspires us; and—when the Islamists or their apologists accuse us of being "anti-Islam"—their agreement legitimates us.

Prove will. Islamists see the West, for all its apparent strength, as weak-willed; it reminds them of the shah's regime in Iran—rich, vain-glorious, corrupt, and decayed. 'Ali Akbar Mohtashemi, the Iranian hard-liner, disdained the United States as "a hollow paper tiger with no power or strength."[36] To be sure, it disposes of wealth and missiles, but these cannot stand up to faith and resolve. Islamists don't even bother to hide their contempt for Western countries. Iran's Ayatollah Ahmad Jannati, for example, publicly asserted in 1993 that "The British today are on their death bed. Other Western countries too are in a similar state."[37]

Such contempt obliges the West to act even more strongly and decisively than otherwise might be the case. Tough positions are needed both as an end in themselves and to show that we are not the flabby degenerates of the militant Islamic imagination. The U.S. gov-ernment has to prove, however absurd it may sound, that Americans are not weaklings addicted to pornography and drugs. Quite the con-trary, they are a healthy people, resolute and ready to protect them-selves and their ideals. Islamists are so enthralled by their own views of the West that these simplistic points have to be made over and over again. Soheib Bencheikh, a former Islamist himself, explained that the West must give them some of their own medicine: "To fight the fun-damentalists one has to have been a bit so oneself."[38]

Better the left than the right. Until 1990, the left had a global network that threatened American interests, while the right consisted of isolated and mostly weak regimes. It incontrovertibly made sense to work with the friendly tyrants of the right against the Marxist-Leninist complex on the left. Since 1990, these roles have, roughly speaking, been reversed, especially in the Muslim world. Today, the left consists of the odd shipwreck of a regime: the National Liberation Front (FLN) in Algeria or a General Dostam in Afghanistan. These governments stand for no ideas or visions; their leaders merely want to stay in power. However corrupt, however nasty, they pose fewer dangers to the Mid-dle East or to the United States than do their militant Islamic coun-

terparts. Further, as mere tyrannies, they have a better chance of evolv-
ing in the right direction than do intensely ideological regimes.

Instead, it is the right, made up mainly of Islamists, which has built
what Prime Minister Rabin of Israel called "an international infrastructure."[39] The network sends out practical aid; for example, the Iranians are reliably said to provide arms, money, cadres, political
counseling, military training, diplomatic support, and intelligence to
the Sudan. This also provides important psychological support.
Islamists feel much stronger for being part of a surging international
alliance, somewhat as Marxist-Leninists did in previous years. This
new network, like that old one, has the United States of America in
its sights. For these reasons, the U.S. government should—carefully,
intelligently, selectively—join with the left against the right whenever
circumstances suggest doing so.

What to Do

Turning to specific policy recommendations, the overriding goal of
U.S. policy must be to keep Islamists from seizing power.[40] Once they
take over, as the mullahs in Tehran have so clearly shown, they will
hold on tenaciously. Here, then, are some ideas on preventing Islamists
from taking power.

Do not engage in official or public dialogue: It would almost
always be better not to work with militant Islamic groups, the only
exceptions being those of dire necessity. Dialogue sends signals that
undercut existing governments without bringing any gains. President
Husni Mubarak of Egypt counseled Washington along these lines. "To
engage in dialogue with radical fundamentalists is a waste of time."[41]
Actually, it is worse than that because engaging in such dialogue works
both to legitimize Islamists and to confirm their belief in Western
weakness. The U.S. government ought not to talk to militant Islamic
groups, much less ally with them; meetings with Palestinian, Egyptian,
and Algeria Islamists should stop.

Do not appease: As a former CIA specialist on Iran noted, "fundamentalism is a war fought primarily in Muslim imaginations. Private
and collective dreams are not amenable to negotiations."[42] Like other
totalitarians, Islamists respond to appeasement by demanding more

concessions. Saïd Sadi, the Algerian secularist, advised his fellow countrymen not to give in to the Islamists, "because if we made the slightest concession, all our freedoms would be threatened."[43] Again, Mubarak has it right: "I can assure you," he says, militant Islamic groups will "never be on good terms with the United States."[44] A change in foreign policy will not suffice because Islamists despise the West not for what it does but for who it is. Short of adopting their brand of Islam, there is no hope of satisfying them.

Do not help Islamists: With the Cold War now well behind, this goal should be easier to achieve. To get Pakistani permission to arm the Afghan *mujahidin* against Soviet forces in the 1980s, the CIA had disproportionately to supply the Islamists. Washington did as bidden, and rightly so, for it meant aligning with the lesser evil against the greater one. Now that militant Islam is the greater evil—or, at least, the more dynamic one—this conundrum is less likely to arise. It is hard to imagine any scenario today in which the U.S. government should help Islamists.

Press militant Islamic states to reduce aggressiveness: The West should pressure militant Islamic states—Iran, Sudan—to reduce their aggressiveness and the aid they supply to ideological brethren in such countries as Turkey, Jordan, Egypt, and Algeria, as well as to Palestinians. The U.S. government and its allies have a wide range of commercial and diplomatic tools at their disposal with which to confront militant Islamic aggression, with a military option always reserved in the background if needed.

Support those confronting militant Islam: Governments in combat with the Islamists deserve U.S. help. We should stand by the non-Islamists, even when that means accepting, within limits, strong-arm tactics (Pakistan, Egypt, the PLO), the aborting of elections (in Algeria), and deportations (Israel). It also means supporting Turkey in its conflict with Iran and India against Pakistan on the Kashmir issue.

The same applies to institutions and individuals. As a curtain of silence and terror comes down around them, non-Islamists in the Middle East are losing their voice. To be celebrated by Americans would greatly boost their morale and prestige; receiving funds from the U.S. government and private sources would do much good. Again, this means working with some less than Jeffersonian organizations, notably the People's Mojahedin of Iran, despite the controversy that would probably arouse.

Urge gradual democratization: Finally, the U.S. government must be very careful how it presses for democracy. Unfortunately, it has become common to identify democracy with elections, leading to a single-minded emphasis on elections as an end in themselves. In fact, by "democracy," most Americans include liberty and a hefty set of political precepts, not just a means to elect a government.

Quick elections solve little. Often they make matters worse by strengthening militant Islamic elements, these usually being the best organized and the citizenry not being ready to make fully informed electoral decisions. Instead, Washington should press for more modest goals: political participation, the rule of law (including an independent judiciary), freedom of speech and religion, property rights, minority rights, and the right to form voluntary organizations (especially political parties). The goal, in short, is the formation of a civil society. Elections are not the start of the democratic process but its capstone and finale, the signal that a civil society has indeed come into existence. As Judith Miller of *The New York Times* summarized this point in 1993, it should be "Elections tomorrow and civil society today."[45]

5

DOES POVERTY

CAUSE MILITANT ISLAM?

W hat causes some Muslims to turn to militant Islam?

Most analysts assume that socioeconomic distress is the key factor. In the aftermath of September 11, 2001, for example, some analysts noted the poverty of Afghanistan and concluded that herein lay the problem. Susan Sachs of *The New York Times* writes that "Predictably, the disappointed youth of Egypt and Saudi Arabia turn to religion for comfort."[1] Jessica Stern of Harvard University finds that the United States "can no longer afford to allow states to fail" but had better devote a much higher priority to health, education and economic development, "or new Osama [bin Laden]s will continue to arise."[2] Others more colorfully advocated bombarding Afghanistan with foodstuffs rather than explosives.

The evidence, however, does not support this expectation. A survey finds that militant Islam is not a response to poverty or impoverishment; not only are Chad and Iraq not hotbeds of militant Islam, but militant Islam has often surged in countries experiencing rapid economic growth. The factors that cause militant Islam to decline or flourish appear to have more to do with issues of identity than with economics.

"All Other Problems Vanish"

The conventional wisdom—that economic stress causes militant Islam and economic growth is needed for it to subside—has a lot of well-placed adherents.

To begin with, some Islamists themselves accept this connection. In the words of a fiery sheikh from Cairo, "Islam is the religion of bad times."[3] A Hamas leader in Gaza, Mahmud az-Zahar, says that "It is enough to see the poverty-stricken outskirts of Algiers or the refugee camps in Gaza to understand the factors that nurture the strength of the Islamic Resistance Movement."[4] In this spirit, militant Islamic organizations offer a wide range of welfare benefits in an effort to attract followers.[5] They also promote what they call an "Islamic economy" as the panacea for all problems facing Muslims, a third way which offers a far more just and productive path to financial well-being than do either the capitalist or socialist routes. This ambition has spanned a large literature and many institutions since the mid-1970s.[6]

Secular Muslims stress militant Islam's resulting from poverty as an article of faith. Süleyman Demirel, the former Turkish president, says that "As long as there is poverty, inequality, injustice, and repressive political systems, militant Islamic tendencies will grow in the world."[7] Turkey's former prime minister Tansu Çiller finds that Islamists did so well in the 1994 elections because "People reacted to the economy."[8] The chief of Jordanian Army Intelligence holds that "Economic development may solve almost all of our problems [in the Middle East]." Including militant Islam? he was asked. Yes. "The moment a person is in a good economic position, has a job, and can support his family, all other problems vanish."[9]

Leftists in the Middle East concur, interpreting the militant Islamic resurgence as "a sign of pessimism. Because people are desperate, they are resorting to the supernatural."[10] Social scientists sign on too; Hooshang Amirahmadi, an academic of Iranian origins, argues that "the roots of Islamic radicalism must be looked for outside the religion, in the real world of cultural despair, economic decline, political oppression, and spiritual turmoil in which most Muslims find themselves today."[11]

Western politicians find the militant-Islam-from-poverty argument compelling. For former president Bill Clinton, "These forces of reaction feed on disillusionment, poverty and despair," and he advocates a socioeconomic remedy: "spread prosperity and security to all."[12] Edward Djerejian, once a top State Department figure, reports that "political Islamic movements are to an important degree rooted in worsening socio-economic conditions in individual countries."[13] Martin Indyk, another former ranking diplomat, warns that those wishing to reduce the appeal of militant Islam must first solve the economic, social, and political problems that constitute its breeding grounds.[14]

Militant Islam reflects "the economic, political, and cultural disappointment" of Muslims, according to Klaus Kinkel of Germany, then foreign minister of Germany.[15] Former interior minister Charles Pasqua of France finds that this phenomenon "has coincided with despair on the part of a large section of the masses, and young people in particular."[16] Prime Minister Eddie Fenech of Malta draws an even closer tie: "Fundamentalism grows at the same pace as economic problems."[17] Israel's Foreign Minister Shimon Peres flatly asserts that "Fundamentalism's basis is poverty"[18] and that it offers "a way of protesting against poverty, corruption, ignorance, and discrimination."[19]

On occasion, businessmen make investments with an eye to political amelioration. The Virgin Group's chairman, Richard Branson, declared as he opened a large music store in Beirut: "The region will become stable if people invest in it, create jobs and rebuild the countries that need rebuilding, not ignore them."[20]

The academy, with its Marxist disposition and disdain for faith— "religion is not the cause of conflicts but provides a rallying point for conflicts that are basically economic or political"[21]—of course accepts this militant-Islam-from-poverty thesis with near unanimity. Ervand Abrahamian holds that "the behavior of Khomeini and the Islamic Republic has been determined less by scriptural principles than by immediate political, social and economic needs."[22] Ziad Abu-Amr, author of a book on militant Islam (and a member of the Palestine Legislative Council), ascribes a Palestinian turn toward religiosity to "the sombre climate of destruction-war, unemployment, and depression [which] cause people to seek solace, and they're going to Allah."[23]

"Somewhere near the Stratosphere"

The record finds little correlation, however, between economics and militant Islam. Wealth and economics fail as predictors of where militant Islam will be strong and where not.

On the level of individuals, conventional wisdom points to militant Islam attracting the poor, the alienated, and the marginal—yet research finds precisely the opposite to be true. To the extent that economic factors explain who becomes Islamist, they tend to be fairly well off. Take Egypt as a test case. In a 1980 study, the Egyptian social scientist Saad Eddin Ibrahim interviewed Islamists in Egyptian jails and found that the typical member was "young (early twenties), of rural or small-town background, from the middle or lower middle class, with high achievement and motivation, upwardly mobile, with science or engineering education, and from a normally cohesive family." In other words, Ibrahim concluded, these young men were "significantly above the average in their generation"; they were "ideal or model young Egyptians."[24] In a subsequent study, he found that out of thirty-four members of the violent group At-Takfir wa'l-Hijra, fully twenty-one had fathers in the civil service, nearly all of them middle-ranking.[25] More recently, the Canadian Security Intelligence Service found that the leadership of the militant Islamic group Al-Jihad "is largely university educated with middle-class backgrounds."[26] These are not the children of poverty or despair.

Other researchers confirm these findings for Egypt. Galal A. Amin, an economist at the American University in Cairo, in a study on the country's economic troubles, concludes by noting "how rare it is to find examples of religious fanaticism among either the higher or the very lowest social strata of the Egyptian population."[27] When her assistant in Cairo turned Islamist, the journalist Geraldine Brooks tells of her surprise: "I'd assumed that the turn to Islam was the desperate choice of poor people searching for heavenly solace. But Sahar [the assistant] was neither desperate nor poor. She belonged somewhere near the stratosphere of Egypt's meticulously tiered society."[28] And note this account by the talented Hamza Hendawi: In Egypt, "a new breed of preachers in business suits and with cellular phones are attracting increasing numbers of the rich and powerful away from Western lifestyles and into religious conservatism. The modern imams hold their seminars over banquets in some of Cairo's most luxurious homes and in Egypt's seaside resorts to appeal to the wealthy's sense of style and comfort."[29]

What is true of Egypt holds equally true elsewhere: Like fascism and Marxism-Leninism in their heydays, militant Islam attracts highly competent, motivated, and ambitious individuals. Far from being the laggards of society, they are its leaders. Brooks, a much traveled journalist, found Islamists to be "the most gifted" of the youth she encountered. Those "hearing the Islamic call included the students with the most options, not just the desperate cases. . . . They were the elites of the next decade: the people who would shape their nations' future."[30]

Islamists who make the ultimate sacrifice and give up their lives also fit this pattern of financial ease and advanced education. A disproportionate number of terrorists and suicide bombers have higher education, often in engineering and the sciences. This generalization applies equally to the Palestinian suicide bombers attacking Israel and the followers of Osama bin Laden who hijacked the four planes on September 11. In the first case, a researcher found by looking at their profiles that "Economic circumstances did not seem to be a decisive factor. While none of the 16 subjects could be described as well-off, some were certainly struggling less than others."[31] In the second case, as the Princeton historian Sean Wilentz humorously put it, judging by the biographies of the September 11 killers, terrorism is caused by "money, education and privilege."[32]

More generally, Fat'hi ash-Shiqaqi, founding leader of the arch-murderous Islamic Jihad, once commented that "Some of the young people who have sacrificed themselves [in terrorist operations] came from well-off families and had successful university careers."[33] This makes sense, for suicide bombers who hurl themselves against foreign enemies offer their lives not to protest financial deprivation but to change the world.

Those backing militant Islamic organizations also tend to be well off. They come much more from the richer city than the poorer countryside, a fact that Khalid M. Amayreh, a Palestinian journalist, says "refutes the widely-held assumption that Islamist popularity thrives on economic misery."[34] And they come not just from the cities but from the upper ranks. At times, an astonishing one quarter of the membership in Turkey's leading militant Islamic organization, now called the Saadet Party, have been engineers. Indeed, the typical cadre in a militant Islamic party is an engineer in his forties born in a city to parents who had moved from the countryside.[35] Amayreh finds that in the Jordanian parliamentary elections of 1994, the Muslim Brethren did as well in middle-class districts as in poor ones. He generalizes from this that "a substantial majority of Islamists and their supporters come from the middle and upper socio-economic strata."[36]

Martin Kramer, the historian and editor of the *Middle East Quarterly*, goes further. He sees militant Islam as

> the vehicle of counter-elites, people who, by virtue of education and/or income, are potential members of the elite, but who for some reason or another get excluded. Their education may lack some crucial prestige-conferring element; the sources of their wealth may be a bit tainted. Or they may just come from the wrong background. So while they are educated and wealthy, they have a grievance: their ambition is blocked, they cannot translate their socio-economic assets into political clout. Islamism is particularly useful to these people, in part because by its careful manipulation, it is possible to recruit a following among the poor, who make valuable foot-soldiers.

Kramer cites the so-called Anatolian Tigers, businessmen who have had a critical role in backing Turkey's militant Islamic party, as an example of this counter-elite in its purest form.[37]

"Not a Product of Poverty"

The same pattern exists on the level of societies:

- **Wealth does not inoculate against militant Islam.** Kuwaitis enjoy a Western-style income, and owe their state's very existence to the West, yet Islamists generally win the largest bloc of seats in parliament (at present, twenty out of fifty). The West Bank is more prosperous than Gaza, yet militant Islamic groups usually enjoy more popularity in the former than the latter. Mil-

40%

itant Islam flourishes in Western Europe and North America, where Muslims have an economic level higher than the national averages. And of those Muslims, as Khalid Durán points out, Islamists have the generally higher incomes: "In the United States, the difference between Islamists and common Muslims is largely one between haves and have-nots. Muslims have the numbers; Islamists have the dollars."[38]

- **A *flourishing* economy does not inoculate against radical Islam.** Today's militant Islamic movements took off in the 1970s, precisely as oil-exporting states enjoyed extraordinary growth rates. Mu'ammar al-Qadhdhafi developed his eccentric version of proto-militant Islam then; fanatical groups in Saudi Arabia violently seized the Great Mosque of Mecca; and Ayatollah Khomeini took power in Iran (though, admittedly, growth had slacked off several years before he overthrew the shah). In the 1980s, several countries that excelled economically experienced a militant Islamic boom. Jordan, Tunisia, and Morocco all did well economically in the 1990s—as did their militant Islamic movements. Turks under Turgut Özal enjoyed nearly a decade of particularly impressive economic growth even as they joined militant Islamic parties in larger numbers.

- ***Poverty* does not generate militant Islam.** There are many very poor Muslim states, but few of them have become centers of militant Islam—not Bangladesh, not Yemen, and not Niger. As an American specialist rightly notes, "economic despair, the oft-cited source of political Islam's power, is familiar to the Middle East";[39] if militant Islam is connected to poverty, one wonders why it was not a stronger force in years and centuries past, when the region was poorer than today.

- **A *declining* economy does not generate militant Islam.** The 1997 crash in Indonesia and Malaysia did not spur a large turn toward militant Islam. Iranian incomes have gone down by half or more since the Islamic Republic came to power in 1979: yet, far from increasing support for the regime's militant Islamic ideology, impoverishment has caused a massive alienation from Islam. Iraqis have experienced an even more precipitous drop in living standards: Abbas Alnasrawi estimates that per capita income has gone down since 1980 by nearly 90 percent, returning it to where it was in the 1940s.[40] While the country has witnessed an increase in personal piety, militant Islam has not surged, nor is it the leading expression of antiregime sentiments.

Noting these patterns, at least a few observers have drawn the correct conclusion. Saïd Sadi of Algeria flatly rejects the thesis that poverty spurs militant Islam: "I do not adhere to this view that it is widespread unemployment and poverty which produce terrorism."[41] Likewise, Amayreh finds that militant Islam "is not a product or by-product of poverty."[42]

"Providing a Decent Living"

If poverty causes militant Islam, economic growth is the solution. And indeed, in countries as varied as Egypt and Germany, officials argue for a focus on building prosperity and fostering job formation to combat militant Islam. At the height of the crisis in Algeria, during the mid-1990s, when the government pled for Western economic aid, it implicitly threatened that without this, the Islamists would prevail. This interpretation has practical results: for example, the government in Tunisia has taken some steps toward a free market but has not privatized, fearful that the swollen ranks of the unemployed would provide fodder for militant Islamic groups. The same goes for Iran, where Europe and Japan mold policies premised on the notion that their economic ties to the Islamic Republic tame it and discourage military adventurism.

This emphasis on jobs and wealth creation transformed efforts to end the Arab-Israeli conflict during the Oslo era. Prior to 1993, Israelis had insisted that a resolution would require Arabs to recognize that the Jewish state is a permanent fact of life. Achieving that was thought to lie in winning acceptance of the Jewish state and finding mutually acceptable borders. Then, post-1993, came a major shift: increasing Arab prosperity became the goal, hoping that this would diminish the appeal of militant Islam and other radical ideologies. A jump start for the economy was expected to give Palestinians a stake in the peace process, thereby reducing the appeal of Hamas and Islamic Jihad. In this context, Serge Schmemann of *The New York Times* wrote, without citing sources, that Arafat "knows that eradicating militancy will ultimately depend more on providing a decent living than on using force."[43]

The Israeli analyst Meron Benvenisti agreed: Islam's "militant character derived from its being an expression of the deep frustration of the underprivileged. . . . Hamas's rise was directly linked to the wors- ening economic situation and to the accumulated frustration and degradation of the ongoing occupation."[44] As did Shimon Peres: "Islamic terror cannot be fought militarily but by eradicating the hunger which spawns it."[45] Guided by this theory, the Western states and Israel contributed billions of dollars to the Palestinian Authority. Even more remarkably, the Israeli government fought back efforts by pro-Israel activists in the United States to make American aid to the PLO contingent on Arafat's fulfilling his promises to Israel.

At this late date, one hardly needs to point out the falsehood of the Oslo assumptions. Wealth does not resolve hatreds; a prosperous enemy may simply be one more capable of making war. Westerners and Israelis assumed that Palestinians would make economic growth their priority, whereas this was a minor concern of theirs. Instead, what counted were questions of identity and power. So strong is the belief in militant-Islam-from-poverty that Oslo's failure has not managed to dis- credit the faith in prosperity. Thus, in August 2001, a senior Israeli officer endorsed the building of a power station in northern Gaza on the grounds that it would supply jobs, "and every [Palestinian] working is one less pair of hands for Hamas."[46]

If poverty is not the driving force behind militant Islam, several policy implications follow. First, prosperity cannot be looked to as the solution to militant Islam and foreign aid cannot serve as the outside world's main tool to combat it. Second, Westernization also does not provide a solution. To the contrary, many outstanding militant Islamic leaders are not just familiar with Western ways but are expert in them. In particular, a disproportionate number of them have advanced degrees in technology and the sciences.[47] It sometimes seems that Westernization is a route to hating the West. Third, economic growth does not inevitably lead to improved relations with Muslim states. In some cases, for example Algeria, it might help; in others, such as Saudi Arabia, it might hurt.

An Opposite Argument

It could be, quite contrarily, that militant Islam results from wealth rather than poverty. Possibly. First, there is the universal phenomenon that people become more engaged ideologically and active politically only when they have reached a fairly high standard of living. Revolutions take place, it has often been noted, only when a substantial middle class exists. Birthe Hansen, an associate professor at the University of Copenhagen, hints at this when she writes that "the spread of free market capitalism and liberal democracy . . . is probably an important factor behind the rise of political Islam."[48]

Secondly, there is a specifically Islamic phenomenon of the faith having been associated with worldly success. Through history, from the Prophet Muhammad's time to the Ottoman Empire a millennium later, Muslims usually had more wealth and more power than other peoples, and were more literate and healthy. With time, Islamic faith came to be associated with worldly well-being. This connection appears still to hold. For example, as noted in the formulation known as Issawi's Law ("Where there are Muslims, there is oil; the converse is not true"), the 1970s oil boom mainly benefited Muslims; it is probably no coincidence that the current wave of militant Islam began then. Seeing themselves as "pioneers of a movement that is an alternative to Western civilization,"[49] Islamists need a strong economic base. As Galal Amin points out, "There may be a strong relationship between the growth of incomes that have the nature of economic rent and the growth of religious fanaticism."[50]

Conversely, poor Muslims tend to be more impressed by alternative affiliations. Over the centuries, for example, apostasy from the religion has mostly occurred when things go badly. That was the case when Tartars fell under Russian rule or when Sunni Lebanese lost power to the Maronites. It was also the case in 1995 in Iraqi Kurdistan, a region under double embargo and suffering from civil war: "Trying to live their lives in the midst of fire and gunpowder, Kurdish villagers have reached the point where they are prepared to give up anything to save themselves from hunger and death. From their perspective, changing their religion to get a visa to the West is becoming an increasingly more important option."[51] There are, in short, ample rea-

sons for thinking that militant Islam is more an outlook connected to
success than failure.

"The Elevator to Take Power"

When seeking the causes of militant Islam, it is probably more fruitful
to look less to economics and more to other factors. Although material reasons deeply appeal to a Western sensibility,[52] they offer little
guidance in this case. In general, Westerners attribute too many of the
Arab world's problems, observes David Wurmser of the U.S. Department of State, "to specific material issues" such as land and wealth.
This usually means a tendency "to belittle belief and strict adherence
to principle as genuine and dismiss it as a cynical exploitation of the
masses by politicians. As such, Western observers see material issues
and leaders, not the spiritual state of the Arab world, as the heart of
the problem."[53] Or, in Osama bin Laden's ugly but not inaccurate formulation, "Because America worships money, it believes that people
think that way too."[54]

Indeed, if one turns away from the commentators on militant
Islam and instead listens to the Islamists themselves, it quickly
becomes apparent that they rarely talk about prosperity. As Ayatollah
Khomeini memorably put it, "We did not create a revolution to lower
the price of melon." If anything, they look at the consumer society of
the West with distaste. Wajdi Ghunayim, an Egyptian Islamist, sees it
as "the reign of décolleté and moda [fashion],"[55] whose common
denominator is an appeal to the bestial instincts of human nature. Economic strength for Islamists represents not the good life but added
strength to do battle against the West. Money serves to train cadres
and buy weapons, not to buy a bigger house and late-model car. Wealth
is a means, not an end.   *Except for the Taliban*

Means toward what? Toward power. Islamists care less about material strength than about where they stand in the world. They talk
incessantly about this. In a typical statement, 'Ali Akbar Mohtashemi,
the Iranian hard-liner, predicted that "Ultimately Islam will become
the supreme power."[56] Similarly, Mustafa Mashhur, an Egyptian
Islamist, declared that the slogan "God is Great" will reverberate "until
Islam spreads throughout the world."[57] Abdessalam Yassine, a Moroccan Islamist, asserted: "We demand power";[58] and the man standing in

his way, the late King Hassan, concluded that for Islamists, Islam is "the elevator to take power."[59]

By reducing the economic dimension to its proper proportions, and appreciating the religious, cultural, and political dimensions, we may actually begin to understand what causes militant Islam.

6

THE GLORY OF
ISLAMIC ECONOMICS

Samih 'atef El-Zein, a prolific Lebanese Shi'i writer on Islamic sub-jects, has unwittingly done a great service to those who argue that militant Islam the modern ideology has little to do with Islam the tra-ditional religion. El-Zein has written a substantial tract entitled *Islam and Human Ideology* that makes this very point in many ways, color-fully, in detail, and with verve.[1]

Originally published in Arabic some years ago,[2] his book offers a most useful, if disorganized, summation of some common themes in current militant Islamic thinking.[3] Like all pious Muslims, El-Zein makes the sacred laws of Islam paramount over all humans and all institutions. He claims to base all his thinking on three of the standard sources of Islam: the Qur'an; the *hadith* (accounts of the Prophet Muhammad's sayings or actions); and the judgment of jurists.

The Best Ideology

El-Zein sees Islam as not merely a faith but an explicit rival to the world's great ideologies: "There are three types of principles in the

world: the capitalist-democratic, communist-socialist and Islamic."
With unconditional certainty, he declares the superiority of Islam. It
"presents the most gracious system of solidarity in a society. Under
such a system, the honourable do not fall, the honest do not perish, the
needy do not suffer, the handicapped do not despair, the sick do not die
for lack of care, and people do not destroy one another."

Given the poor showing of the Communist system, he wastes little ink on it, but instead concentrates his attack on the capitalist-
democratic foe. Ironically, he denounces this enemy in ways vaguely
reminiscent of Moscow's. Capitalism he dismisses as an "erroneous
approach" that makes "production the basis of the economy while
completely neglecting the question of the distribution of wealth
among the individuals of the society." In El-Zein's rather primitive (or
is it bookish?) understanding, "the capitalist system does not concern
itself at all with providing funds necessary for fulfilling their necessary
needs such as housing, food and clothing, as this is not relevant at all
to those who are in charge of the system." He paints the capitalist
countries as suffering from a great number of economic woes—cheat-
ing, lying, gambling, monopolizing, and the charging of usury. Most
basically, El-Zein finds that in the West, "the purpose of life is profi-
teering." This ruthless materialism naturally causes Westerners to
ignore all moral, spiritual, and human values. From this, he concludes
that Western civilization "should not be adopted, because it is in total
contrast with Islamic culture." Quite the reverse: the West (and the
rest of the world) would do well "to emulate this lofty, Islamic ideology."

And what precisely is this lofty ideology? A body of ideas and precepts that derive from the Shari'a. "No problem can occur or event
take place for which there is not an explanation in Islamic law." In
common with other Islamists, El-Zein extends the Shari'a far beyond
its traditional bounds; in particular, he finds a vast body of alleged
Islamic precepts that pertain to the realms of economics and politics.

Islam's Economic System

El-Zein makes many high-minded statements of a general nature about
Islam and economics, for example: "The economic viewpoint in Islam
is summed up by saying that the economy is for the benefit of humanity not the individual." But his most interesting assertions are the spe-

cific ones. To begin with, he pronounces on those practices that an Islamic economy rejects and those it accepts. On the negative side, all forms of insurance are illegal, as are cooperatives, monopolies, and any form of price-fixing by the state. Selling short is out, as is speculation in gold and silver.

In contrast, El-Zein accepts private property, but within strict limits. Human beings "are appointed as Allah's deputies in the ownership of items," implying that they must behave in accord with divine wishes. In particular, both "wastefulness and parsimony are prohibited." Fortunately for the *suq* tradition, bargaining is legal. Somewhat unexpectedly, he finds some credit arrangements legal, as well as the practice of setting different prices for cash and for deferred payment. El-Zein deems corporations legal in general, while severely condemning joint stock corporations, for in collecting capital from individuals but not labor they contradict Islamic law: "labour or personal effort is the basis for developing property and for obtaining funds."

Islamic law famously and emphatically prohibits usury; El-Zein interprets this to mean a proscription on all forms of interest. But, he quickly assures the anxious capitalist, that presents no problem, for "a society in which Islamic laws are implemented will have no need for usury." Indeed, eliminating interest has the happy result of rendering banks unnecessary, except for a single state-run bank which offers interest-free loans "for the common good of the community." The ban on interest has another positive consequence: no more foreign loans, the accepting of which El-Zein sees as "the most dangerous course a country may take." He even sees American loans as a conspiracy by which the United States hopes to "take control" over other countries.

Alms (*zakat*) are integral to this system. In contrast to traditional Islam, which left alms up to the individual, El-Zein would have the state organize and administer these contributions, in the course of which he changes what had once been a pious and voluntary offering into a compulsory payment: a tax. The advantages of this appropriation are great indeed; alms not only redistribute wealth from those who do not need it, but they even (rather magically) provide protection against inflation.

In El-Zein's pie-in-the-sky view, an Islamic system means "injustice is non-existent due the State's provision for the well-being of all people"; this in turn implies there is "no need" for trade unions. And should employer and worker disagree on compensation? Here El-Zein seems to contradict himself. In one place, he decides that "the experts" will determine the proper compensation; in another, he declares that the state "determines wages for all employees." This casual inconsistency points to a larger consistency—that some authority, and not the negotiating process will make this decision from an Olympian height. Unlike traditional Islamic notions, which gave the state almost no role in private commerce, El-Zein grants nearly unlimited powers to government officials. And once workers receive their just rewards, El-Zein sees "no need" for retirement benefits, bonuses, or other supplements to the basic wage; nor does he see any role for annual raises, which he scorns as "part of the capitalist system" and "a form of deception." To sum up, "in Islam there are no labour problems."

Interestingly, many of El-Zein's dicta reflect Marxist-Leninist thinking. He holds that the state must own mines, oil wells, pastures, city squares, seashores, river straits, and other properties; it must guarantee work for all who seek it; and it must provide to all both basic subsistence—food, clothing, accommodation—as well as free medical care and education. Should the state lack the means to pay for these many obligations, it may "appropriate those funds that exceed the basic and luxury needs of the population." In plain English, it may seize whatever it likes. Again, this reflects far more the customs of twentieth-century authoritarianism than the precepts of traditional Islam.

Also in a quaintly socialist vein, El-Zein believes that the only way to industrialize is establishing a heavy equipment industry, as though Stalin pursued the only possible method of economic growth. "There is no way the country can be industrialized except through giving heavy industrialization priority over everything else and establishing no new factories except with equipment manufactured in the country." El-Zein even finds in the Islamic holy books a precept requiring industrial self-sufficiency. (Which might remind an American of the Supreme Court finding in the U.S. Constitution a right to abortion.)

Summing up, a devout Muslim may not join a trade union, put his money in a bank or buy stocks, speculate in the commodity markets, own seashore property, or buy any form of insurance. In return for giving up these rights, he gets no inflation, no poverty, perfect equity, and an abundance of material goods.

Islam's Political System

El-Zein takes up political issues almost as an afterthought to his lengthy discussion of economics. Consistent with militant Islamic ideology, he declares that "there are no minorities in Islam." Muslims are one people, under a single ruler; he waves aside all differences that do exist—cultural, linguistic, ethnic, national, doctrinal—as irrelevant. El-Zein envisions a single Muslim polity stretching from Morocco to Indonesia, though he does not explain how this huge state will be achieved or maintained.

In contrast, he does focus on the question of who is to rule this monster state. No kings, presidents, or emirs need apply; the caliph, or vice-regent of God, is the only legitimate Islamic ruler. Though the last caliph who truly ruled lived about a millennium ago, this poses no obstacle to our author, who fantasizes in some detail about resurrecting a caliphal system. Nominees for the top position are to be selected by a council of wise men (*majlis ash-shura*) and then voted on by the population. The caliph then rules for life, on the condition that he personally lives by the Islamic law and enforces it throughout his universal Muslim domain. So long as the caliph fulfills his duties, he is proof against *coups d'état*, for Muslims "are enjoined by a divine decree to obey the government." Those who revolt will rot in hell. El-Zein envisions the caliph in a paternal role highly reminiscent of fascism: "the prince of the believers will act as father to children when their father is away from them."

Do not count El-Zein among those mealy-mouthed apologists who claim that *jihad* means moral self-improvement; he's a red-blooded sort of fellow who sees *jihad* as a mandatory military obligation on all Muslim men and (showing his modernity) women. Nor does he pretend to support democracy. Instead, he candidly subordinates the popular will to God's: "the Islamic religion with its texts and evidence does not require that the opinion of the majority be respected unless it is in agreement with the law."

Stupidity Can Do Damage

El-Zein's study prompts three thoughts. First, his is a sure prescription for poverty and dictatorship, if not totalitarianism. Second, it contains hardly an original thought, but derives in its near entirety from the corpora of Marxism-Leninism and fascism. Even the ban on interest leads to a monopolistic state banking system that sounds very similar to that which existed in the People's Democracies. Third, El-Zein writes in apparently complete ignorance of modern history. He dismisses the successes of the West (capitalism, the separation of powers) as blithely as he learns nothing from the tragedies of totalitarianism (assuming that a better society can be constructed by glossing over rivalries and other differences).

Although El-Zein is but an intellectual theorist with little chance of becoming a Lenin or Hitler who applies his own ideas, he is part of a wave of thinkers who cumulatively exert enormous influence on politics in the Muslim world. In other words, the hypothetical nature and shoddy quality of El-Zein's thinking does not diminish its potential importance. As the twentieth century many times witnessed, inferior minds can do extraordinary damage.

7

THE WESTERN MIND
OF MILITANT ISLAM

Fat'hi ash-Shiqaqi, a well-educated young Palestinian living in Damascus, once boasted of his familiarity with European literature. He told an interviewer how he had read and enjoyed Shakespeare, Dostoyevsky, Chekhov, Sartre, and T. S. Eliot. He spoke of his particular passion for Sophocles' *Oedipus Rex*, a work he read ten times in English translation "and each time wept bitterly."[1] Such acquaintance with world literature and such exquisite sensibility would not be of note except for two points—that Shiqaqi was an Islamist and that, until his assassination in Malta in late 1995, he headed Islamic Jihad, the arch-terrorist organization that has murdered dozens of Israelis.

Shiqaqi's familiarity with things Western fits a common pattern. His successor as head of Islamic Jihad was Ramadan 'Abdullah Shallah, a scholar who had previously lived in Britain and the United States for nine years and at the time of Shiqaqi's death taught political science at the University of South Florida in Tampa. Eyad Ismoil, one of the 1993 World Trade Center bombers, also had a special affection for the United States. According to his brother, "He loved everything American from cowboy movies to hamburgers."[2] His sister recalled how keen he was for U.S. television and his having announced, "I want to live in America forever." The family, she commented, "always considered him a son of America."[3] His mother confirmed that "he loves the United States."[4]

Islamist intellectuals are also very much at home in the West. Hasan at-Turabi, for some years the effective ruler of Sudan, the man behind the notorious "ghost houses" and the brutal persecution of his country's large Christian minority, often flaunts his knowledge of the West. He told a French interviewer that most Islamist leaders, like himself, are "from the Christian, Western culture. We speak your languages."[5]

This pattern points to a paradox: the very intellectuals intent on marching the Muslim world back to the seventh century also excel in Western ways and seem very much to appreciate at least some of them. How does this happen and what does it indicate about their present strengths and future course?

Islamists Are Westernized

Islamist leaders tend to be well acquainted with the West, having lived there, learned its languages, and studied its cultures. Turabi of the Sudan has advanced degrees from the University of London and the Sorbonne; he also spent a summer in the United States in 1961, touring the country on a U.S. taxpayer–financed program for foreign student leaders. Abbasi Madani, a leader of Algeria's Islamic Salvation Front (FIS), received a doctorate in education from the University of London. His Tunisian counterpart, Rashid al-Ghannushi, spent a year in France and since 1993 makes his home in Great Britain. Necmettin Erbakan, Turkey's former prime minister, studied in Germany. Mousa Mohamed Abu Marzook, the head of Hamas's political committee, has a doctorate degree in engineering from the University of Louisiana, and lived in the United States from 1980 until his extradition in 1997 with his wife and six children.[6]

Indeed, the experience of living in the West often turns indifferent Muslims into Islamists. Discussing Mehdi Bazargan, an Iranian engineer who spent the years 1928–35 in France, Hamid Dabashi dissects the process many Muslim students undergo:

Beginning with the conscious or unconscious, articulated or mute, premise that they ought to remain firmly attached to their Islamic consciousness, they begin to admire "The Western" achievements. . . . They recognize a heightened state of ideological self-awareness on the part of "The West" that they identify as the source and cause of its achievements. They then look back at their own society where such technological achievements were lacking, a fact they attribute, in turn, to the absence of that heightened state of ideological self-awareness.[7]

The key notion here, the French analyst Olivier Roy explains, is the rather surprising notion that ideologies are "the key to the West's technical development." This assumption leads Islamists "to develop a modern political ideology based on Islam, which they see as the only way to come to terms with the modern world and the best means of confronting foreign imperialism."[8]

Some leading Islamists fit this pattern. The Egyptian Sayyid Qutb went to the United States in 1948 as an admirer of things American, only to "return" to Islam during his two years resident there,[9] becoming one of the most influential Islamist thinkers of our time. 'Ali Shari'ati of Iran lived five years in Paris, 1960–65; from this experience came some key ideas of the Islamic revolution. In other cases, Islamist thinkers do not actually live in the West but absorb its ways at a distance by learning a Western language and immersing themselves in Western ideas, as did the Indo-Pakistani journalist, thinker, and politician Sayyid Abul A'la Mawdudi (1903–1979). In still other cases, reading Western works in translation serves just as well. Morteza Motahhari, a leading acolyte of Khomeini's, made as thorough a study of Marxism as possible in the Persian language.

Many of militant Islam's intellectual lights share a background of technical accomplishment. Erbakan quickly rose to the top of the engineering profession in Turkey as a full professor at Istanbul Technical University, director at a factory producing diesel motors, and even head of the country's Chamber of Commerce. His political party is known sometimes as "the engineers' party." Layth Shubaylat, a Jordanian firebrand, is also president of the Jordanian Engineers Association. These men take special pride in being able to challenge the West in the area of its greatest strength.

Actual terrorists also tend to be science-oriented, though less accomplished. Ramzi Yusuf, the convicted mastermind of the 1993 World Trade Center bombing, is an electronics engineer and explosives expert with an advanced degree from the Swansea Institute in South Wales;[10] Nidal Ayyad was an up-and-coming chemical engineer at Allied Signal; and Eyad Ismoil studied computers and engineering at Wichita State University. This same pattern holds in the Middle East: Salah 'Ali 'Uthman, one of three terrorists who attacked a bus in Jerusalem on July 1, 1993, was a student of computer science at the University in Gaza. One of the most notorious anti-Zionist terrorists was Yahya 'Ayyash, nicknamed "The Engineer." Many Islamist Egyptians who engage in violence against the regime have science degrees, including the leader of the gang that assassinated Anwar el-Sadat in 1981. The leadership of Al-Qaeda, including Osama bin Laden himself and nearly all of the leadership, boasted a high degree of technical proficiency.

Islamist knowledge of the West seems to focus on engineering and comedies, but it is not limited to that. In a statement of beliefs from his Manhattan jail cell, Ramzi Yusuf cited the *Encyclopaedia Britannica* and *The New York Times*, as well as one of Newton's laws of physics;[11] this man is no bumpkin. One of his friends says that the remarkable thing about Ramzi Yusuf was his apparent pleasure in learning about new languages, cultures, and peoples, then proceeding to blow them up.[12]

So much knowledge of the West points to Islamists who are not peasants living in the unchanging countryside but modern, thoroughly urbanized individuals, many of them university graduates. Notwithstanding all their talk about recreating the society of the time of Muhammad, Islamists are modern individuals at the forefront of coping with modern life. These are women struggling to keep their virtue on extremely packed buses, entrepreneurs attempting to live by the Qur'anic strictures on usury, and engineers working out the spiritual significance of the computer.

Ignorance of Traditional Islam

In contrast to this ostentatious familiarity with Western ways, Islamists are distant from their own culture. Turabi admitted to a French interviewer, "I know the history of France better than the history of Sudan.

I love your culture, your painters, your musicians."[13] He offered no comparable praise for Sudanese painters and musicians. Having found Islam on their own as adults, many Islamists are ignorant of their own history and traditions. Some of "the new generation of Islamic fundamentalists," Martin Kramer notes, "are born-again Muslims, ill-acquainted with Islamic tradition, who often see Islam only as an ideology of power."[14] Tunisia's minister of religion Ali Chebbi goes further, saying that "They ignore the fundamental facts of Islam."[15] Like Mawdudi, these autodidacts mix a bit of this and that, as Seyyed Vali Reza Nasr of the University of California at San Diego explains:

> Mawdudi's formulation was by no means rooted in traditional Islam. He adopted modern ideas and values, mechanisms, procedures, and idioms, weaving them into an Islamic fabric . . . he sought not to resurrect an atavistic order but to modernize the traditional conception of Islamic thought and life. His vision represented a clear break with Islamic tradition and a fundamentally new reading of Islam which took its cue from modern thought.[16]

On reflection, this lack of knowledge should not be surprising. Islamists are individuals educated in modern ways in search of solutions to modern problems; of course they know the West's ways better than their own country's traditions. The Prophet may inspire, but they approach him through the filter of their own time. In the process, they unintentionally substitute Western ways for those of traditional Islam.

Traditional Islam—the immensely rewarding faith of nearly a billion adherents—developed a civilization that for over a millennium gave order to the lives of young and old, rich and poor, sophisticate and ignorant, Moroccan and Malaysian. Alienated from this tradition, Islamists dispense with it in the chimerical effort to return to the pure and simple ways of Muhammad. To connect spiritually to the first years of Islam, when the Prophet was alive and the faith was new, they seek to skip back fourteen centuries. The most mundane issues inspire them to recall the Prophet's times. Thus, one author portrays the "survival tactics" employed by Muslim students at American universities to retain their Islamic identity as being "much like [those of] the early Muslims during the Hijra [from Mecca to Medina]."[17]

Islamists take pride in seeing themselves not as tradition-bound but rather as engaged in a highly novel enterprise. According to Iran's spiritual leader, 'Ali Hoseyni Khamene'i, "The Islamic system that the imam [Khomeini] created . . . has not existed in the course of history, except at the beginning [of Islam], and does not exist elsewhere in the world today."[18] Similarly, Ghannushi asserts that "Islam is ancient but the Islamist movement is recent."[19] In rejecting a whole millennium of culture and tradition, Islamists throw out a great deal of their own legacy, from the great corpus of Qur'anic scholarship to the finely worked interpretations of law. They are not absorbed by the splendors of mosque architecture. On the contrary, they admire efficient factories and armies. For them, no less than for a Swedish aid official, the Muslim world is backward, and they too urgently seek its overhaul through the application of modern means. When this process goes slowly, they blame the West for withholding its technology. Thus, 'Ali Akbar Mohtashemi, the Iranian arch radical, bemoans that "the United States and the West will never give us the technology" to pursue what he quaintly calls "the science of industrialization."[20]

When it comes to understanding history, traditional Muslims saw the world either as static or as steadily in decline. The era of Muhammad, which lasted from 610 to 632, was the best, and every generation since has witnessed degeneration. The idea of progress, so endemic to the modern West, is alien. In this worldview, "there is no place for development, progress or social advancement and improvement."[21] In contrast, the Islamists assume profound changes are underway, and very possibly for the better. Sayyid Qutb, one of the most influential Islamist thinkers, accepted the Marxist notion of stages of history, adding only an Islamic stage. Around 1950, he predicted the twentieth century would witness the demise of the capitalism in the West and the blossoming of communism. But communism, although it would satisfy material needs, would not fulfill the spiritual side. "At that stage, Qutb argued, Islam would be the only candidate for the leadership of humanity."[22] Well, Qutb had a few details wrong, but what is of special interest is how he accepts the Marxist (and very un-Islamic) notion of history unfolding in stages.

The Islamists' goal turns out to be not a genuinely Islamic order but an Islamic-tinted version of Western reality. This is particularly apparent in four areas: religion, daily life, politics, and the law.

I. IMITATING CHRISTIANITY

It was certainly not their intent, yet Islamists have introduced some distinctly Christian notions into their Islam.

Churchlike structure. Traditional Islam was characterized by informal organizations. Virtually every major decision—establishing a canonical text of the Qur'an, excluding philosophical inquiry, or choosing which religious scholars to heed—was reached in an unstructured and consensual way. This has been the genius of the religion, and it meant that rulers who tried to control the religious institution usually failed.

Islamists, ignorant of this legacy, have set up churchlike structures. The trend began in Saudi Arabia, where the authorities built a raft of new institutions. Already in 1979, Khalid Durán wrote about the emergence of a "priestly hierarchy with all its churchly paraphernalia":

> A number of religious functionaries have come into being whose posts were previously unheard of, for example: the Secretary of the Muslim World League, the Secretary General of the Islamic Conference, the Rector of the Islamic University in Medina, and so [on] and so forth. For the first time in history the imam of the Ka'ba has been sent on tour of foreign countries as if he were an Apostolic Nuntius.[23]

The Islamic Republic of Iran soon followed the Saudi model and went beyond it, Shahrough Akhavi explains, to institute a Catholic-style control of the clergy:

> the centralization that has occurred in the religious institution in Iran is unprecedented, and actions have been taken that resemble patterns in the ecclesiastical church tradition familiar in the West. For example, in 1982, Khomeini encouraged the "defrocking" and "excommunication" of his chief rival, Ayatollah Muhammad Kazim Shari'atmadari (d. 1986), although no machinery for this has ever existed in Islam. Other trends, such as centralized control over budgets, appointments to the professoriate, curricula in the seminaries, the creation of religious militias, monopolizing the representation of interests, and mounting a Kulturkampf in the realm of the arts, the family, and other social issues tell of the growing tendency to create an "Islamic episcopacy" in Iran.

Even more striking, Akhavi notes, is how Khomeini made himself into a kind of pope:

> Khomeini's practice of issuing authoritative fatwas, obedience to which is made compulsory, comes close to endowing the top jurist with powers not dissimilar to those of the pope in the Catholic church. After all, compliance with a particular cleric's fatwas in the past had not been mandatory. In creating this faux Christian hierarchy, fundamentalists invented something more Western than Islamic.[24]

Friday as Sabbath. In similar confusion, Islamists have turned Fridays into a Sabbath, something it had not previously been. Traditionally, Friday was a day of congregating for prayer, not a day of rest. Indeed, the whole idea of Sabbath is alien to the vehemently monotheistic spirit of Islam, which deems falsely anthropomorphic the notion of God needing a day of rest. Instead, the Qur'an (62:9–10) instructs Muslims to "leave off business" only while praying; once finished, they should "disperse through the land and seek God's bounty"—in other words, engage in commerce. A day of rest so much mirrors Jewish and Christian practice, some traditional Islamic authorities actually discouraged taking Friday off. In most places and times, in fact, Muslims did work on Fridays, interrupted only by the communal service.

In modern times, Muslim states imitated Europe and adopted a day of rest. The Ottoman Empire began closing government offices on Thursday, a religiously neutral day, in 1829. As Christian imperialists imposed Sunday as the weekly day of rest throughout their colonies, Muslim rulers adopted this practice as well. For example, the Republic of Turkey did so in 1935, responding in large part to business interests that preferred the European calendar. Upon independence, virtually every Muslim government inherited the Sunday rest and maintained it. S. D. Goitein, the foremost scholar of this subject, notes that Muslim states did so "in response to the exigencies of modern life and in imitation of Western precedent."[25]

Recently, as the Sunday Sabbath came to be seen as too Western, Muslim rulers asserted their Islamic identities by instituting Friday as the day off. Little did they realize that, in so doing, they perpetuated a specifically Judeo-Christian custom. And as Fridays have turned into a holiday (for family excursions, spectator sports, etc.), Muslims have imitated the Western weekend.[26]

In other ways, too, Muslims have become Christianized. With the solitary exception of the Isma'ilis, traditional Muslims did not organize to spread Islam; missionary work was undertaken by individuals such as merchants. Only in the nineteenth century, when faced with organized Christian missionary work, did Muslims respond in kind. This description of athletic games sponsored by an offshoot of Hamas within Israel proper was part of an effort to make sure apprentice Islamists get trained in the martial arts: "Games are always preceded by prayer and proceed without any interruptions, in perfect sportsmanship, without any cursing and bickering between players and fans. Players wear long trousers, and after the games the members of each team embrace their opponents, enjoy a festive meal, and conduct a joint prayer for both teams."[27]

II. Feminism

Perhaps the most striking Westernisms of daily life that Islamists have introduced are associated with women. Taking up the veil and separating women from men may appear to be an archaism, and that is certainly how the Islamists see these acts. Yet Islamists actually espouse an outlook more akin to Western-style feminism than anything in traditional Islam.

Traditional Muslim men took pride in their women staying home; in well-to-do households, they almost never left its confines. Hasan at-Turabi has something quite different in mind: "Today in Sudan, women are in the army, in the police, in the ministries, everywhere, on the same footing as men."[28] Turabi proudly speaks of the Islamic movement having helped "liberate women."[29] Following the adage that "the best mosque for women is the inner part of the house," traditional women prayed at home, and female quarters in mosques were slighted; but Islamist women regularly attend public services and new mosques consequently allot far more space to women's sections.

Traditional Muslim men did not take pride in the freedom and independence of their women, but Islamists do. Ahmad al-Banna, son of the founder of Egypt's Muslim Brethren, adopts a feminist outlook that leads him to reinterpret Muslim history according to Western standards: "Muslim women have been free and independent for fifteen centuries. Why should we follow the example of Western women, so dependent on their husbands in material matters?"[30]

For centuries, a woman's veil served primarily to help her retain her virtue; today, it serves the feminist goal of facilitating a career. Muslim women who wear "Islamic dress," writes a Western analyst, are usually well educated, often in the most prestigious university faculties of medicine, engineering, and the sciences, and their dress signifies that although they pursue an education and career in the public sphere, they are religious, moral women. Whereas other women are frequently harassed in the public sphere, such women are honored and even feared. By the late 1980s, Islamic dress had become the norm for middle-class women who do not want to compromise their reputation by their public activities. Boutiques offer Parisian-style fashions adopted to Islamic modesty standards.[31]

If the veil once symbolized a woman's uncontrollable sexuality, Islamists see it as the sign of her competence. Turabi declares, "I am for equality between the sexes," and goes on to explain how covering up helps achieve this key feminist goal: "A woman who is not veiled is not the equal of men. She is not looked on as one would look on a man. She is looked at to see if she is beautiful, if she is desirable. When she is veiled, she is considered a human being, not an object of pleasure, not an erotic image."[32]

The establishment of an Islamic order in Iran has, ironically perhaps, opened many opportunities outside the house for pious women. Sayyid Muhammad Khatami, the president of Iran, has proudly declared that "Under the Islamic Republic, women have full rights to participate in social, cultural, and political activities."[33] Women do work in the labor force and famously serve in the military. A parliamentary leader boasts, not without reason, about Iran having the best feminist record in the Middle East, and points to the number of women in higher education.[34] In keeping with this spirit, one of Khomeini's granddaughters attended law school and then lived in London with her husband, a cardiac surgeon in training; another organizes women's sporting events.

Curiously, some Islamists see the veil representing not careers and equality but something quite different: positive sexuality. Samira Isma'ili, a woman in Sharjah, hints at this when she points out an implication of being completely covered: "Being anonymous gives me freedom."[35] Shabbir Akhtar, the British writer, is more explicit. For him, the veil serves "to create a truly erotic culture in which one dispenses with the need for the artificial excitement that pornography provides."[36] Traditional Muslims, it hardly needs emphasizing, did not see veils as a substitute for pornography.

III. Turning Islam into Ideology

Traditional Islam emphasized man's relations with God while playing down his relations to the state. Law loomed very large, politics small. Over the centuries, pious Muslims avoided the government, which meant almost nothing to them but trouble (taxes, conscription, corvée labor). On the other hand, they made great efforts to live by the Shari'a.

Infected by the twentieth-century disease, Islamists make politics "the heart" of their program.[37] They see Islam less as the structure in which individuals make their lives and more as an ideology for running whole societies. Declaring that "Islam is the solution," they hold with Khamene'i of Iran that Islam "is rich with instructions for ruling a state, running an economy, establishing social links and relationships among the people and instructions for running a family."[38] For Islamists, Islam represents the path to power. As a very high Egyptian official observed, to them "Islam is not precepts or worship, but a system of government."[39] Olivier Roy finds the Islamist inspiration to be far more mundane than spiritual: "For many of them, the return to religion has been brought about through their experience in politics, and not as a result of their religious belief."[40]

Revealingly, Islamists compare Islam not to other religions but to other ideologies. "We are not socialist, we are not capitalist, we are Islamic," said the Malaysian militant Islamic leader Anwar Ibrahim.[41] This comparison may seem overblown—socialism and capitalism are universal, militant Islam limited to Muslim—yet it is not, because Islamists purvey their ideology to non-Muslims too. We have noted the striking instance of Khomeini in January 1989 imploring the Soviet president not to turn westward to replace his failing ideology but rather to Islam. Turabi of the Sudan came to a similar conclusion: "Now that socialism has disappeared, there is a great void that only Islam can fill."[42]

IV. OVERHAULING THE SACRED LAW

Even as Islamists pay homage to Islam's sacred law, they turn it into a Western-style code, causing three age-old characteristics of the Shari'a to disappear: its elaboration by independent scholars; its precedence over state interests; and its application to persons rather than territories.

Developed by the state. Through the centuries, jurists (*faqihs*) wrote and interpreted the Islamic law on their own, with little control by governments. These jurists established early on that they were answerable to God, not to the prince. Joseph Schacht, a leading scholar of this subject, explains: "the caliph, though otherwise the absolute chief of the community of Muslims, had not the right to legislate but only to make administrative regulations with the limits laid down by the sacred Law."[43] Rulers did on occasion try to dictate terms to jurists but they invariably failed. Most significantly, in the years A.D. 833–49, four successive caliphs imposed their understanding of the Qur'an's nature (that it was created by God, as opposed to the religious scholars, who said it had always existed). Despite energetic attempts by the caliphs, which included the flogging of a very eminent religious authority, the effort failed, and with it the pretensions of politicians to define the contents of Islam.

The jurists retained full control of Islamic law until the nineteenth century, when the British, French, and other European rulers codified the Shari'a as a European-style body of state law. Independent Muslim states, such as the Ottoman Empire, followed the European lead and also codified the Shari'a. With independence, all the Muslim rulers maintained the European habit of keeping the law firmly under state control; by the 1960s, only in Saudi Arabia did it remain autonomous.

In 1969, Mu'ammar al-Qadhdhafi of Libya started the new wave of expanding the Shar'i content of state laws (e.g., in the criminal statutes). He did so as ruler, using the state apparatus to compel jurists to carry out his orders. Islamists in many countries then emulated Qadhdhafi, giving the state authority over the Shari'a even as they extended its purview. They made no effort to revert to the jurists' law of old but continued practices begun by the European powers.

When Islamists on rare occasions protest this state domination of the law, it carries little conviction. Turabi may have remarked that "Islamic government is not total because it is Islam that is a total way of life, and if you reduce it to government, then government would be omnipotent, and that is not Islam,"[44] but Turabi's enormous power in the Sudan makes it hard to take this critique seriously. Islamists accept Western ways because, first, they know the imperial system far better than the traditional Muslim one, and so perpetuate its customs. Second, reverting to the traditional Muslim way would, as Ann Mayer of the Wharton School points out, "entail that governments relinquish the power that they had gained over legal systems when European-style codified law was originally adopted,"[45] and they have little incentive to do that.

More generally, it had been the case that only highly qualified jurists could rule on the law. Now anyone with political power—voter, parliamentarian, or military despot—has potential authority over the outcome. This inevitably leads to the law becoming a tool of state power.

State interests take priority. The state takeover invariably causes problems. Perhaps most important is that, in the traditional arrangement, the jurists jealously maintained their independence in interpreting the law. They insisted on God's imperatives taking absolute priority over those of the ruler. Such acts as prayer, the fast of Ramadan, or the pilgrimage to Mecca, they maintained, must never be subjected to the whims of despots. Jurists got their way, for hardly a single king or president, not even so ardent a secularist as Turkey's Kemal Atatürk, had the temerity to interfere with the Lord's commandments.

But Ayatollah Khomeini did. In January 1988, he issued an edict flatly contravening this ancient Islamic assumption. In a remarkable but little noted document, the ayatollah asserted that "The government is authorized unilaterally to abolish its lawful accords with the people and . . . to prevent any matter, be it spiritual or material, that poses a threat to its interests." This means that, "for Islam, the requirements of government supersede every tenet, including even those of prayer, fasting and pilgrimage to Mecca."[46] Subordinating these acts to *raisons d'état* has the effect of diminishing the Shari'a beyond recognition.

Khomeini—a classical educated scholar, an authority on Islamic law,[47] and an eminent religious figure—justified this edict on the grounds that the interests of the Islamic Republic were synonymous with the interests of Islam itself. But this hardly explains so radical and unprecedented a step. The real reason lies in the fact that, like count-less other twentieth-century rulers, he sought control of his country's spiritual life. Hitler, Stalin, and Mao subordinated religion to the state, and Khomeini too. His edict subordinated Islam to the total state. Khomeini may have looked medieval, but he was a man of his times, deeply affected by the totalitarian ideas that flourished in his younger years.

Applies to geographic jurisdictions. In traditional Islam, as in Judaism, laws apply to the individual, not as in the West to the terri-tory. It matters not whether a Muslim lives here or there, in the home-land or in the diaspora; he must follow the Shari'a. Conversely, a non-Muslim living in a Muslim country need not follow its directives. For example, a Muslim may not drink whisky whether he lives in Tehran or Los Angeles; and a non-Muslim may imbibe in either place. This leads to complex situations whereby one set of rules applies to a Muslim thief who robs a Muslim, another to a Christian who robs a Christian, and so forth. The key is who you are, not where you are.

In contrast, European notions of law are premised on jurisdictions. Commit a crime in this town or state and you get one punishment, another in the next town over. Even highways have their own rules. Where you are, not who you are, is what counts.

Ignorant of the spirit underlying the Shari'a, Islamists enforce it along territorial, not personal lines; Turabi declared that Islam "accepts territory as the basis of jurisdiction."[48] As a result, national differences have emerged. The Libyan government lashes all adulterers. Pakistan lashes unmarried offenders and stones married ones. The Sudan imprisons some and hangs others. Iran has even more punishments, including head-shaving and a year's banishment.[49] In the hands of Islamists, the Shari'a becomes just a variant of Western, territorial law.

This new understanding most dramatically affects non-Muslims, whose millennium-old exclusion from the Shari'a is over. Now they must live as virtual Muslims. Omar Abdel Rahman, the Egyptian sheikh in an American jail, is adamant on this subject: "it is very well known that no minority in any country has its own laws."[50] 'Abd al-'Aziz bin Baz, the Saudi religious leader, called on non-Muslims to fast during Ramadan. In Iran, foreign women may not wear nail polish—on the grounds that this leaves them unclean for (Islamic) prayer.

Entering the country, the authorities provide them with petrol-soaked rags and insist they wipe clean their varnished nails. A militant Islamic party in Malaysia wants to regulate how much time nonrelated Chinese men and women may spend alone together.

This new interpretation of Islamic law creates enormous problems. Rather than fairly much leaving non-Muslims to regulate their own conduct, as did traditional Islam, militant Islam seeks to intrude into their lives, fomenting enormous resentment and sometimes leading to violence. Palestinian Christians who raise pigs find their animals mysteriously poisoned. The million or two Christians living in the northern, predominantly Muslim, Sudan must comply with virtually all the Shar'i regulations. In the southern Sudan, Islamic law prevails wherever the central government rules, although "certain" Shar'i provisions are not applied there;[51] should the government conquer the whole south, all the provisions would probably go into effect, an expectation that does much to keep alive nearly half a century of civil war.

In brief, militant Islam has adopted so many European legal notions that the details of its program may be Islamic but its spirit is Western.

Militant Islam Is Not Transitory

Despite themselves, Islamists are Westernizers. Whichever direction they turn, they end up going west. Even in rejecting the West, they accept it. This has two implications. First, however reactionary in intent, militant Islam imports not just modern but Western ideas and institutions. The Islamist dream of expunging Western ways from Muslim life, in short, cannot succeed.

Second, the resulting hybrid is more robust than it seems. Opponents of militant Islam often dismiss it as a regressive effort to avoid modern life and comfort themselves with the prediction that it is doomed to be left behind as modernization takes place. But this expectation seems mistaken. Because militant Islam appeals most directly to Muslims contending with the challenges of modernity, its potential grows as do their numbers. Current trends suggest that militant Islam will remain a force for some time to come.

That is not to say that it will permanently endure, for it will wither just as surely as did the other radical utopian ideologies of the last century, fascism and communism. But this process may take decades rather than years and cause great damage in the process. Opponents of militant Islam, Muslim or non-Muslim, cannot afford the luxury of sitting back and awaiting its collapse.

8

ECHOES OF THE
COLD WAR DEBATE

As Americans discuss militant Islam, it is striking to see how they do so in ways that resemble the prior great ideological battle—how to deal with Marxism-Leninism. They recapitulate roughly the same arguments as existed during the Cold War, dividing along the familiar liberal and conservative lines. Liberals say co-opt the radicals. Conservatives say confront them. As usual, the conservatives are right. More striking yet, the same individuals hold generally the same positions. A left-wing Democrat like David Bonior advocates a soft line, now as then. A right-wing Republican like John Ashcroft argues for a tough line, now as then.

Analytic Differences

There are many parallels between the two debates.

Causes: The left, in keeping with its materialist outlook, sees Communist and militant Islamic ideologies as cover for a deeper economic motivation. The Russian Revolution expressed deep-seated class grievances; militant Islamic violence in Algeria, the State Department told us in 1994, expresses "frustration arising from political exclusion and economic misery."[1] In contrast, the right sees radical utopian ideology as a powerful force in itself, not an expression for socioeconomic woes. Ideas and ambitions count at least as much as the price of wheat: visions of a new order go far to account for the revolutions of 1917 and 1979.

Solutions: If misery causes radicalism, as the left argues, then the antidote lies in economic growth and social equity. The West can help in these areas through aid, trade, and open lines of communication. But if, as the right believes, ambitious intellectuals are the problem, then they must be battled and defeated. In both cases, liberals look to cooperation, conservatives to victory.

The West's responsibility: The left sees Western hostility as a leading cause for things having gone wrong. It's the old liberal "blame America first" attitude: just as Americans were responsible for every Soviet trespass from Stalin to the arms race, so they are now answerable for the appearance of Ayatollah Khomeini (due to U.S. support for the shah) and for the many Arab militant Islamic movements (due to U.S. support for Israel). Thus, according to one journalist, the West "made its own sizable contribution" to causing the current crisis in Algeria.[2] The right adamantly denies Western culpability in both cases, for that would absolve tyrants of their crimes. The U.S. government makes mistakes, to be sure, but that's because it finds it hard to contend with radical utopian movements. Along these lines, Arnold Beichman argues that "We are at the beginning of what promises to be a long war in which new moral complexities . . . will present themselves as once they did in the days of Soviet communism."[3]

A single source: When the State Department disclaimed "monolithic international control being exercised over the various Islamic movements,"[4] it used almost the same words as it once used to speak of Marxism-Leninism. For decades, American "progressives" insisted that Communist organizations around the world had indigenous sources and did not owe anything to Moscow (a claim easier to make so long as Moscow's archives remained closed). To which conservatives have long replied: Of course, there's no "monolithic international control," but there is an awful lot of funding and influence. Tehran administers a network akin to a militant Islamic Comintern, making its role today not that different from Moscow's in the past.

The antis: For many decades, the left saw those Russians, Chinese, and Cubans whose firsthand experience turned them into anti-Communists as marginal elements. In similar fashion, the left today looks at anti-Islamists as unauthentic or sellouts. Churches are among the worst offenders here. For example, in one 1991 analysis, a German priest presented the extremist element as the Muslim community per se.[5] The right wholeheartedly celebrates both types of antis as brave individuals bringing advance word of the terrors that result from efforts to radically remake society.

Do moderates exist? The left distinguishes between those ideologues willing to work within the system, deemed acceptable, and those who rely on violence and sabotage, deemed unacceptable. This meant accepting Italian Communists but not Stalin, or accepting the Turkish Islamists but not the Iranian ones. The right acknowledges differences in tactics but perceives no major difference in goals. Accordingly, it tends to lump pretty much all Communists or Islamists together.

Motives: When the other side strikes out in an aggressive way, the left often excuses its acts by explaining how they are defensive in nature. Invasions by Napoleon and Hitler accounted for the Soviet presence in Angola; the legacy of European colonial oppression accounts for the depths of militant Islamic rage. The right concludes from events like the downing of a Korean Airlines flight or the 2001 World Trade Center attack that the other side has offensive intentions, and has no patience with attempts to explain these away.

Fighting words: The two sides draw contrary conclusions from aggressive speech. Liberals tend to dismiss the barrage of threats against the West as mere rhetoric. Conservatives listen carefully and conclude that the West needs to protect itself (France's Interior Minister Charles Pasqua in 1994: militant Islamic groups "represent a threat to us").[6]

Threat to the West: If they are only approached with respect, Marxist-Leninists and Islamists will leave us alone, says the left. Don't treat them as enemies and they won't hurt us. The right disagrees, holding that all revolutionaries, no matter what their particular outlook (fascist, Communist, militant Islamic), are deeply anti-Western and invariably target the West. Their weaponry ranges from ICBMs to truck bombs to passenger jet airliners, but their purpose is the same: to challenge the predominance of modern, Western civilization.

And if truck bombs threaten less than missiles, it needs to be noted that Islamists challenge the West more profoundly than do Communists. The latter disagree with the West's politics but not its whole way of life (how could they, even as they pay homage to Dead White Males like Marx and Engels?). In contrast, Islamists despise the entire Western way of life, including the manner of dressing, mating, and praying. To appease Communists means changing the political and economic spheres; to appease Islamists means women taking up the veil or *burqa*, the scuttling of nearly every form of diversion, and an overhaul of the judicial system.

Future prospects: In the 1940s, the left portrayed Marxism-Leninism as the wave of the future; today, some leftists ascribe the same brilliant prospect to militant Islam. These radical ideologies are an unstoppable force; stand in their way and you'll not only get run over but you might even spur them on. Conservatives see utopianism enjoying only a temporary surge. The effort to remake mankind, they say, cannot work; like communism, militant Islam will surely end up in the dustbin of history.

Summing up, the left is more sanguine than the right about both communism and militant Islam. It is hard to imagine a conservative calling Ayatollah Khomeini "some kind of saint," as did Andrew Young, Jimmy Carter's ambassador to the United Nations. It is about as unlikely to hear a liberal warning, along with France's former defense minister, François Leotard, that "Islamic nationalism in its terrorist version is as dangerous today as National Socialism was in the past."[7] On the scholarly level, a liberal democrat like John Esposito publishes a book in 1992 entitled *The Islamic Threat: Myth or Reality?*[8] and concludes that the threat is but a myth. In complete contrast, Walter McDougall, the historian and sometime assistant to Richard Nixon, sees Russia helping the West in "holding the frontier of Christendom against its common enemy," the Muslim world.[9]

Policy Differences

These contrary analyses lead, naturally, to very different prescriptions for U.S. policy. The Left believes that dialogue with the other side, Communist or Islamist, has several advantages: it helps to understand their legitimate concerns, signals them that the West means them no harm, and reduces mutual hostility. Beyond dialogue, the West can show goodwill by reducing or even eliminating its military capabilities. Roughly speaking, this was the Clinton administration position vis-à-vis Algeria, where it hoped to defuse a potential explosion by urging the regime to bring in militant Islamic leaders who reject terrorism, thereby isolating the violent extremists.

The right has little use for dialogue and unilateral disarmament. Communists and Islamists being invariably hostile to a whole way of life, the West should show not empathy but resolve; not goodwill but willpower. The best way to display these intentions is with armed strength. Conservatives prefer to think in terms of containment and rollback. Algeria fits into the tradition of friendly tyrants—states where the rulers treat their own population badly but who help the United States fend off a radical ideology. It makes sense to stand by Algiers (or Cairo) just as it earlier made sense to stick by Saigon or Pinochet in Chile.

Of course, the schema presented here does not align perfectly. In its confusion, the Reagan administration searched for "moderates" in Iran, an effort led by none other than the very conservative Oliver North. The Bush administration of 1989–93 enunciated a soft policy toward militant Islam. The Clinton administration pursued a more resolute policy toward Iran than either of its predecessors, a policy the second Bush kept fairly much in place. Interests sometimes seem to count more than ideology. The liberal Clinton administration spoke out against a crackdown on Islamists in Algeria, where the stakes were low for Americans, but accepted tough measures in Egypt, where the United States had substantial interests. The conservative French government bemoans the crackdown in Egypt (not so important for it) but encourages tough measures in Algeria (very important).

Still, the basic pattern is clear. And as the lines of debate sort themselves out, the two sides are likely to stick more consistently to their characteristic positions. This suggests that while Marxism-Leninism and militant Islam are very different phenomena, Americans respond in similar ways to the parallel ideological challenges that they present.

They do so owing to a profound divide in outlook. Liberals believe in the peaceful and cooperative nature of mankind; when confronted with aggression and violence, they tend to assume it is motivated by a just cause, such as socioeconomic deprivation or exploitation by foreigners. Anger cannot be false, especially if accompanied by the high-minded goals of Communists or Islamists. Less innocently, conservatives know the evil that lurks in men's hearts. They understand the sometimes important roles of fanaticism and hatred. Just because an ideology has utopian aims does not mean that its adherents have lofty motives or generous ambitions.

The left's soft approach to militant Islam predominated in the Clinton administration, the universities, the churches, and the media. Indeed, to recall one of the left's favorite phrases, it became the hegemonic discourse in the United States. On the other side stood nothing but a handful of scholars, some commentators and politicians, and the great common sense of the American people. Americans know an opponent when they see him, and are not fooled by the left's theoretical arguments. That common sense prevailed in the Cold War and no doubt will suffice yet again to wrestle down the new follies of the New Class.

9

THE U.S. GOVERNMENT,
PATRON OF ISLAM?

with Mimi Stillman

I slam has dominated American public life on two occasions, once during the period of the Iranian hostage crisis from 1979 to 1981, and more recently since the attacks against the World Trade Center and the Pentagon on September 11, 2001. In both instances, Americans responded with outrage and puzzlement to the sight of ostensibly pious individuals—Ayatollah Khomeini then, Osama bin Laden now—sponsoring unprovoked violence against American civilians. Each time, Islam became one of the most discussed topics in American public life.

The U.S. government, however, responded very differently to the Islamic dimension of these two episodes. In that first round, it stayed aloof from the debate, limiting itself to policy pronouncements on Iran. Islam was mentioned hardly if ever, in keeping with the time-honored and correct practice of U.S. officials saying little about matters of faith. After all, these were politicians and diplomats, not scholars of religion. "Discoursing" on Islam was not exactly their specialization, and they were humble enough to know it.

But the reticence ran deeper: as spokespersons for the U.S. government, a constitutionally secular institution, they knew not to articulate views on the truth or falsehood of specific religions. In some contexts, that tradition is still a strong one. When the "Real IRA" killed twenty-eight at a fair in Omagh, Ireland,[1] the U.S. president did not seize the opportunity to ruminate on the true nature of Catholicism. Baruch Goldstein's murderous rampage in Hebron spurred no commentary on Judaism by the secretary of state. The Bharatiya Janata Party, with its Hindu nationalist outlook, prompted no high-level analyses of Hinduism on its coming to power in India.

The same used to be the case with Islam. In theory, anyway, it still is. At a festive dinner she held for American Muslims in 2000, Madeleine K. Albright as secretary of state informed her guests that "Of course, the United States doesn't have a political policy towards Islam."[2] One of her staff confirmed this on the operational level: "Islam is not a factor in our policymaking."[3]

But this is simply not true any more. Islam, the most political of religions, now enjoys a privileged place in Washington, just as it does in almost every capital around the world. The first Bush administration began the discussion of Islam in June 1992. On coming to office in 1993, the Clinton administration developed a fairly subtle policy toward Islam. Policy formulation accelerated in the present Bush administration. And since September 11, the president and his team have devoted intensive efforts to explaining what role Islam did and did not play in the recent tragedy. "Islam" now trips off the tongues of American statesmen, politicians, and diplomats with an almost dizzying frequency.

While the intensity of the current debate is new, the substance of current U.S. government statements on Islam is not. The latest statements develop the themes and arguments of a policy articulated over the past decade. That policy has four main elements, each of which has become a policy mantra: There is no clash of civilizations. Terrorism is not Islamic. Islam is compatible with American ideals and adds to American life. Americans must learn to appreciate Islam.

Clash of Civilizations

The first and most urgent task that government spokesmen tackle is contradicting the idea that the Cold War has been replaced by a "clash of civilizations." Samuel Huntington of Harvard first proposed the idea in 1993; in his catalogue of possible conflicts, a "clash of civilizations" between Islam and the West loomed large.[4] Over and over again, officialdom asserts the falseness of this idea. President Clinton himself argued with Huntington, declaring it "terribly wrong" to believe in "an inevitable clash" between the West and Islam. To support his point, he called on the authority of American Muslims, who "will tell you there is no inherent clash between Islam and America."[5] More disdainfully, Albright noted that "The United States has no interest in the 'clash' with Islam that some commentators have predicted."[6] To the contrary, there is "no inherent conflict between Islam and the United States."[7] Assistant to the President for National Security Affairs Samuel R. Berger echoed the theme: "There is no clash of civilizations."[8]

Whenever the topic came up, the lesser ranks dutifully lined up behind their superiors. Deputy Assistant Secretary of State Ronald Neumann found "no inherent conflict between Islam and the West. We do not see any 'clash of civilizations.' "[9] Special Adviser to the Secretary of State John Beyrle found that "it makes no sense to see America as a nation 'in conflict' with Islam."[10] According to a State Department fact sheet, "Islam and the West are not in confrontation."[11] Even the Department of Defense, not usually concerned with such matters, had an opinion: according to Deputy Assistant Secretary Bruce Riedel, "The Pentagon rejects the argument that a clash of civilizations is imminent between Islam and the West."[12]

As a corollary, officialdom argued against the idea that Islam had been promoted to the status of enemy. "We should not accept the notion," said R. James Woolsey, former director of the Central Intelligence Agency, that "the 'Red Menace' that dominated our lives for nearly a half a century is now being replaced by a 'Green Menace' sweeping throughout the Arab world."[13] Assistant Secretary of State for Near Eastern Affairs Edward Djerejian asserted that the U.S. government "does not view Islam as the next 'ism' confronting the West or threatening world peace."[14] Martin Indyk, at the time serving on the National Security Council staff, broadened the point: "We do not regard Islam as a threat."[15] The only crack in the facade was provided after September 11, when Deputy Secretary of Defense Paul Wolfowitz implied that Samuel Huntington did not create the problem, he only diagnosed it: "These criminals . . . want to inflame a war of the cultures, and we should avoid that."[16]

Terrorism Is Not Islamic

The second task the U.S. government has taken upon itself is severing the common association Americans make between Islam and terrorism. Officialdom does not deny that devout-seeming Muslims are constantly trying to kill Americans, but it vociferously denies their connection to Islam.

President Clinton complained about "so many people" unfairly identifying "the forces of radicalism and terrorism" with Islam.[17] As he acknowledged, "we have had problems with terrorism coming out of the Middle East," but he then insisted that this "is not inherently related to Islam, not to the religion, not to the culture."[18] A Department of State fact sheet echoed the president: "Terrorism is not a principle of any major religion, including Islam."[19] And the department's coordinator for counterterrorism, Philip Wilcox, Jr., went still further: "Islam, like Christianity and Judaism, preaches peace and nonviolence."[20]

Some Muslims may preach nonviolence. But politicians and diplomats must account for the stubborn fact that Muslim radicals have attacked Americans in such diverse locales as Lebanon, Yemen, Kenya, the Philippines, New York City, and Washington, D.C. They do so by deeming such attacks not inspired by Islam but contrary to Islam. In 1994, Clinton criticized "the forces of terror and extremism, who cloak themselves in the rhetoric of religion and nationalism but behave in ways that contradict the very teachings of their faith and mock their patriotism."[21] He returned to this topic in 1998, accusing Osama bin Laden and his associates of engaging in "a horrible distortion of their religion to justify the murder of innocents." He dismissed them as "fanatics and killers who wrap murder in the cloak of righteousness, and in so doing, profane the great religion in whose name they claim to act."[22]

The president's men dutifully followed suit. National Security Adviser Anthony Lake denounced "militants who distort Islamic doctrines and seek to expand their influence by force."[23] A violent Islamic group in Algeria was acting against "the principles of Islam," according to Robert Pelletreau, who also moonlighted as assistant secretary of state.[24] Woolsey considered it "a major mistake" to blame Islam for the state of affairs in Iran today, and specifically for the choice of its leaders to rely heavily on terror. He argued that "a few men" who had broken with Islamic traditions alone were responsible for the situation in Iran.[25] Michael A. Sheehan, the State Department's coordinator for counterterrorism, called terrorism "a perversion of the teachings of Islam."[26] Beyrle checked his copy of the Qur'an and concluded that "extremism is not truly Islamic."[27] "Terrorists who claim to speak for Islam," averred Wilcox, "are abusing their faith."[28]

The events of September 11, 2001, brought this issue to center stage. Interestingly, while all government officials agreed that the four hijackings could not be ascribed to Islam, they differed among themselves on the question of whether it was simply, as Wolfowitz put it, "not an Islamic act"[29] or something done in actual contravention of Islam.

President George W. Bush's speech to Congress pointed to the first interpretation: "The terrorists practice a fringe form of Islamic extremism that has been rejected by Muslim scholars and the vast majority of Muslim clerics; a fringe movement that perverts the peaceful teachings of Islam. . . . [Islam's] teachings are good and peaceful, and those who commit evil in the name of Allah blaspheme the name of Allah. . . . The terrorists are traitors to their own faith, trying, in effect, to hijack Islam itself."[30]

But the second interpretation surfaced in President Bush's speech to a Muslim audience during his visit to the Islamic Center in Washington: "These acts of violence against innocents violate the fundamental tenets of the Islamic faith. . . . The face of terror is not the true face of Islam. That's not what Islam is all about."[31] The White House press secretary, Ari Fleischer, went further, calling the attacks "a perversion of Islam."[32] Secretary of State Colin L. Powell made the same point even more emphatically, casting the hijackers not only out of Islam but even out of Arabdom, and seeming to imply that Muslims definitionally cannot be terrorists; their acts, he argued, "should not be seen as something done by Arabs or Islamics; it is something that was done by terrorists."[33]

This distinction between Islam and terrorism, however it is made, has a profound implication for the post–September 11 concept of the enemy: The United States is fighting a war "on terror," not on militant Islam or any type of Muslims. President Bush told congressional leaders, "we don't view this as a war of religion, in any way, shape or form."[34] According to Powell, "this is not a conflict against Arabs or Muslims or those who believe in one particular religion."[35] Terrorism "is a threat not only to our civilization but to theirs as well," explained Department of State spokesman Richard Boucher. "We don't see this as an effort against Arabs; we don't see this as an effort against Muslims."[36] More succinctly, Deputy Secretary Wolfowitz declared that "our enemy is terrorism, not Islam."[37]

Even the judicial branch now has views about terrorism not being Islamic. At the sentencing of Ramzi Yusuf, Judge Kevin Duffy berated the defendant: "Ramzi Yusuf, you are not fit to uphold Islam. Your God is death. Your God is not Allah. . . . What you do you do not do for Allah; you do it only to satisfy your own twisted sense of ego."[38]

To sum up, in the words of the State Department's John Beyrle: "Some believe that . . . the Cold War has been replaced by a clash of civilizations. Others, including some in my own country, believe that terrorism is somehow related to Islam. They are both wrong."[39]

Islam, a Positive Force

Islam, then, is not an enemy or a source of terrorism. But officials do not leave it at that. They even postulate two positive features of the religion: its compatibility with American ideals and its potential benefits for the United States.

There is nothing in the religion of American Muslims, Bill Clinton averred, "that would divide us, that would promote terrorism, that would be destructive of our values."[40] He and other officials then specified where exactly Islam complemented American values: "Devotion to family and to society, to faith and good works—are in harmony with the best of Western ideals."[41] John Beyrle found no conflict between Islam and "such Western ideals as personal freedom or individual choice."[42] A Department of State fact sheet announced that "most Americans and most Muslims share fundamental values such as peace, justice, economic security, and good governance."[43] The most colorful and specific formulation came from Deputy Secretary of Defense John

J. Hamre: "Quoting from the Preamble to the U.S. Constitution—
'We, the people of the United States, in order to form a more perfect
union, establish justice, ensure domestic tranquility, provide for the
common defense, promote the general welfare and secure the blessings
of liberty to ourselves and our posterity'—There isn't a word here that
a good Muslim wouldn't fight for."[44]

Better yet, Islam is declared to be a force for good in the United
States. Some officials content themselves with vague encomia. Djerejian called Islam "a historic civilizing force among the many that have
influenced and enriched our culture."[45] Likewise, his successor Pelletreau deemed Islam "a great civilizing movement."[46]

But on occasion, officials got specific. "We welcome Islam in America," said President Clinton, attributing to it three virtues: "It enriches
our country with Islam's teachings of self-discipline, compassion, and
commitment to family."[47] In another statement, he reiterated two of
these virtues and changed the third one: "America is made stronger by
the core values of Islam—commitment to family, compassion for the
disadvantaged, and respect for difference."[48] Albright ascribed a quite
different triad of virtues to Islam, "a faith that honors consultation,
cherishes peace, and has as one of its fundamental principles the inherent equality of all who embrace it."[49] Hillary Rodham Clinton found
yet other reasons to praise Islam: for its "universal values—love of family and community, mutual respect, education, and the deepest yearn-
ing of all—to live in peace . . . values that can strengthen us as a people
and strengthen the United States as a nation."[50]

John Hamre dispensed with the laundry list of virtues and instead
zeroed in on one in particular when he addressed a military group as it
broke the Ramadan fast: "In an America that sometimes is too busy
worrying about the latest fad in clothes, or the newest model of car or
other material things, it is good to be with people who think in a
broader way, who think about their relationship to God, who think
about charity, alms giving, as one of the central mandates of life. This
is a great thing. You're a great people to be with."[51]

Americans: Appreciate Islam!

But there is a fly in the ointment: the American "street" views Islam
less enthusiastically than do official spokesmen, and the discrepancy is

an embarrassment to the officials. Sometimes they simply ignore it. President Clinton reported variously that "Americans respect and honor Islam"[52] and "the United States has great respect for Islam,"[53] statements that he and his staff often repeated almost word for word. In a rare example of greater specificity, William Milam, the U.S. ambassador to Pakistan, wished to "lay to rest the myth that the United States is hostile to Islam and Islamic peoples"[54] and reported that "most of the American people" understand that there is no connection between terrorism and Islam.[55]

But the penitential confession, to the effect that Americans are biased against Islam, receives about equal time. Albright spoke of Americans' "appalling degree of ignorance" about Islam.[56] Hillary Clinton wrote that "we, as a society, too often mischaracterize Islam and those who adhere to its teachings."[57] Ambassador Robert Seiple spoke about modern Islam being "so terribly misconstrued."[58] Jeremy Gunn of the Office of International Religious Freedom was especially candid: "The religion of Islam has been the victim of unfortunate stereotypes in the United States."[59]

The picture is confusing. Is there "respect and honor" for Islam or is the religion "so terribly misconstrued"? The solution: Blame the media for blocking the positive image of Islam purveyed by the officials. A Department of State fact sheet rues the "sometimes-distorted portrayal of Islam in Western media" while promising that "the United States continues to address" this problem.[60] "The United States" here, of course, means the U.S. government, which is the source of truth and light, while the media is the source of the problem. It comes in for special criticism. Hillary Clinton fretted that "news stories about Muslims often focus on extremists like those responsible for the [1993] World Trade Center bombing and other acts of terrorism."[61] Albright waxed indignant about stereotypes applied "to a quarter of the globe's people." These figured "every day in the press, in public discussions, and even among those who consider themselves knowledgeable and fair-minded."[62] In short, there is a battle over U.S. opinion, and officialdom has the duty of enlightening a benighted populace.

Samuel Berger alluded to this when he explained why his boss, Bill Clinton, spoke so often on this subject: because "many Americans are naive about Islam." The president, he said, "made a conscious effort to dispel the old stereotypes of Islam . . . as a hotbed of fanaticism and terrorism . . . to overcome such prejudices and forge common cause for the things we all care about in the future: peace, self-respect, and coop-eration."[63]

U.S. officials are at pains to distance themselves from the great unwashed, those everyday people who watch the news and associate Islam with violence. According to Milam, "there are unfortunately some ill-informed . . . Americans who fear Islam . . . [who] confuse Islam with terrorism. I can tell you, without fear of contradiction, that the U.S. government does not share this confusion."[64] As a State Department fact sheet candidly reveals, "Whatever distortions exist, President Clinton, our diplomats, and others responsible for our offi-cial dealings with the Islamic world generally have a clear understand-ing and deep respect for Islam."[65]

This attitude explains why the State Department sees the educa-tion of Americans about Islam as part of its mission. "We should encourage Americans to learn more about Islam," wrote Albright.[66] Her staff advanced several proposals on how to achieve this. Ambas-sador Seiple deemed it "important to make sure that the State Depart-ment provides a point of learning and dialogue and exchange."[67] Gunn said the U.S. government needs "to do what it can to promote under-standing, dialogue and communication on issues."[68] A Department of State fact sheet sees a remedy "through education, people-to-people exchanges, and by encouraging responsible reporting in the mass media and accurate portrayal in the movie industry."[69]

Fortunately, officialdom hints, another party can help educate Americans about Islam: U.S. Muslims, whose presence, Bill Clinton said, has the virtue of deepening "America's respect for Muslims here at home and around the world."[70] Addressing an audience of Muslims, George W. Bush said roughly the same: "By educating others about your religious traditions, you enrich the lives of others in your local communities."[71] The Department of State fact sheet is less coy: "As the number of American Muslims continues to increase, and as that com-munity develops its domestic political visibility—through gaining elective office and founding effective political action committees—we will no doubt begin to see more consistently objective portrayals of Muslims in our media."[72]

Continuing a Tradition

One cannot but wonder what the objective of these officials might be. Why go to such lengths to pronounce Islam a faith completely unblemished by the violence of some of its practitioners? And why hold up Islam as an exemplar of American values?

This exercise has a patently practical objective: it is designed to lessen Muslim hostility to the United States. The chain of reasoning goes as follows: (1) Many Muslims crave Western respect for Islam and recognition of its virtues. (2) The U.S. government in turn yearns for acceptance by Muslims. (3) Therefore, Washington gives Muslims the acknowledgment they seek. (4) Grateful Muslims diminish their hostility to the United States. (5) Washington can realistically demand that those same Muslims come to the defense of the United States against the more radical Muslims who still oppose it. (In addition, some of this rhetoric serves domestic purposes, to assuage the U.S. Muslim population.)

Seen in this diplomatic context, the origins in 1992 of this official U.S. tradition of vocal support for Islam make sense, for it was in the aftermath of the Kuwait War that radical groups such as Osama bin Laden's began to make more headway in the Middle East and throughout the Muslim world.

One speculates whether this strategy will work. For perspective, it helps to look at two prior efforts along similar lines. "People of Egypt," Napoleon proclaimed upon his entry to Alexandria in 1798, "You will be told that I have come to destroy your religion; do not believe it! Reply that I have come to restore your rights, to punish the usurpers, and that more than the Mamluks, I respect God, his Prophet, and the Qur'an."[73] One of his generals, Jacques Ménou, even converted to Islam.

The history of Europe is replete with such statements. After Britain secured its rule over India, its officials made repeated professions of respect for Islam, so as to diminish Muslim hostility to their rule. During World War I, the Germans, who were allied with the Ottomans, proclaimed themselves the one European power sympathetic to Islam. A particularly bizarre instance dates to 1937, when the Italian dictator Benito Mussolini arranged for Muslim notables from

Italian-ruled Libya to gird him with the "sword of Islam" during a visit to Tripoli. "Muslims may rest assured," Mussolini intoned on that occasion, "that Italy will always be the friend and protector of Islam throughout the world." His foreign minister declared Muslim values perfectly compatible with fascism: "The Islamic world, in accordance with its traditions, loves in the Duce the wisdom of the statesman united to the action of the warrior."[74]

The analogies are admittedly not perfect, as none of the Joint Chiefs of Staff has yet converted to Islam; nor has President Bush girded himself with any swords. But he did visit a mosque, accept a Qur'an as a gift, and convene a *diwan* (assembly) of Muslim representatives at the White House. More deeply, U.S. objectives are nearly identical with those of Napoleon and Mussolini—to curry favor with a basically hostile population.

Implications Spelled Out

The earlier Western efforts to pander to Muslim sentiments came up short, as the Muslim leaders of Egypt fought Napoleon with all they had, while Mussolini failed to find the widespread Muslim support he had hoped to win. So too, the American effort will no doubt end in failure. It is nearly inconceivable that moderate Muslims will have any influence over their more radical coreligionists.

Practicalities aside, American officials would do well to ask whether their statements on Islam do not conflict with their government's basic principles. The United States has a message for the world, and that message is not Islam. The message, it hardly needs pointing out, is one of individualism, freedom, secularism, rule of law, democracy, and private property.

Finally, federal officials may not realize the implications of their scolding of Americans who are apprehensive about Islam, and their noisy espousal of that religion's virtues. Here, then, it is spelled out for them: In adopting a determinedly apologetic stance, they have made themselves an adjunct of the country's Islamic organizations. By dismissing any connection between Islam and terrorism, complaining about media distortions, and claiming that America needs Islam, they have turned the U.S. government into a discreet missionary for the faith.

Without anyone quite realizing it, the resources of the federal government have been deployed to help Muslims spread their message, and, in effect, their faith. If the "war on terror" is to have any larger purpose, it must be to free people from the yoke of politicized Islam. There can be no better place to begin than right at home.

10

A MONUMENT OF

APOLOGETICS

The *Oxford Encyclopedia of the Modern Islamic World* is a modern work in two senses.[1] First, and more plainly, it deals primarily with topics of the past two centuries. Unlike the *Encyclopaedia of Islam*—the mammoth reference work published by E. J. Brill and thirty-five years into the project only halfway done—with its concentration on matters medieval, the *Oxford Encyclopedia* not only provides entries on up-to-date topics (such as surrogate motherhood and the Muslim Brethren), but it also follows up old institutions (inheritance, *waqf*) into modern times. Particularly helpful is the serious coverage of new Muslim communities in the West and of twentieth-century Islamic thinkers (among the more interesting: Mohammed Arkoun and Hasan Hanafi, an Algerian and an Egyptian).

Edited by John Esposito of Georgetown University, one of the most articulate scholars of Islam, the *Oxford Encyclopedia* provides thoughtful and even coverage on many of these matters. Some entries deal with ambitious subjects, such as book publishing, dance, and economic development, and convey a sense of the topic in just a few paragraphs. Others deal with arcane topics, such as Islam in Suriname, the Hujjatiya school of thought, that otherwise would be beyond the reach of most readers. An interested reader might spend hours leafing through the four volumes, and he will consistently find well-presented and informative articles.

Of course, no matter how complete, some subjects will mysteriously be absent. The Alevis of Turkey, millions strong, seem not even to rate a mention. Saddam Husayn, though hardly a pious Muslim, would seem to deserve an entry given his Ba'th ideology, his war against Iran, and his appeal to the Islamists in 1990–91. The intriguing issue of predestination and fatalism (*jabriya, jahmiya*) is inexplicably absent, as is taxation deemed illegal by the laws of Islam (*maks*), an important issue for its role in inspiring revolts against Muslim authorities.

The *Oxford Encyclopedia* is modern in a second sense, too: in spirit. Like many other reference works in the age of deconstruction, it faces problems of identity and purpose. An encyclopedia used to be a straightforward compendium of known and useful facts. But when scholars increasingly agree that truth depends on one's vantage point (and especially one's gender, race, and class), the encyclopedic function becomes far less obvious. A large number of the 450 contributors to this work would seem to accept the modern notion that objectivity being unobtainable, there's little point in even trying. Instead of aspiring to objective, hard knowledge, one contributor after another offers essays—highly opinionated articles about such subjects as Islamic studies and feminism. Some go further and write naked diatribes. The entry on health care, for example, rails against "Eurocentric scholarship" and interprets the advent of European medicine as a "mechanism of social control in colonized Islamic societies."

Political Correctness Reigns

As this example suggests, political correctness reigns in the *Oxford Encyclopedia*. Thus, of the two articles that make up the entry on Arabic literature, one is an overview and the other an analysis of "Gender in Arabic Literature." An essay in the entry on "Women and Islam" is supposed to inform about the role and status of women in Islamic law, but it tells much less about this than about the author's feminist reinterpretation of that law. "Although certain social and economic regulations in the scripture seemingly favor men," she tells us, "the conditions prevailing at the time of the revelation, which seemed to justify such inequality, have lapsed." Over and over again, we learn a scholar's views of how things should be, not how they are.

Political correctness extends to the theological realm as well. Citing a 1969 book, *Muhammad's Thoughts on Death: A Thematic Study of the Qur'anic Data*, a contributor apologizes about the "unfortunate title and the assumptions behind it." (The title implies, contrary to Islamic tenets, that the Qur'an came from Muhammad, not God.)

Zionism and Israel, as might be expected, fare poorly in a reference work where objectivity is not the goal. In the entry on terrorism, we learn that "Arguably, the first modern act of political terrorism in the region was the bombing of the King David Hotel in 1947." Arguably, it's not: many incidents of terrorism preceded it. Most famously, the Armenian Dashnak Party captured the Imperial Ottoman Bank's office in Istanbul in August 1896, threatening to kill their hostages unless certain demands were met. Four people died directly as a result of this incident and some six thousand Armenians lost their lives in the resulting massacres. The article on the Arab-Israeli conflict reads like a screed from the PLO, with not even an attempt to appear unbiased. It tells volubly of Palestinians suffering at the hands of Israelis (discrimination, death) but never the reverse problem. Only one Israeli author—the arch anti-Zionist Simha Flapan—is permitted into the bibliography.

The tyranny that is most important in this encyclopedia, however, is the apologetic one. The crisis of the Muslim world—attested to by every serious analyst of the subject—can hardly be found in the *Oxford Encyclopedia*. Instead, this is a formal presentation for outsiders, hoping they will come away with a good impression. The entry on games and sport offers so unrelentingly upbeat a vision ("Women are sure to be spectators of sports on television in the privacy of their own homes"), even someone who knows nothing about the subject must realize he's being sold a piece of goods.

Hajj Amin al-Husayni, the midcentury Palestinian leader, gets whitewashed in the *Oxford Encyclopedia*: the entry for Husayni says, for example, that he tried "to persuade Hitler to pledge support for Arab independence." Really? In a letter dated January 20, 1941, and addressed to Hitler, Husayni appealed for aid to the Arabs to fight Zionists on the grounds that this would "cause the Jews to lose heart," especially in the United States, and that in turn would prompt Roosevelt to abandon his support for Britain. In other words, please help the Arabs and the Axis wins the war. That's a lot more than an appeal for help with Arab independence.

Time and again, contributors shield their subjects from criticism. Abbasi Madani, founder of Algeria's radical militant Islamic Salvation Front, is "known for his moderation." Rashid al-Ghannushi, the radical Tunisian thinker, is not criticized for his murderous plans but praised for his "masterly understanding of western and Islamic philosophies and a genuine concern for reconciling the basic tenets of Islam with modernity and progress." Better yet, he is lauded for his "important intellectual contribution" in "linking westernization with dictatorship"! If an unfortunate phenomenon simply cannot be hidden, it might be explained away. Take the case of violent militant Islamic groups: "The number of *jihad* organizations has been increasing in the Arab world, and indeed in much of the Islamic world. This fact does not say as much about Islam, as is often assumed in the West, as it says about desperate attempts to exploit Islam politically." Murderers in the name of Islam, in other words, reflect badly not on Muslims but on the West.

Less serious but still revealing is the fact that sources deemed politically incorrect simply do not turn up in the bibliographies. Of three recent biographies in English on Hajj Amin al-Husayni, two favorable ones, by Taysir Jbara and Philip Mattar, are listed, while the critical one—*The Grand Mufti*, by Zvi Elpeleg—is not. The entry on Ayatollah Khomeini omits a 349-page biography by Amir Taheri, *The Spirit of Allah*, presumably because it is unfriendly to that Iranian "saint." In a similar spirit of subjectivity, a son of Elijah Muhammad wrote the biography of Malcolm X. Odder yet is inviting individuals associated with certain Islamic organizations (the Institute of Muslim Minority Affairs or the International Islamic University at Kuala Lumpur) to compose the entries about themselves; of course, their entries read like press releases. These entries implicitly signal the message that there is no such thing as objective knowledge, so there is no point even to pretend to try for it.

Vanity bibliographies (in which authors refer to their own writings) further confirm this pattern of excluding unwanted information. One contributor cites himself in five out of ten bibliographic references. Others mention their own work in three out of six items, three out of five, and even three out of four. One author lists no less than seven of his own writings. In one case, a contributor has the amusing gall to call his book "my epic." It's hard to imagine such indulgences in the *Britannica* Eleventh.

A Frank Word

The occasional frank word comes as a relief amid this ocean of excuses and evasions. The entry on financial interest does not laud Islamic banking as a brilliant breakthrough but handles the subject skeptically: outside Iran and Pakistan, we learn, "where Islamic banks exist, their operations tend to rely almost exclusively on camouflaged interest." Maryam Jameelah, the impassioned Jewish convert to militant Islam, it is admitted, distanced herself from the movement when she realized the depth of its borrowing from the West.

Apologetics, once the preserve of Islamic polemicists, has invaded the universities; that is the unhappy message of the *Oxford Encyclopedia*. The base of knowledge is formidable, but the political constraints are stifling. If only the editor had the wisdom and discipline to rule out politically tinged submissions from his contributors, the *Oxford Encyclopedia* would be an excellent tome. But then, that would be asking for a very different academy from the one we actually have.

PART II

ISLAM REACHES AMERICA

�֍֎

The arrival of Taliban prisoners to the U.S. military base at Guantánamo Base in Cuba led to the odd situation in which American troops were guarding the very most fanatical of Al-Qaeda prisoners, one of whom can be seen on the left. The American authorities did their best to accommodate their prisoners religiously, including a sign, in Arabic, pointing the *qibla* (direction to Mecca) so that they can direct their prayers in the right direction. (REUTERS)

11

"WE ARE GOING TO
CONQUER AMERICA"

In the aftermath of the violence on September 11, American politicians from George W. Bush on down have tripped over themselves to affirm that the vast majority of Muslims living in the United States are just ordinary folk. Here is how the president put it on a visit to a mosque on September 17, 2001: "America counts millions of Muslims amongst our citizens, and Muslims make an incredibly valuable contribution to our country. Muslims are doctors, lawyers, law professors, members of the military, entrepreneurs, shopkeepers, moms and dads."[1] Two days later, he added that "there are millions of good Americans who practice the Muslim faith who love their country as much as I love the country, who salute the flag as strongly as I salute the flag."[2]

These soothing words were obviously appropriate for a moment of tension and mounting bias against Muslims living in the United States. And it is absolutely true that the number of militant Islamic operatives with plans to carry out terrorist attacks on the United States is a statistically tiny proportion of the Muslim population as a whole.

The situation, nonetheless, is more complex than the president would have it. The Muslim population is not like any other, for it harbors a substantial body—one many times larger than the agents of Osama bin Laden—who have worrisome aspirations for the United States. Although not responsible for the atrocities in September, these people share important goals with the suicide hijackers: both despise the United States and ultimately wish to transform it into a Muslim country. However bizarre this goal, the killing of over three thousand Americans requires that it be noted and seriously worried about.

An Ambition to Rule

Siraj Wahhaj, for example, is a black convert to Islam, the recipient of some of the Muslim community's highest honors, and called "one of the most respected Muslim leaders in America."[3] In June 1991, he enjoyed the honor of being the first Muslim to deliver the daily prayer invocation for the U.S. House of Representatives, at which time he recited from the Qur'an and appealed to the Almighty to guide American leaders "and grant them righteousness and wisdom."[4]

With this background, what does one make of his vision of Muslims taking over the United States, articulated to an audience of New Jersey Muslims in late 1992? "If we were united and strong, we'd elect our own emir [leader] and give allegiance to him . . . take my word, if 6–8 million Muslims unite in America, the country will come to us."[5] If Muslims were more clever politically, Wahhaj told his listeners, they could take over the United States and replace the constitutional government with a caliphate. Wahhaj openly calls for replacing the U.S. government with a caliphate.[6] He also served as a character witness for Sheikh Omar Abdel Rahman in the trial that found him guilty of conspiracy to blow up a number of New York City landmarks as part of a campaign to overthrow the government of the United States. In addition, the U.S. attorney for New York listed Wahhaj as one of the "unindicted persons who may be alleged as co-conspirators" in the sheikh's case.[7]

The contrast between Wahhaj's quiet appearance in the House and militant Islamic hope to dispatch the U.S. government fits into a larger pattern common to the American Muslim scene: speaking moderately to the general American public and radically to Muslim-only audiences.[8] This means that anyone who would understand the real views of American Muslims must delve deeper than the surface of their public statements.

The ambition to take over the United States is hardly a new one. The first Islamic missionaries from abroad arrived in the 1920s and unblushingly declared: "Our plan is, we are going to conquer America."[9] The audacity of this and other statements of intent did not go unnoticed, as a 1922 newspaper commentary shows:

> To the millions of American Christians who have so long looked eagerly forward to the time the cross shall be supreme in every land and the people of the whole world shall have become the followers of Christ, the plan to win this continent to the path of the "infidel Turk" will seem a thing unbelievable. But there is no doubt about its being pressed with all the fanatical zeal for which the Mohammedans are noted.[10]

Such hopes have become commonplace in recent years, as shown by Siraj Wahhaj's vision of an Islamic America. The key figure here was Isma'il Al-Faruqi, a Palestinian immigrant who taught for many years at Temple University and founded the International Institute of Islamic Thought. Called "a pioneer in the development of Islamic studies in America" by John Esposito,[11] he was the first theorist of a United States made Muslim. "Nothing could be greater," Al-Faruqi has written, "than this youthful, vigorous, and rich continent [of North America] turning away from its past evil and marching forward under the banner of Allahu Akbar [God is great]."[12] Zaid Shakir, formerly the Muslim chaplain at Yale University, has said that Muslims cannot accept the legitimacy of the secular system in the United States, for it "is against the orders and ordainments of Allah . . . the orientation of the Qur'an pushes us in the exact opposite direction as the forces that are at work in the American political spectrum."[13] Ahmad Nawfal, a leader of the Jordanian Muslim Brethren who frequently speaks at American rallies, has denigrated the United States as a country that "has no doctrine and no ideology, no thought, no values and no ideals," then goes on to say that if Islamists "stand up, with the ideology that we possess, it will be very easy for us to preside over this world once again."[14] Masudul Alam Choudhury, a Canadian professor of business, writes matter-of-factly about the "Islamization agenda in

North America,"[15] and Shamim A. Siddiqi even writes of the establishment of "Islamic rule" (Iqamat ad-Din) in the United States.[16]

For a full exposition of this outlook, one can do no better than to turn to a 1989 book written by Siddiqi, an influential commentator on American Muslim issues, and published in Brooklyn. Cryptically entitled *Methodology of Dawah Ilallah in American Perspective* (which can be more idiomatically rendered as *The Need to Convert Americans to Islam*), this 168-page study is nearly unavailable to a general audience (neither amazon.com nor bookfinder.com listed it over a period of months), but is widely found on militant Islamic Web sites and has a faithful readership among their visitors.[17] Siddiqi lays out a detailed justification and plan for Islamists to take over the United States that bears close attention.

Siddiqi argues that Muslims taking control of the United States has more importance than such goals as sustaining the Iranian revolution or destroying Israel, for it has greater impact on the future of Islam. The centrality of America hinges not on the reasons one might expect—its large population, wealth, or cultural influence—but on three other arguments:

- The perception of Washington as the premier enemy of militant Islam (or, possibly, Islam itself). In Siddiqi's colorful language, whenever Muslims move toward the emergence of an Islamic state, the "treacherous hands of the secular West are always there in the Muslim world to bring about the defeat of the Islamic forces." Muslim rulers are no help, for they are "all in the pockets of the Western powers."[18] To permit Islam to attain its rightful place requires that the "ideology of Islam prevail over the mental horizon of the American people."[19] The future of the Muslim world, Siddiqi concludes, "now depends on how soon the Muslims of America are able to build up their own indigenous movement."[20]

- Establishing militant Islam in America would signal the triumph of this ideology over its only rival, the bundle of Christianity and liberalism that constitutes Western civilization. (So much for Fukuyama's "end of history" thesis, which also appeared in 1989.)

- Joining Islam and the United States makes for an ideal team, Siddiqi wrote in a subsequent article. The United States is more successful than any country with a Muslim majority, but it lacks a guiding ideology and is decaying morally. Bringing together this successful country with that "superb ideology"[21] makes for an extraordinary combination.

Contemplating the implications of a militant Islamic victory in the United States, Siddiqi can hardly contain his enthusiasm, finding that this could mean that the establishment of "God's Kingdom" on earth no longer is "a distant dream."[22]

This dream, however, will just not happen by itself. To achieve it, Muslims must devote "all of their energies, talents and resources in building and strengthening the Islamic Movement of America."[23] American Muslims, in other words, have the paramount responsibility of bringing Islam to power in their country. Indeed, this will be how they are assessed on Judgment Day: "Every Muslim living in the West will stand in the witness box in the mightiest court of Allah . . . in Akhirah [the Last Day] and give evidence that he fulfilled his responsibility . . . that he left no stone unturned to bring the message of the Qur'an to every nook and corner of the country where he used to live [i.e., in the West]."[24]

Revolution or Evolution

If Islamists agree on the need to take over in Washington, they disagree on how to do so, whether through revolution or evolution.

Revolution. There are some—most famously Osama bin Laden—who see the United States as an "enemy of Islam"[25] that must be destroyed through violence. This outlook was forged by the sending of American troops to protect Saudi Arabia during the Kuwait crisis of 1990–91, when militants like bin Laden discerned a parallel between this and the Soviet occupation of Afghanistan (1979–89). As *The New Yorker* writer Mary Anne Weaver explains, to them, "the United States had become to Saudi Arabia what the Soviet Union had been to Afghanistan: an infidel occupation force propping up a corrupt, repressive and un-Islamic government."[26] That the Islamists in Afghanistan, by defeating the Soviets, had had a role in the collapse of the Soviet Union, made the notion of bringing down the United States that much more plausible. Innocent of any deeper understanding of how the two countries differed, the Islamists vaguely thought they could repeat their Soviet success in America.

The blind sheikh, Omar Abdel Rahman, may be the second most famous enemy of the United States. He calls on Muslims to "conquer the land of the infidels";[27] in his understanding, bombing the World Trade Center in 1993 was part of a revolutionary strategy of defeating America on the battlefield: as some of his followers put it, the goal was to "bring down their highest buildings and the mighty constructions they are so proud of, in order thoroughly to demoralize them."[28] Even some native-born Americans converted to Islam adopted this approach. One of them explained his goal in America to be akin to his efforts helping defeat the Soviets in Afghanistan by force of arms: "it is the duty of all Muslims to complete the march of *jihad* until we reach America and liberate her. And I will be a guide for them."[29]

There are, however, several problems with this head-on assault against the United States. First, Islamists have a caricatured vision of American life and hence completely misunderstand the impact of their assault. Attacks such as those on September 11 are intended to demoralize, prompt civil unrest, and weaken the country. In fact, as we have seen, they brought Americans together in a way not witnessed for years, showing a patriotism and sense of purpose. Second, Abdel Rahman is sitting out a life sentence in a federal penitentiary, his campaign of violence stillborn; Osama bin Laden became the target of a massive military campaign launched to get him "dead or alive." More broadly, it is very hard to see how the use of force against the United States can succeed in wearing down the country, much less leading to a change in government.

Third, violence implies looking at the United States as a whole as the enemy, thereby alienating the allegiance of most Muslims resident in the country. According to preliminary estimates compiled by Muslim groups, several hundred Muslims died in the World Trade Center collapse. This anti-Americanism especially puts off some converts to Islam. One of them, Jeffrey Lang, writes of his dismay attending a lecture in a San Francisco mosque not long after his conversion and hearing an immigrant medical student issue a seditious call to arms:

we must never forget—and this is extremely important—that as Muslims, we are obligated to desire, and when possible to participate in, the overthrow of any non-Islamic government—anywhere in the world—in order to replace it by an Islamic one.

But calling on Muslims to overthrow the U.S. government, Lang protested to the lecturer, means that accepting Islam was tantamount to an act of political treason. "Yes, that's true," the lecturer blithely replied.[30] The convert was appalled.

Evolution. The nonviolent approach has a brighter future. It is legal and it does not alienate loyal Americans. It implies an optimism about the United States; rescue it rather than destroy it. It works with Americans, not against them. These features make it both more attractive and realistic than revolution.

Most Islamists have adopted this approach. They present Islam as a way to "bring extremely beneficial things to this society."[31] As a teacher at an Islamic School in Jersey City, across the Hudson from New York, explains, the school's "short-term goal is to introduce Islam. In the long term, we must save American society."[32] A Pakistan-born professor of economics and finance explains that Muslims "have the opportunity and the responsibility to offer an alternative model"[33] to what exists in America. Isma'il Al-Faruqi, the professor of religion, held that propagating true faith is a step toward transforming "the unfortunate realities of North America" into something acceptable in God's eyes.[34]

Practically speaking, though, the key question is how Muslims establish an Islamic state in the United States through nonviolence. By two goals, comes the answer: increasing the numbers of American Muslims, and establishing Islamic law, the Shari'a.

GOAL 1: MORE AMERICAN MUSLIMS

Increasing the number of Muslims is the first priority, the basis for all else. Islamists aspire to transform American Islam, a new presence in the United States and just 1 to 2 percent of the population, from an exotic growth into a majority. Here is Wahhaj, explaining what this will mean:

I have a vision in America, Muslims owning property all over, Muslim businesses, factories, *halal* meat, supermarkets, all these buildings

owned by Muslims. Can you see the vision, can you see the Newark
International Airport and a John Kennedy Airport and LaGuardia
having Muslim fleets of planes, Muslim pilots? Can you see our
trucks rolling down the highways, Muslim names? Can you imagine
walking down the streets of Teaneck, [seeing] 3 Muslim high schools,
5 Muslim junior high schools, 15 public schools? Can you see the
vision, can you see young women walking down the street of Newark,
New Jersey, with long flowing *hijab* and long dresses? Can you see the
vision of an area of no crime, controlled by the Muslims?[35]

There are three possible means to increase Muslims numbers to
achieve this dream: immigration, reproduction, and conversion. Sens-
ing that overwhelming the country with immigrants would provoke a
backlash and that reproduction will take a long time, Islamists focus
most of their efforts on conversion.

Indeed, they see converting Americans to Islam as the central fact
of Muslim life in the United States. Al-Faruqi argued that it is the only
possible justification for Muslims to live in the United States. Whatever their reason for being there—economic opportunity, political
refuge, conversion, or accident of birth—living in America imposes on
them a "duty to call all non-Muslims to Islam."[36] Siddiqi says American Muslims have no choice in the matter—they are "ordained by
Allah" to do it,[37] adding hyperbolically that Muslims living in the
United States "have no right even to breathe" unless they help replace
Evil with Good.[38] Wahhaj, a convert, agrees: "Wherever you came
from, you came to America. And you came for one reason—for one
reason only—to establish Allah's *din* [faith], as a servant of Allah."[39]

Espoused too by other authoritative figures, these ideas have been
widely adopted. Many Muslims attest to the sense of responsibility in
their daily lives that comes from being an "ambassador for Islam,"
always mindful of the importance of winning new adherents to Islam.
The Muslim Student Association, a leading militant Islamic organization, heavily promotes such ideas.

Islamists are optimistic about their chances of success. How could
it be otherwise, given the truth of their message and the depravity of
modern American culture? Siddiqi sees circumstances in America as
"better and more conducive" for militant Islam than anywhere else.[40]
Abul Hasan Ali Nadwi, an important Indian Islamist, is certain that

"A life of Taqwah [piety] will immediately attract non-Muslims towards Islam."[41]

The Islamists have a point, for the more Islam is present, the more its message is available, leading to more converts. To make serious headway in the United States, Islam depends on hands-on contact and a personal experience with Muslims.[42] A survey of American conversions to Islam finds that over two thirds did so under the influence of a Muslim friend or acquaintance.[43] "Islam's increasing numbers in recent years could be a sign that attempts at educating the American public about Islam by several American-based Muslim organizations have been working," observes Anayat Durrani.[44] Converts often feel alienated from their own society ("America is sick")[45] and are looking for something to fill the gap; they usually discover Islam via a spouse, through a long religious search, or chance contact with a Muslim who impresses them.

GOAL II: APPLYING ISLAMIC LAW

Numbers and percentages of Muslims are necessary but not sufficient for Islamists; such countries as Turkey, Egypt, and Algeria have overwhelmingly Muslim populations, yet militant Islam is suppressed by their governments. Indeed, from a militant Islamic point of view, the situation in Turkey is far worse than in the United States, both because the rulers crack down harder on militant Islam and because it is worse to reject the divine message than to be ignorant of it. In addition to building up Muslim numbers, therefore, Islamists must also prepare the United States for their own brand of ideology. This means effecting a number of changes connected to applying Islamic law and creating a militant Islamic environment.

The changes fall into three main categories. The first pertains to forwarding Islamic rituals and customs: Permit recitation of the *basmallah* ("In the name of God, the Merciful, the Compassionate") in public situations. Win the right to broadcast the five daily Islamic calls to prayer (*adhan*) over loudspeakers. Gain facilities for Muslim prayers in public institutions such as schools and airports. Win public recognition of the Islamic holidays. Promote the Arabic language. Gain the right to slaughter a sheep or other animal on the Feast of the Sacrifice (*'Id al-Adha*) without heeding hygienic or other regulations. Segregate children by sex in school. Tolerate polygamy. Apply lenient or no pun- ishments to perpetrators of "honor" killings (against women deemed to have soiled their families' honor).

The second implies special privileges for Islam: Provide public financial support for Islamic schools, mosques, and other institutions. Recognize Islam in government settings (commemorative postage stamps, invocations at public events, celebration of Islamic holidays, library displays). Establish special quotas for Muslim immigrants. Restrict law enforcement's ability to deal with Muslims and militant Islamic organizations. Permit disrespect for national symbols. Institute affirmative action for Muslims. Force corporations to make special allowances for Muslims.

Finally, the Islamists seek to restrict or disallow what others may do: Punish activities offensive to Islam such as drinking liquor and gambling. Punish disrespect toward those religious figures whom Islam deems holy—especially the Prophet Muhammad, but also Moses, Jesus, Mary, and others. Punish criticism of Islam, militant Islam, or Islamists. Restrict anything construed as anti-Islamic. Close down the critical analysis of Islam. Disallow a public presence for other religions (e.g., singing Christmas carols in school).

What may be a puzzling list of goals should be understood in the light of a few comments. First, each of these steps in itself is relatively minor, implying no drastic changes. But cumulatively, they have the effect of establishing Islamic law and changing the American whole way of life by making Islam a public presence, ensuring that the work- place and the educational system accommodate Islam, adapting family customs to Islam, and winning it a privileged position in American life. Second, whereas most Westerners would look at this list and see that permitting such changes expresses an open-mindedness toward Islam, Islamists see these same acts as a way to whittle away at the existing order. Third, these steps would surely be followed by others that would sharpen the militant Islamic order: the prohibition of con- version out of Islam, criminal punishments for adultery, inequality in the treatment of men and women, banning the consumption of pork, and enhanced legal rights for Muslims.

Taking Over

Siddiqi provides the most detailed public analysis on the matter of how Muslims will actually take over. He assumes that bringing Islam to the United States will not be easy. Just as the Prophet Muhammad confronted die-hard opponents in pagan Mecca, so pious Muslims in America will face opponents, led by the "secular press cum media, the agents of capitalism, the champions of atheism (Godless creeds) and the [Christian] missionary zealots."[46] Doing battle with them demands focus, determination, and sacrifice, far more so than American Muslims have shown until now. Immigrants have the additional challenge of having to detach themselves from too much concern with their countries of origin (Egypt, Pakistan, and the like) and focusing instead on the United States.

It will be tough, but Siddiqi sees Muslims disposing of two great advantages. First, Americans are hungry for the militant Islamic message that "pinpoints the shortcoming of capitalism, elaborates the fallacies of democracy [and] exposes the devastating consequences of the liberal life-style."[47] Add in the dedication of militant Islamic cadres, and Siddiqi estimates that Muslims can prevail with just one tenth of the resources of their opponents; he specifically estimates that $10 million per year will suffice to achieve these hugely ambitious goals—though that sounds like far less than one tenth of the other side's resources.

Second, the United States permits Islamists to transform the country in a legal fashion. They never need to challenge the existing political order, but can achieve all their goals "without disturbing or violating the constitution of the U.S.A."[48] Indeed, because that Constitution guarantees complete government neutrality toward religion, Siddiqi finds that the existing system can be used to further militant Islamic aims. Democratic means can be used to spread the message—for example, by developing a lobby, cultivating politicians, and electing Muslim representatives. Nearly a million legal immigrants arrive in the country each year, as well as many more through the long coastlines and porous land borders. Courts are an important vehicle. Conversion to Islam is not just perfectly legal but happening in substantial numbers. These are advantages, it hardly needs stressing, that did not exist in Muhammad's Mecca or in any other society outside the contemporary West.

Yet things will not be completely smooth. A delicate point will be reached as society polarizes between the Muslim and non-Muslim camps and this becomes "visible in every walk of life."[49] At that point, the struggle between Truth and Error "acquires momentum and the tension increases along with it." Seeing the balance tip against them, the "Wrong Doers" will likely take desperate steps to "eliminate the Islamic Movement and its workers by force."[50] Islamists must tread very carefully to get past this point, taking care not to alienate the non-Muslim population.

Siddiqi happily speculates that the point will be navigated and eventually there will be what he calls a "Rush-to-Islam" that finds most Americans embracing Islam.[51] The process will culminate in a change of leadership. Muslims will find themselves not just enfranchised but actually running the show: with due representation in Congress and throughout American life, "they will be able to create a strong lobby in Washington for the promotion of Islam and its cause in this country as well as elsewhere in the world."[52]

Support for an Islamic America

A Muslim majority and Islamic law applied in the United States? It sounds far-fetched, yet Islamists are optimistic. Wahhaj finds that implementation of the Shari'a in the United States "appears to be approaching fast."[53] Siddiqi sees Islamists in power in Washington before 2020.[54]

Of course, Islamists are deluding themselves if they think that today's newborns will be going to college in an Iranian-style United States. But this does not mean their effort is entirely quixotic: their devotion, energy, and skill give them a real chance to move the country in their preferred direction.

Despite the complaints of bias—more voluminous than ever in the wake of the airplane hijackings on September 11—American Muslims have built an enviable record of socioeconomic accomplishment, they have wide public acceptance for their faith, and they have managed to

make it particularly difficult for anyone to criticize their faith or customs. The American Muslim community is in a position, especially as
its numbers grow, to affect the country's public life.

And if the institutions that dominate the community continue to
espouse the militant Islamic outlook they do today, that influence will
surely be in the militant Islamic direction. A survey of American Islam
finds that most of the organized Muslim community in the United
States agrees with the dream of turning the United States into an
Islamic country. With varying degrees of explicitness, most Muslim
spokesmen indicate that they hope to build an Islamic state in America. Muhammad Hisham Kabbani of the Islamic Supreme Council of
America estimates that "extremists" with this outlook have "taken
over 80 percent of the mosques" in the United States.[55] And not just
mosques: publications, schools, youth groups, community centers,
political organizations, professional associations, and commercial
enterprises also tend to share a militant Islamic outlook extremely hostile to the prevailing U.S. culture and wanting to replace it with an
Islamic order.

(Of course, that leaves 20 percent of the institutions and many
individual Muslims who reject the idea of turning the United States
into a Muslim country. Turks and those who flee militant Islamic states
like Iran and Sudan usually want nothing to do with Islamic politics,
nor do Sufis. Kabbani himself, for example, repudiates the application
of Islamic law in the United States, saying that "America was founded
on the principle of a separation between church and state. Therefore,
I presume it is not legally possible by virtue of the Constitution of this
country.")[56]

Nonetheless, many individuals and some organizations do express
a hope that one day Muslims will take over in the United States. For
example, the International Institute of Islamic Thought in Herndon,
Virginia, aims for nothing less than "the Islamization of the humani-
ties and the social sciences." But the best known Muslim political organizations—the ones whose members are invited to offer prayers and
invocations before the Congress, the president, and the two political
parties—are publicly coy about the full extent of their agendas, knowing full well that broadcasting aspirations to "conquer America" harms
them. So they announce arch-respectable goals: the American Muslim

Council works "towards the political empowerment of Muslims in America";[57] the Council on American-Islamic Relations is "putting faith into action";[58] and the Muslim Public Affairs Council seeks just to make American Muslims "an influential component in US public affairs."[59]

These modest aims notwithstanding, everything about the leading organizations points to their agreement with the "conquer America" agenda. But their leadership—people like Al-Faruqi and Shakir—on occasion explicitly raise this goal. Wahhaj is a top figure in many of the leading militant Islamic organizations (vice-amir of the Council of Muslim leaders of New York City, vice president of the Islamic Society of North America, a member of the North American Islamic Trust's board of advisers, as well as on the board of the Council on American-Islamic Relations and associated with the Muslim Alliance in North America and the Muslim Arab Youth Association), so his outspoken views contaminate every one of them.

Preservation of the Existing Order

That a significant movement in this country aspires to erode its bedrock social and legal arrangements, including the separation of church and state, and has even developed a road map toward that end, poses a unique dilemma, especially at this moment. Every responsible public official, and every American of good faith, is bent on drawing a broad distinction between terrorists operating in the name of Islam and ordinary Muslim "moms and dads." It is a true and valid distinction, but it goes much too far, and if adhered to as a guideline for policy, it will cripple the effort that must be undertaken to preserve our institutions.

What such an effort would look like is a subject unto itself, but at a minimum it would have to entail the vigilant application of social and political pressure to ensure that Islam is not accorded special status of any kind in this country; the active recruitment of moderate Muslims in the fight against Islamic extremism; a keener monitoring of Muslim organizations with documented links to Islamist activity, including the support of terrorism; and the immediate reform of immigration procedures to prevent a further influx of visitors or residents

with any hint of Islamist ideology. Wherever that seditious and totalitarian ideology has gained a foothold in the world, it has wrought
havoc, and some societies it has brought to their knees. The preserva-
tion of our existing order can no longer be taken for granted; it needs
to be fought for.

12

CONVERSION AND

ANTI-AMERICANISM

An odd political controversy briefly dominated the sports pages in March 1996. A black twenty-seven-year-old player in the National Basketball Association, Mahmoud Abdul-Rauf, refused to follow the NBA rule requiring players to stand in a "dignified posture" while the American national anthem plays. Instead, since the beginning of the 1995–96 season, he had decided to sit out the rendition of "The Star-Spangled Banner" that precedes each game. Born a Baptist in Mississippi and a convert to Islam in 1991, Abdul-Rauf declared that as a Muslim, he could not pay homage to the American flag, which he found a "symbol of oppression, of tyranny." More than that, he argued the flag directly contradicted his Islamic faith: "This country has a long history of [oppression]. I don't think you can argue the facts. You can't be for God and for oppression. It's clear in the Qur'an. Islam is the only way."[1]

The NBA responded firmly, suspending Abdul-Rauf until he changed his mind and obeyed league rules. He missed one game, then came around. Two factors probably weighed most heavily on him: losing $31,707 for each game not played, and facing wide opposition by other Muslims to his decision. If Abdul-Rauf agreed to stand during the anthem, he did not completely capitulate: while standing, he insisted he would "offer a prayer, my own prayer, for those who are suffering. Muslim. Caucasian. African-American. Asian."[2]

Though brief-lived and soon forgotten, this act of anti-American defiance raised important questions. When a young man earning almost $3 million a year and enjoying wide adulation talks publicly of hating his own country, something is afoot. What that might be is hinted at by a similar case a whole generation earlier, that of the boxer Muhammad Ali. After his conversion in 1960 to a form of Islam (Elijah Muhammad's Nation of Islam, then often called the Black Muslims), the former Cassius Clay adopted a set of intensely anti-American attitudes. Most famously, he refused to be drafted by the U.S. military, which led to the forfeiture of his heavyweight title. As Muhammad Ali later put it, he stood against "the entire power structure" in the United States, one dominated by Zionists who "are really against the Islam [sic] religion."[3]

Stories such as these have given American converts to Islam a reputation for hating their own country. Is this accurate?

Militant Islam and Anti-Americanism

Although numbers about religious affiliation in the United States are soft, Americans who have converted to Islam (plus their descendants) probably number up to 1 million. This makes them by far the largest convert population of Muslims in the Western world, though a distinct minority of the immigrant Muslims (and their descendants) in the United States. Of this million, the overwhelming majority are black; whites number maybe 50,000.

A convert's attitude toward the United States depends on what sort of Islam he adopts. If it is a tolerant and moderate form of the religion, then he probably has mild views. His Islam will be an act of private faith with few political consequences. This moderate spirit is widely found among the (mostly female) "Cupid's Muslims" who marry immigrant Muslims and the (mostly white) converts attracted to Sufism, the mystical dimension of Islam. The same goes for converts drawn to Islam as an old-fashioned way of life or for its emphatic monotheism. In short, there is nothing inherently antagonistic between the faith of Islam and good American citizenship.

Well-known moderate Muslim converts include Kareem Abdul-Jabbar, the basketball player, who has a positive view of the United States and a constructive attitude toward its problems. Mike Tyson, for all his troubles with the law (raping a woman, biting a rival boxer's ear), has found in Islam a soothing and civilizing influence (Islam, he says, is "going to make me a better person").[4] On a more elevated level, Robert Crane, a onetime foreign policy adviser to Richard Nixon, holds that the U.S. Constitution and the Bill of Rights were implicitly based on the Islamic principles of equality and justice for all. He concludes from this that the United States and Islam are totally compatible: "To be the best Muslim is to be a good American, and to be the best American is to be Islamic." In fact, "both paradigms, the overtly Islamic and the traditionalist American, are the same."[5]

Things are less positive if a convert adopts two specific types of Islam: the Nation of Islam (NoI), the black nationalist sect that originated in 1930 in Detroit, or the militant Islam brought from the Middle East and South Asia. In these cases, he will likely turn against his own country.

The Nation of Islam from its inception has forwarded a black nationalist outlook hostile to mainstream American culture and politics. "You are not American citizens," Elijah Muhammad, its longtime leader, told his people.[6] He completely disengaged from American political life, going to jail rather than enlist to fight in World War II and even disallowing NoI members from taking Social Security numbers. Malcolm X, his famous disciple, contrasted the pure evil of America with the pure good of Islam, saying that the American passport "signifies the exact opposite of what Islam stands for."[7] Continuing in this anti-American spirit, NoI's current leader, Louis Farrakhan, threatened back in the 1980s to "lead an army of black men and women to Washington, D.C., and we will sit down with the President, whoever he may be, and will negotiate for a separate state or territory of our own."[8] Farrakhan's weekly newspaper, *Final Call*, characterizes life in the United States as living in "the Belly of the Beast."[9] More directly, sitting among the America-haters in Tehran, Farrakhan declared in February 1996 that "God will destroy America at the hands of Muslims."[10]

Many black Americans leave the NoI and join normative Islam; should they become Islamists, they are likely to continue radically to disassociate themselves from everything around them. Even after his break with the NoI, for example, Malcolm X announced, "I'm not an American."[11] We have already noted the case (in chapter 11) of Siraj Wahhaj, who on one day opens a session of the U.S. Congress and on other days serves as a character witness for Omar Abdel Rahman when the latter is on trial for (and found guilty of) conspiracy to blow up New York bridges and buildings. Similarly, the onetime radical H. Rap Brown, now known as Jamil Al-Amin, declares that "When we begin to look critically at the Constitution of the United States . . . we see that in its main essence it is diametrically opposed to what Allah has commanded."[12] Ihsan Bagby, a prominent black American convert to Islam, says of Muslims: "Ultimately we can never be full citizens of this country . . . because there is no way we can be fully committed to the institutions and ideologies of this country."[13]

Black converts who went to fight the Soviets in Afghanistan in the 1980s may have proved to be the most extreme in their hatred of America. Having imbibed there the *mujahidin* vision of destroying both the Soviet Union and the United States, they vowed to do their part on return home. Other converts went further and actually acted on this vision, as an account in the British newspaper *The Guardian* explains: "When Clement Rodney Hampton-el, a hospital technician from Brooklyn, New Jersey, returned home from the war in Afghanistan in 1989, he told friends his only desire was to return. Though he had been wounded in the arm and leg by a Russian shell, he said he had failed. He had not achieved martyrdom in the name of Islam. So he found a different theatre for his holy war and achieved a different sort of martyrdom."[14] That "different theatre" was helping set off the February 1993 explosion at the World Trade Center in New York.

White Islamists have a similar outlook. They typically condemn American immorality, consumerism, tolerant social policies, and warm relations with Israel. They talk about "our society's unrelenting greed" and its neglect for the downtrodden.[15] The prolific Islamist author Maryam Jameelah, a convert from Judaism, in a book entitled *Islam versus the West* writes that "The country which a century ago produced an Abraham Lincoln now has little better to offer the world than Coca-Cola, chewing gum, vulgar songs and filthy pictures."[16]

In some cases, converts become actively disloyal, to the point of associating with hostile governments versus their fellow Americans. Mohammad Al-Asi, leader of the Washington Mosque, explicitly called on Muslims to vanquish the United States during the Kuwait crisis of 1990–91 (note how he uses the pronoun "we"): "If the Americans are placing their forces in the Persian Gulf, we should be creating another war front for the Americans in the Muslim world—and specifically where American interests are concentrated. In Egypt, in Turkey, in the Indian subcontinent, just to mention a few. Strike against American interests *there*."[17]

Accounting for This Pattern

Two factors mainly account for the bile of converts toward their country: personal temperament and the immigrant Muslim milieu. Americans drawn to militant Islam tend to be discontented with their lives or alienated from their society. For them, Islam's reputation as Christianity's historic arch rival is an attraction; accepting Muhammad and the Qur'an offers a protest vehicle that is far larger than themselves and much deeper than politics. (This helps explain why blacks are so very much more likely to convert; as the most downtrodden and discontented element in American society, Islam offers an ultimate expression for their anger.)

Converts are also influenced by the contempt for America that many immigrant Muslims bring from their homelands. Because accepting Islam is a very large step, one that often means breaking with family and friends, the new Muslim typically feels vulnerable and particularly in need of his new community's favor. This weakness makes him susceptible to the views of immigrants, including their negative outlook on America. Immigrants, to be sure, do appreciate America's economic opportunities and political freedom, but survey research suggests that at least half of them, and usually the more pious among them, despise American politics and ethics.[18] If anything, their first-hand experience in the United States enhances an assumption that Christian America has lost its faith and lacks moral strength. This outlook affects the new convert. Jeffrey Lang, a white professor of mathematics at the University of Kansas, candidly admits how, in an effort to win acceptance from his new coreligionists, he became "a passionate denouncer of everything American and a staunch defender of Middle-Eastern culture." In this spirit, he propagated conspiracy theories about the United States before taking hold of himself and going back to his old self.[19]

Reflections and Recommendations

Militant Islam—and to a lesser degree, the Nation of Islam—presents a great challenge to the United States. It turns significant numbers of Americans, plus potentially their progeny, against their country. No other body of ideas claims, as the militant Islamic ones do, blanket superiority over the culture, customs, laws, and policies of the United States; even the fascist and Marxist-Leninist ideologies dealt only with politics. Nothing in U.S. history prepares Americans for this challenge; no wonder the vast majority of them are happily unaware of the Islamist danger.

What is to be done? The priority is for journalists, intellectuals, clergy, and specialists to wake Americans up to this still incipient but rapidly growing problem.

Once awakened, the remedy is clear. With all due respect for the fact that turning against one's own country is legal (though acting on this hatred, through sedition or treason, is not), Americans must combat this self-hatred. Precisely because sitting out the national anthem or defaming the Constitution falls under the category of protected speech, combating it is less a matter of law enforcement and more one of moral suasion; less a burden on the government and more one on the citizenry. Yes, politicians should use their bully pulpits to decry such sentiments and government-run institutions—such as schools, the armed forces, prisons—can combat Islamist influence.

But private institutions, which are not subject to the full range of First Amendment and other constraints, have the major role here. (The government, for instance, could not have compelled Abdul-Rauf to stand for the anthem as did the NBA.) There's a place for nearly everyone—business executives, union leaders, Hollywood producers, investigative journalists, columnists, scholars and teachers, clergy—to debate with the self-hating Americans and the organizations they form. These must not be invited to the White House, consulted by the Department of State, quoted as authorities by the media, or hired by Wall Street firms. They should be combated, not legitimated.

One might think it obvious that life in the United States is immeasurably preferable to what one finds in Iran, Sudan, or Afghanistan of the Taliban. But clearly not everyone knows that. Those Americans who understand this simple truth must explain it to their fellow citizens.

13

FIGHTING MILITANT
ISLAM, WITHOUT BIAS

The entire United States, and New York City especially, has an urgent new question to deal with in the aftermath of September 11, 2001: How to view and deal with the Muslim populations living in one's midst?

The question, of course, is prompted by the fact that a militant Islamic network organized the hijackings and crashes and that these were carried out exclusively by Arabic-speaking Muslims resident in North America.

Initial reactions have been very varied. As noted in chapter 11, elite opinion, as voiced by President George W. Bush, rushed to disassociate any connection between the horrid events and the resident Muslim population. Other officials—Secretary of State Powell, Attorney General John Ashcroft, Governor George Pataki, Mayor Rudolph W. Giuliani—closely echoed these comments.

This approach may have made sense as a way to calm the population and stave off attacks against Muslims, but it clearly failed to convince everyone. Representative John Cooksey (Republican of

Louisiana) said on a radio show that anyone wearing "a diaper on his head and a fan belt wrapped around the diaper" ought to be "pulled over" for extra questioning at airports.[1] Survey research has consistently shown that Americans do tie Islam and Muslims to the horrifying events of early September. One poll found 68 percent of respondents approving "randomly stopping people who may fit the profile of suspected terrorists."[2] Another found 83 percent of Americans favoring stricter controls on Muslim entry into the country and 58 percent wanting tighter controls on Muslims traveling on airlines or trains.[3] Remarkably, 35 percent of New Yorkers favor establishing internment camps for "individuals who authorities identify as being sympathetic to terrorist causes."[4] Consistent with this, 31 percent of Americans in a national poll favor detention camps for Arab-Americans "as a way to prevent terrorist attacks in the United States."[5]

What in fact are the connections between the atrocities and the Muslim minority resident in the United States and Canada? What policies can be adopted to protect the country from attack while also protecting the civil rights of Muslims?

What Is Militant Islam?

The problem at hand is not the religion of Islam but the totalitarian ideology of militant Islam. Islam is one of the world's major religions in terms of duration, extent, and numbers of adherents; as a faith, it has meant very different things over fourteen centuries and several continents. If one were very broadly to generalize, something called "traditional Islam" was forged in the medieval period and it has inspired Muslims to be bellicose and quiescent, noble and not. There is simply no way to generalize over such a large canvas. Two common points one can note are that: Islam is, more than any other major religion, deeply political in the sense that it pushes its adherents to hold power; and once Muslims gain power, there is a strong impetus to apply the laws of Islam, the Shari'a.

Militant Islam goes back to Egypt in the 1920s, when the organization called the Muslim Brethren first emerged, though there are other strains as well, such as the Iranian one (largely formulated by Ayatollah Khomeini) and the Saudi one (the one to which the ruling Taliban in Afghanistan and Osama bin Laden both belong).

Militant Islam differs in many ways from traditional Islam. It is faith turned into ideology, and radical ideology at that. When asked, "Do you consider yourself a revolutionary?", Hasan at-Turabi of Sudan immediately replied, "Completely."[6] Whereas traditional Islam places the responsibility on each believer to live according to God's will, militant Islam makes this duty something the state is responsible for. If the first focuses on the individual, the second looks to the society. The one is a personal belief system, the second a state ideology.

Apologists would tell us that militant Islam is a distortion of Islam, or even that it has nothing to do with Islam, but that is not true; it emerges out of the religion, constituting a radically new interpretation. It adapts an age-old faith to the political requirements of our day by adopting some of the key premises of earlier totalitarianisms, fascism and Marxism-Leninism. It is an Islamic-flavored version of radical utopianism. Islamists constitute a small but significant minority of Muslims, perhaps 10 to 15 percent of the total population. They may appear law-abiding and reasonable, but they are part of a totalitarian movement and as such must be considered potential killers.

Traditional Muslims, usually the first victims of militant Islam, understand this ideology for what it is and respond with fear and loathing. The Egyptian writer Naguib Mahfouz said to his country's prime minister and interior minister as they were opposing militant Islam: "You are fighting a battle for the sake of Islam."[7] Other traditional Muslims concurred with Mahfouz, with one terming militant Islam "the barbaric hand of terrorism"[8] and another calling for all extremists to be "hanged in public squares."[9] In Tunisia, Minister of Religion Ali Chebbi says that Islamists belong in the "garbage can."[10] Algeria's interior minister Abderrahmane Meziane-Cherif concludes that "You cannot talk to people who adopt violence as their credo; people who slit women's throats, rape them, and mutilate their breasts; people who kill innocent foreign guests."[11] If Muslims feel this way, non-Muslims may as well; being antimilitant Islam in no way implies being anti-Islam.

Militant Islamic Violence

Islamists of all stripes have a virulent attitude toward non-Muslims and have a decades-long history of fighting with the British and French colonial masters and non-Muslim governments such as those of India, Israel, and the Philippines. It is vital to note that they also have had long and bloody battles against Muslim governments which reject the militant Islamic program. Perhaps the most spectacular such battle is the one still going on in Algeria, where more than 100,000 persons are said to have lost their lives in a decade's fighting, but others include Tunisia, Egypt, Syria, Turkey, and Pakistan.

Militant Islamic violence is a global phenomenon. During the first week of April 2001, for example, relying only on news agency stories, which are hardly exhaustive, I counted up the following incidents: Court judgments were issued against radical Muslims in Yemen, Jordan, Turkey, France, Germany, Italy, and in the United States. Deaths due to violent action occurred in Algeria (forty-two persons), the West Bank (one), Kashmir (seventeen), Bangladesh (two), and the southern Philippines (three). And assorted violence has occurred in many other countries, including Nigeria, Sudan, Afghanistan, and Indonesia. Islamists are well organized, to the point that fully eleven of the twenty-nine groups that the U.S. Department of State defines as "foreign terrorist organizations" are Islamist. Likewise, fourteen out of twenty-one groups outlawed by the Home Office in the United Kingdom are Islamist.

Starting in 1979, Islamists have felt confident enough to extend their fight against the West. The new militant Islamic government assaulted the U.S. Embassy in Tehran at the end of that year and held nearly 60 captives for 444 days. Eight American soldiers (the first casualties in this war) died in the failed U.S. rescue attempt in 1980. Violence against Americans began in earnest in 1983 with the attack on the U.S. Embassy in Lebanon, killing sixty-three. Then followed a long sequence of assaults on Americans in embassies, ships, planes, barracks, schools, and elsewhere.

Starting in 1979, Islamists also began targeting Americans on their own soil. Here is a rundown of militant Islamic violence in the United States prior to September 2001 that has led to deaths:

- the July 1980 murder of Iranian dissident Ali Akbar Tabataba'i by David Belfield, an agent of the Iranian government, in the Washington, D.C., area;
- the January 1990 murder of Egyptian Rashad Khalifa, a bio-

chemist and Islamic freethinker, in Tucson, Arizona;

- the November 1990 assassination of Rabbi Meir Kahane by the Egyptian El-Sayyid Nossair, in New York City;
- the February 1991 murder of Mustafa Shalabi in Brooklyn, New York, an Egyptian who ran the Al-Kifah Refugee Center, in a feud over control of the center;
- the January 1993 attack on CIA personnel, killing two, by the Pakistani Mir Aimal Kansi, outside CIA headquarters in Langley, Virginia;
- the February 1993 World Trade Center bombing by Sheikh Omar Abdel Rahman and his henchmen from many countries, including Sudan and the United States;
- the March 1994 shooting at a van of Orthodox Jewish boys, killing one, by the Lebanese Rashid Baz on the Brooklyn Bridge;
- the February 1997 murder atop the Empire State Building of a Danish tourist by the Palestinian Ali Hasan Abu Kamal; and
- the October 1999 crash of an EgyptAir flight near New York City, killing 217, possibly with an intent to wreck havoc on solid ground (the flight fell into the sea).[12]

(It bears noting that six out of the above nine incidents took place in the New York City region, as did most of the deaths in September 2001; and that between them, the New York and Washington areas account for all but one death on U.S. soil.) This listing does not include near misses, most especially the "day of terror" planned for June 1993 that would have witnessed the simultaneous bombing of the United Nations and the Lincoln and Holland tunnels. Lesser foiled plans include the letter bomb sent to the federal prison in Kansas where Sheikh Omar Abdel Rahman is incarcerated, bombs exploding during Seattle's millennial celebrations, and the botched effort to blow up a pipe bomb on New York's B subway line.

In short, the killing of three thousand Americans in September 2001 was not the start of something new but the escalation of a militant Islamic violence against the United States that has gone on for over two decades.

Islam in the United States

No one knows how many Muslims there are in the United States—the estimates range widely and are prone to exaggeration—but their numbers are clearly in the several millions. The body of faithful divides into two main components, immigrants and converts, with the former two to three times larger in size than the latter. Immigrants come from all over the world, but especially from South Asia, Iran, and the Arabic-speaking countries. Converts tend overwhelmingly to be African-American.

This community faces a profound choice in the United States, one likely to have a large significance for both the United States and Islam: It can integrate or it can be Islamist.

Muslims who integrate can live simultaneously as patriotic Americans and as committed Muslims. Integrationist Muslims, whether pious believers or not, do not have a problem giving allegiance to a government that is primarily non-Muslim. They teach that what American culture calls for—respect for one's neighbor, hard work, honesty—is compatible with the norms of Islam. In turn, they see Islam enhancing American values. Integrationists accept that the United States is not a majority Muslim country and seek ways to live successfully within its constitutional framework, keeping their personal customs to the extent they wish but foregoing the political dimensions of the Islamic message. Symbolic of this positive outlook, the Islamic Supreme Council of America displays an American flag on its Internet home page.

If Muslims go the Islamist route, they will reject the prevailing American civilization, based as it is on a mix of Christian and Enlightenment values, both of which they reject. As Islamists, they believe that their ways are superior and want to impose these on the country as a whole. In the short term, they promote Islam as the solution to the social and moral ills; in the long term, they work to turn the United States into not just a Muslim country but one run along militant Islamic lines (see chapter 11). However outlandish this goal, it is one which in militant Islamic circles is widely assumed and much discussed.

Integrationists tend to be people thankful to live in the United States, with its rule of law, democracy, and personal freedoms. Islamists despise these attributes and long to bring the ways of Iran or Afghanistan. The one seeks to create an American Islam; the other wants an Islamic America. Integrationists can take part in American life as do peoples from every other background. Islamists cannot. Which of these outlooks prevails obviously has great importance for the United States.

The Great Conundrum

The inescapable and painful fact is that only Muslims are tempted by militant Islam. This creates a moral, legal, and political challenge. While anyone might become a fascist or Communist, only Muslims become Islamists. And if it is true that most Muslims are not Islamists, it is no less true that all Islamists are Muslims.[13]

This has many implications. Police searching for suspects after militant Islamic violence takes place will not spend much time checking out churches, synagogues, or Hindu temples, but they will be visiting mosques. Immigration officials will look only at Muslim applicants for signs of militant Islamic fervor. Airport security will pay particular attention to passengers bearing Arabic names. Guards at government buildings will more likely question pedestrians who sport beards or wear headscarves.

Because these steps have an admittedly prejudicial quality to them, the authorities have shown great reluctance to focus particularly on Muslims. Islamists and their apologists (some Arab groups, academics, politicians, and lawyers) have taken advantage of this sensitivity to stifle any attempts to single out Muslims. Thus, when Muslims are involved in crime, officials bend over backwards to disassociate their motives from politics, and especially from militant Islam. Two examples, both in New York City:

- A Lebanese cab driver with a well-documented fury at Israel and Jews rained a hail of fire on a van full of Hasidic Jewish boys driving across the Brooklyn Bridge, killing one; in response, the FBI ascribed his motive to "road rage." Only after persistent efforts by the murdered boy's mother did the FBI finally relent and, almost seven years after the killing, agree to classify the case as "the crimes of a terrorist."[14]

- A Palestinian gunman killed one person at the top of the Empire State Building, then left a suicide note in which he accused the United States of using Israel as "an instrument" against Palestinians.[15] Steven Emerson, a former Senate aide and investigative reporter for such media as *U.S. News & World Report* and CNN, has written that "Although not publicly revealed, law enforcement officials found out that Abu Kamal had received assistance from members of a Florida mosque. These members helped him get his gun, accompanied him on target practice, and escorted him on a planned but aborted shooting in Miami."[16] But New York City officials dismissed the gunman as "one deranged individual working on his own" (Police Commissioner Howard Safir)[17] and a "man who had many, many enemies in his mind" (Mayor Rudolph Giuliani).[18]

It may be unpleasant to focus in on militant Islam and Muslims, but there is no longer a choice. Airline security personnel once looked especially hard at Arabs and Muslims until the lobbies raised such a fuss about "airline profiling," on the grounds that this practice "unfairly singles out" minorities, that it was effectively abandoned. Current policy remains "vigilant in ensuring that the airport security procedures, mandated by FAA and implemented by the airlines, are not unlawfully discriminatory."[19] The airlines themselves now heartily endorse this policy.[20] Yet the absence of ethnic profiling on airplanes meant that nineteen Arab Muslims could board four separate flights on September 11 and commandeer all four planes. The reluctance to come to terms with militant Islam is understandable but unrealistic. Pretending this ferocious ideology does not exist is a form of self-sacrifice.

The focus on Muslims must go well beyond the airport to touch on any and all facets of life. The four teams of September 11 hijackers showed how deeply the deception can go. As one investigator explained, noting the length of time these hijackers spent in the United States, "These weren't people coming over the border just to attack quickly. . . . They cultivated friends, and blended into American society to further their ability to strike."[21] All Muslims, unfortunately, are suspect.

On the positive side, many Muslims (and Arab-Americans) understand that by accepting some personal inconvenience and even humiliation, they are helping to protect both the country and themselves. Tarek E. Masoud, a Yale graduate student, shows a maturity many of his elders seem to lack: "How many thousands of lives would have been saved if people like me had been inconvenienced with having our bags searched and being made to answer questions? People say profiling makes them feel like criminals. It does—I know this firsthand. But would that I had been made to feel like a criminal a thousand times than to live to see the grisly handiwork of real criminals in New York and Washington."[22]

Two Quite Different Goals

The paramount objective is to achieve two quite different goals simultaneously: safeguard Muslim civil rights and protect the society from militant Islam. My recommendations fall into four general categories.

1. The easiest to deal with are Islamists who happen not to be U.S. citizens:

   - Exclude foreign Islamists, the adherents of a radical ideology. Each Islamist who enters is one more enemy on the home front. It is imperative to keep out visitors and immigrants alike who have Islamist records. Potential visitors or residents need to be vetted for their speech, their associations, and their activities. This may offend some purists (as similar legislation to keep out Marxist-Leninists did in past decades), but taking these steps is clearly legal and it is a simple matter of due diligence and self-protection. Making this easier is the fact that immigration rules already provide for such screening. Though written decades before militant Islam appeared on the scene in the United States, the McCarren-Walter Act of 1952 excludes anyone seeking to overthrow the government. Other regulations permit the exclusion of persons on suspicion of terrorism or "potentially serious adverse foreign policy consequences." These laws exist—they need to be used.

   - Use the "secret evidence" provisions. These permit the Immigration and Naturalization Service to rely on classified evidence to keep foreigners off the streets. The affected persons have a choice to stay incarcerated or leave the country.

- Monitor resident Islamists who are not citizens. They too need to be watched carefully for speech, associations, and activities that indicate militant Islam, with an eye to expulsion. The September 11 hijackers are poster boys for this need.

2. Islamists who are citizens enjoy the full protection of the law but they need to be watched:
- Maintain the utmost respect for individual Muslims, mosques, and other institutions. A time of crisis does not change the assumption that each of us is innocent until proven guilty.
- Avoid making prejudicial statements about Muslims, remembering that a great majority of them are innocent of militant Islam or illegal behavior.
- Provide extra protection to prevent acts of vandalism or hooliganism against Muslim property and individuals.
- Have politicians and other opinion leaders speak out to reinforce these points.
- Distinguish between Islam and militant Islam. It's obvious but it's also easy to forget. The former is the religion of Muslims, the latter is the ideology of Islamists.
- Strengthen airplane-profiling procedures. Just as airport security takes a closer look at twenty-year-olds than octogenarians, so must Middle East–looking types get more attention than Scandinavians. This is a commonsensical measure to keep an especially watchful eye for Islamists.
- Focus on the prospect of militant Islamic "sleepers." These are individuals who go quietly about their business until one day they are called into action. Tarik Hamdi carried a crucial battery to Osama bin Laden in Afghanistan. Ali A. Mohamed, a sergeant in the U.S. Army, used his military skills on bin Laden's behalf. The nineteen hijackers of September 11 had lived normal-seeming lives until the day they were called into action. Sleepers are caught through vigilance at the borders, with good intelligence, and through citizen vigilance.
- Reduce the broader climate of hatred and extremism among American Muslims, for this has led to terrorism. The Lebanese-born driver who killed a Hasidic boy on the Brooklyn Bridge; finds one analyst, "lived in a milieu that cultivated terrorism"

and that "encouraged [him] to perpetrate violence."[23] The government and other institutions need frankly to acknowledge the alienation among resident Muslims and to make it a priority to confront and diminish the antisocial forces at work in this community.

3. Combat the totalitarian ideology of militant Islam:
   • Isolate noisy and vicious militant Islamic institutions such as the Council on American-Islamic Relations, the American Muslim Council, and the Muslim Public Affairs Council. They should be avoided by politicians, the media, corporations, fellow voluntary organizations, and all of mainstream society. More, they should be closely monitored by the tax authorities and other law enforcement, much as the Teamsters are.
   • Shut down Internet sites that promote violence, raise money for this purpose ("Donate money for the military Jihad"), and recruit new members. The U.S. government began this process in September 2001 when it closed down InfoCom, a Dallas-based host for many militant Islamic organizations, some of which were sending money to militant Islamic groups abroad.

4. Finally, society as a whole has to make some changes:
   • Look to moderate (i.e., non-Islamist) Muslims for vital help in the struggle against militant Islam, for both tactical reasons (these are the people first injured by its excesses) and public relations ones (their presence makes the charge of "Islamophobia" much harder to sustain). Listen to their advice and look to them to help penetrate the clandestine militant Islamic organizations.
   • Insist that experts on Islam and Muslims—academics, journalists, religious figures, and government officials—play straight. They have apologized for their subject matter rather than honestly interpreting it, leading to egregious mistakes. As such, they bear some responsibility for the unpreparedness that led to September 2001's disaster.
   • Demand objectivity from the media, which has shamefully covered up what might be criticized about Islam and Muslims. The 2001 PBS documentary *Islam: Empire of Faith* offered, as *The Wall Street Journal* put it, an "uncritical adoration of Islam, more

appropriate to a tract for true believers than a documentary purporting to give the American public a balanced account."[24] Islamists in New York City celebrated the destruction on September 11 at their mosques but journalists refused to report this development, effectively hiding it from the U.S. public.

Implementing these steps permits Americans to be fair toward the moderate majority of Muslims while adopting a very tough stance toward the militant Islamic enemy. This combination requires sensitivity without political correctness—a tough but achievable balance if done honestly and intelligently.

14

CATCHING SOME SLEEPERS

President George W. Bush provided a good definition of sleepers and the problem they pose in his 2002 State of the Union address: "Thousands of dangerous killers, schooled in the methods of murder, often supported by outlaw regimes, are now spread throughout the world like ticking time bombs, set to go off without warning."[1] Sleepers—those seemingly law-abiding individuals who live quietly and inconspicuously near the scene of their future operations, waiting for orders to spring into action—make up one of the leading security problems facing the United States. Indeed, one day after that speech, FBI director Robert S. Mueller expressed his fear that "sleeper cells" exist within the United States and declared that they require the country to remain on extended high alert.[2]

It is important to understand that these sleepers are a vital part of Al-Qaeda's network, much of which exists outside Afghanistan. The author of a best-selling book on the Taliban, Ahmed Rashid, notes that Al-Qaeda "has always been divided into two halves. One is the half which is based in Afghanistan, fighting with the Taliban. And they will certainly be eliminated. But the tens of thousands of al Qaeda militants, usually well-educated, middle class people who have come into Afghanistan, trained and then left, and settled down in many foreign countries, these cells . . . are going to remain."[3] Others estimate that an even smaller proportion—perhaps 20 percent—of Al-Qaeda's assets were ever in Afghanistan. While being secretly recorded by Italian police, a member of Al-Qaeda's Milan cell boasted that his organization is "everywhere."[4] And indeed, according to intelligence sources, as many as seventy thousand agents trained in weapons and explosives remain at large in some fifty countries. What are they doing there?

Preparing for further acts of terrorism, of course. This requires a substantial infrastructure of individuals placed in mosques, Muslim institutions, financial institutions, law firms, government offices, and many other sensitive positions. But the key operatives are the sleepers. Documents found in Afghanistan point to larger numbers of sleepers trained at Al-Qaeda camps in that country than previously imagined. One estimate sees one thousand five hundred of them in North America and Europe.[5] In Los Angeles, for example, the authorities are watching up to thirty individuals.[6] Or this: in mid-September 2001, some 250 members of Al-Qaeda, thought to be sleeper agents, fled Afghanistan to an island in the Indian Ocean off the coast of Africa, from which point they dispersed to parts unknown.[7]

Nor is Al-Qaeda the only source of militant Islamic sleepers. Yonah Alexander of the Potomac Institute for Policy Studies notes that Hizbullah, the militant Islamic organization of Lebanon, "has sent entire families to settle in Latin America, South Africa and Europe. It's a long-term approach that follows the Soviet model to send sleepers."[8]

September 11 showed what damage sleepers can do. Catching them before they wake up is one of the most urgent and most difficult tasks in the war on terrorism.

Dealing with the Problem

U.S. Attorney General John Ashcroft understated the case when he observed in mid-October 2001 that it is "very unlikely" that all of those with a part in the suicide hijackings of September 11 and other "terrorism events" have been apprehended.[9] Indeed, the FBI has initiated at least 150 investigations of suspected sleepers (according to CNN), confirming just how much work remains to be done.[10]

The trouble is, the federal government has a record of proven incompetence at rooting out sleepers going back to the 1980s. The story of Ali Abdelsoud Mohamed, an Egyptian immigrant born in 1952, shows just how deep the rot has gone. An officer in the Egyptian military, Mohamed rose to the rank of major in Egypt's special forces. At some point, he joined the militant Islamic terrorist group that in 1981 assassinated President Anwar Sadat. Under growing suspicion for extremist views, he was cashiered in 1984. A year later he moved to the United States and joined the U.S. military, rising to the rank of supply sergeant as well as lecturer on the Middle East culture at the U.S. Army's special warfare school in Fort Bragg in 1986–89. He also began working for Osama bin Laden then. Mohamed taught his army skills to Al-Qaeda's recruits, translated military manuals from English into Arabic, and, as one of bin Laden's oldest and most trusted aides, helped plan operations. The most important of these was in Kenya, where he admits he "took pictures, drew diagrams, and wrote a report." Bin Laden later "looked at the picture of the American embassy and pointed to where a truck could go as a suicide bomber."[11] His colleagues blew up the embassy in August 1998. Mohamed's case points to a massive failure on the part of both the State Department, which issues visas to foreigners, and the U.S. Army.

More recently, the chance arrest in December 1999 of Ahmed Ressam, an Algerian member of Al-Qaeda, as he was crossing the Canada-U.S. border to bomb Los Angeles International Airport, opened a window into the substantial network of sleeper agents already within the United States. (Information he provided also led to the arrest of sleepers in four European countries.)[12]

How to tell who might be a sleeper? Don't ask the feds; Mohamed himself, when pleading guilty to his crimes, dismissed current profiles of sleepers as "invalid."[13] He was probably referring to the fact that the sixteen men convicted in the 1993 World Trade Center bombing and related conspiracy cases had a specific profile that reigned for many years afterwards: uneducated, "conspicuous hotheads, young immigrant men from the poorest and most radicalized Arab countries, clustered around a fire-breathing preacher at an established mosque," all of them working for a "state sponsor" of terrorism.[14] Other than being young immigrant men, the September 11 hijackers have none of these characteristics.

Nor are other governments better prepared: Hassan Butt, a twenty-two-year-old British Muslim, who claims to have helped recruit more than two hundred British volunteers to fight for the Taliban in Afghanistan, disdained the British ability to protect the society, maintaining that "The security forces and intelligence services within Britain are not competent to deal with sophisticated Mujahideen."[15] Magnus Ranstorp of the University of St. Andrews in Scotland criticizes Western intelligence in the 1990s for having "take[n] the eye off the ball" on the sleeper issue.[16]

For Washington to get serious about this problem requires some substantial changes. In particular, Congress should review current laws to protect the country from them. Here are four specifics that need changing:

- The FBI and CIA face a barrage of regulations restricting their intelligence-collecting abilities actively to collect information on and penetrate hostile groups.
- Immigration law does not consider membership in a terrorist organization, or advocacy of acts of terrorism, as grounds to exclude a foreigner.
- The Department of Transportation instructs airlines "not to target or otherwise discriminate against passengers based on their race, color, national or ethnic origin, religion, or based on passengers' names or modes of dress,"[17] thereby prohibiting the intelligent use of passenger profiling.
- A law dating from 1986 prohibits an employer from requiring specific documentation from would-be employees to prove their right to live and work in the United States. An employer must accept virtually any documents an applicant submits—school report cards, doctors' records, even day care receipts. If the employer, even one with public safety responsibilities, asks to see a passport, green card, or birth certificate, he is liable to be sued by the Department of Justice and to be fined a hefty civil penalty.

Many other institutions besides the government also have a major role in protecting the country, something John Ashcroft recognized when he called for the establishment of a "national neighborhood watch."[18] Some local programs have sprung up, such as the New Jersey–based Community Anti-Terrorism Training, which deputizes community groups and citizens by training them to spot possible dangers by becoming more aware of their environment,[19] but the bulk of the responsibility falls on institutions, especially corporations. Recall how airport security operators, flight instruction companies, and airlines had their shortcomings brutally exposed on September 11. Manufacturers of weaponry and paramilitary equipment have been lax in controlling their sales. Banks have not cracked down on money laundering. Hi-tech firms have scoffed at the need for controls on their products. Educational institutions have taught anyone qualified the secrets of electrical engineering.

Proving that hardly any business is exempt, consider what happened to ABC News when it employed Tarik Hamdi of Herndon, Virginia, to help secure an interview with bin Laden in early 1998. The network transported Hamdi to Afghanistan, unaware of his real purpose in going there—to carry a replacement battery to bin Laden for the satellite telephone he would later use to order the embassy bombings in East Africa.[20]

In some cases, private institutions have done a better job of discerning sleepers than has law enforcement. Most notable is the case of the Pan Am International Flight Academy in Minneapolis, where the flight instructor became immediately suspicious of his student, Zacarias Moussaoui, who showed no interest in basic aviation skills but wanted only to practice on an advanced commercial jet simulator. "Do you realize how serious this is?" the instructor asked an FBI agent. "This man wants training on a [Boeing] 747. A 747 fully loaded with fuel could be used as a weapon!" In this case, at least, the FBI did arrest Moussaoui. But when Pan Am's Phoenix branch called the Federal Aviation Administration (FAA) to report on Hani Hanjour, who later piloted the plane that crashed into the Pentagon, the FAA responded by sending an employee to observe Hanjour. The result? He discussed with Pan Am the issue of Hanjour's poor English and finding someone to help him with this obstacle to his becoming a pilot! "The school was clearly more alert than federal officials," observes Representative Martin Sabo of Minnesota.[21]

Ira A. Lipman of Guardsmark, a leading private security firm, warns that "sleepers are one of the most dangerous elements facing the United States in the years ahead" and argues that private organizations must be vigilant no less than public ones. In particular, he notes the need for comprehensive background investigations and proactive protective systems. Although it is hard to find anyone who will dispute these points post–September 2001, it is true that this good advice is only sometimes implemented in full.

Deception

Granting that sleepers can do terrible damage, how does one recognize them? While the great majority of sleepers to date have been young Middle Eastern Muslim men, this pattern must be used with caution. The fact is, militant Islam is an ideology open to all races, ethnicities, and nationalities. David Belfield, the Iranian agent who assassinated a man outside Washington, D.C., in 1980,[22] and Clement Rodney Hampton-El, a culprit in the first World Trade Center attack, are both African-Americans. A plot in 2001 against the U.S. Embassy in Paris depended in part on so-called white Moors, or French converts to Islam such as the two French brothers, David and Jerome Courtailler.[23] Richard Reid, the would-be shoe bomber, is half-English and half-Jamaican.

Nor does looking piously Islamic offer much of a clue. Most pious Muslims, of course, are not terrorists, a fact that came home when a state trooper on the Pennsylvania Turnpike in September 2001 stopped the car carrying Sheikh Muhammad Hisham Kabbani of the Islamic Supreme Council of America in order to check out what one person called "something fishy."[24] In fact, Kabbani—who wears a flowing robe and has a full beard and is a patriotic citizen—was driving home from a private prayer session with the president of the United States.

The problem, rather, has to do with a person's subscribing to militant Islam, the Islamic-flavored totalitarianism that fuels violent movements from Egypt to the Philippines, that has brought low Iran and Algeria, and has devastated Afghanistan and Sudan. Its adherents seek to bring this radical utopian program not just to majority-Muslim countries but even to Western Europe and North America. About one of every eight Muslims worldwide accepts militant Islam. These today

are the prime threats to the United States and other Western countries. They have proven themselves to be ideologically dedicated, ruthless, and technically sophisticated. They will stop at nothing to harm
or even destroy the countries they hate.

In normal circumstances, militants take pride in making themselves conspicuous through their appearance and clothing, their
actions and statements. For obvious reasons, however, sleepers prefer
to blend into the nonmilitant majority, so they take precautions to
hide themselves. They "don't wear the traditional beards and they
don't pray at the mosques,"[25] Mohamed testified. Al-Qaeda instructs
its agents to wear Western clothes and (advised some poorly spelled
English-language class notes found in a training house in
Afghanistan), "Don't taike any thing wich belong to Islam."[26] A captured Al-Qaeda encyclopedia, *Military Studies in the Jihad Against the
Tyrants*, instructs sleepers to "have a general appearance that does not
indicate Islamic orientation," and specifically mentions the need for
men not to wear a beard. The book also admonishes sleepers not to
denounce the inequity in their midst, not to use common Islamic
expressions such as "peace be on you," nor to frequent Islamic locations, such as mosques.[27]

Sleepers might be married to non-Muslims; indeed, they make a
practice of using their families as cover. "They often avoid Muslim
communities, living blameless lives, paying their taxes, holding down
steady jobs," notes Simon Reeve, the biographer of Osama bin Laden.[28]
And while the leaders live abstemiously and according to Islamic precepts, the lower ranks are more self-indulgent, with a taste for pornography, women, liquor, and drugs. The man accused of planning to ram
an airplane into the fifty-five-story Rialto Towers, Australia's highest
building, often turned up twice a week at the Main Course brothel in
downtown Melbourne, where he became notorious "as a bit of a sneak,
always trying to get more than he paid for."[29]

Such duplicity makes it much harder to discern who should be suspect. "It's like a ghost in front of you," commented a senior French official about the September 11 gang in general.[30] "They didn't do
anything to raise eyebrows," said an acquaintance about two of its
members in particular.[31] For sleepers, this deception also has the
advantage of bringing the Muslim population as a whole under suspi-

cion, which both provides cover and raises questions of bias (often proving an obstacle to effective law enforcement).

Recognizing Sleepers

Despite these difficulties, ways do exist to distinguish the likely sleepers from other Muslims. To begin with, all known sleepers until now have been young men. (The only women arrested for Al-Qaeda activities were two Algerians producing fake credit cards and passports in Leicester, England.) Perhaps the militant Islamic networks will one day go beyond this self-imposed limitation, but for now it appears to be one way of winnowing down the pool of potential suspects.

It is hard for sleepers to maintain a perfect cover. Connections to foreign countries offer one set of warning signals:

- Arrival from countries where violent militant Islamic groups (such as Al-Qaeda) are known to operate;
- Long, unexplained absences; or absences for vague purposes of religious education, charity work, or pilgrimage;
- Travel to hot spots where Muslims are fighting non-Muslims (Bosnia, Chechnya, Lebanon, Kashmir);
- Travel to countries where militant Islam rules (Sudan, Iran, Afghanistan).

Sleepers much prepare themselves for their operations, and this can leave telltale indications:

- Study of technical subjects (such as electrical engineering or computer sciences) that would help pull off an operation.
- Collecting information on subjects (e.g., crop-dusting planes) that could help in carrying out an operation.
- Working in an area (such as import/export) that serves as a cover for preparing for an operation.
- Engaging in para- or military training, perhaps under guise of preparing to do security work (e.g., serving as a bodyguard).
- Physical training.
- Possession of such artifacts as detonators and a protective suit against chemical and biological weapons.

- Purchase of chemicals and other dual-use materials.
- Scouting out military bases, government buildings, and other potential targets; practicing routines; and otherwise rehearsing for an operation.
- Possession of instructions for conducting *jihad* of either a spiritual nature (how to prepare for one's suicide death) or a practical nature (how to smuggle detonators).

Some attitudes raise red flags:

- Support for militant Islamic groups and fronts.
- Outspoken support of Muslims in combat against non-Muslims.
- Excusing violence against Americans on the grounds that American actions provoked the problem.
- Disparagement of Western civilization in favor of Islamic civilization.
- Fury at the West, for reasons ranging from the personal (unemployment) to the global (policy toward Iraq).
- Bigoted statements against non-Muslims in general ("infidels") or specifically against Jews, Christians, or Hindus.
- Seeing moderate Muslims as apostates from Islam.
- Conspiracy theories about Westerners (e.g., the CIA arranged for the 2001 attack on the World Trade Center to boost its funding levels).
- Accusing the West of trying to destroy Islam.
- Hoping to apply Islamic law in the United States.
- Disregard for the U.S. legal system where it prohibits something permitted by Islamic societies (such as polygamy or the "honor" killing of women).

Problems having to do with identity are a further indication:

- Fraudulent personal identities, sometimes with inconsistencies. (Zacarias Moussaoui presented himself as French, but when spoken to in French not only could not reply but became belligerent.)
- A cover story that does not ring true. (A young Arab, recently arrived in Spain, wants to buy a watch repair shop and the owner

agrees to sell, but something seems not right—"He had fat fingers, so how was he going to fix watches?")[32]
- Evasive about his background ("I'm from the Middle East" rather than giving a country name).[33]
- Losing passports or other documentation so as to get new ones.
- Acquisition of multiple identities and their careful use. ("The only time [the shoe-bomber, Richard] Reid appears to have used his real name is when flying.")[34]

Social activities can offer clues:

- Membership in militant Islamic groups or front organizations.
- Financial support for those groups or fronts.
- Active involvement at mosques known for their militant Islamic orientation.
- Close friendships or family ties with other suspects.
- Immersion in a purely Muslim environment.
- Avoiding contact with the larger society: "friendly but standoffish," in the words of a former assistant U.S. attorney. "Say 'hello' but don't talk. Let people see you, but don't bring attention to yourself," in the words of an Al-Qaeda advisory.[35]

Other miscellaneous pointers to look for include:

- Choosing to live in areas where many cultures are represented and an easygoing attitude toward different customs is evident (northern New Jersey, southern Florida, Leicester or Bradford in England, Hamburg in Germany).
- Sending or receiving large amounts of money.
- A preference for cash transactions.
- Criminal activity, especially reliance on counterfeited money and smuggling.
- A promising career that failed, descent into drugs and alcohol, then redemption through Islam.
- An offer to work for the enemy's intelligence services.
- Enrolling in university studies in the liberal arts, then switching to engineering or the sciences.

These are admittedly imprecise indicators; a Muslim who exercises and makes anti-Hindu statements cannot automatically be suspected of planning a suicide operation. Rather, the above signals must be seen in the context of a whole personality and a wider pattern of behavior. Precisely because the legitimate search for sleepers is open to abuse, it requires an unusual degree of common sense, sensitivity, and restraint.

15

ARE AMERICAN MUSLIMS
THE VICTIMS OF BIAS?

President Bill Clinton in early 2000 stated that American Muslims face "discrimination" and "intolerance."[1] Not long after, the U.S. Senate passed a resolution inveighing against "discrimination and harassment" against American Muslims.[2]

These pronouncements did not happen by themselves, but followed on years of effort by organizations claiming to speak on behalf of Muslims living in the United States. Thus, the American Muslim Council (AMC) complained of an "ongoing wave of discriminatory acts."[3] The Council on American-Islamic Relations (CAIR) went further, stating that "discrimination is now part of daily life for American Muslims."[4] And a member of the CAIR board, Mujeeb Cheema, found that Islamophobia, or the hatred of Islam, is "at epidemic levels in the West."[5] But these are mere statements, not proofs of bias. Do American Muslims really face more obstacles than other Americans as they go to school, make a living, and express their faith?

In fact, a review of American Muslim life—based largely on information made available by CAIR and other Muslim organizations—

finds a flourishing community that rightly boasts substantial accomplishments. The picture is far better than the self-appointed Muslim groups would have us believe.

Positive Experience

In socioeconomic terms, Muslims have little to complain about. They boast among the highest rates of education of any group in the United States, with a 1999 survey finding that 52 percent have a graduate degree.[6] Among converts, whites tend to be highly educated, blacks not. That said, Muslims among African-Americans are substantially better educated than their non-Muslim counterparts.

Education translates into prestigious and remunerative work. Immigrant Muslims concentrate in the professional and entrepreneurial vocations, with a specialty in engineering and medicine. A 1970s survey found 17 percent of Muslims in the United States to be engineers and 13 percent in medicine.[7] A 1980s inquiry found a quarter of Muslims working as engineers and 8 percent in medicine.[8] A 1990s survey in Chicago found 17 percent engineers, 8 percent in medicine.[9] A late 1990s national survey found 20 percent engineers and technicians, 14 percent medical.[10] Though the numbers range considerably, they consistently point to a disproportionate number of Muslims in these professions.

More than a few American Muslims have lived out the classic immigrant success story of arriving with a few dollars and building up substantial wealth. Average income for Muslims appears to be higher than the U.S. national average: a 1996 survey found them with a median income of $40,000 (versus $32,000 for the country as a whole); among African-Americans, Muslims have a median income of $30,000 (compared with $23,000 for all blacks); this same research found 70 percent of Muslim with incomes over $70,000.[11] A 1999 survey of 878 Muslims found 38 percent reporting a household income of over $75,000.[12] A year later, the median yearly household income was said to be $69,000.[13] One specialist, Abdulkader Thomas, notes that "As a rule, upper-income Muslim immigrants tend to be conspicuous consumers,"[14] and indeed, Muslim magazines are replete with advertisements for luxurious mansions, stately cars, and fine jewelry.

Business tycoons of note include Bijan (high-end men's clothing),

Rashid A. Chaudhry (personal care products), Ayhan Hakimoğlu (military contracts), Yusef Haroon (consulting and managerial services), Mansoor Ijaz (investment management), Farooq Kathwari (furniture), Nemir Kirdar (venture capitalism), and Safi Qureshey (computers). The very richest American Muslim appears to be a software engineer of Turkish origins, Kenan Şahin, who netted $1.45 billion in 1999 on selling his company, Kenan Systems (which specializes in billing plans), to Lucent Technologies. American Muslims proudly say that theirs is "the richest Muslim society on earth,"[15] and they are right.

These, in short, are not an oppressed people.

Further, the Muslim effort to be accepted in the United States is not a particularly difficult one, for enlightened Americans make persistent efforts to understand Islam and portray Muslims positively. This results from a sense of guilt about past prejudice, plus a multiculturalist impulse. Jewish and Christian groups often join with Muslim counterparts to fight what they perceive as bias. For example, when Representative James Rogan (Republican of California) refused to meet with a Muslim leader, Salam Al-Marayati, on the (correct) grounds that Al-Marayati "seems to be an apologist for Muslim terrorists,"[16] Jewish and Christian organizations rushed to Al-Marayati's defense and held a news conference that was instrumental in prompting Rogan to back down and apologize to Al-Marayati.[17]

Similarly, Muslims in the dock often find themselves benefiting from the pro bono services of non-Muslim lawyers, sometimes eminent ones intent on winning justice for them. And where money is needed, non-Muslim institutions come to their aid; the Becket Fund, "a bipartisan and ecumenical, public-interest law firm that protects the free expression of all religious traditions," helped a Muslim police officer in Newark, New Jersey, win a case in Federal Appeals Court that entitles him to wear a beard.[18]

Less formally, too, one finds innumerable expressions of goodwill. Some citizens delight in the appearance of mosques, for example, as articulated by one resident of Frederick County, Maryland, during a debate about a zoning request for a mosque: he hoped the structure would be built because "a mosque will be an asset for not just the Muslim community, but the entire community."[19] Non-Muslims occasionally even donate funds to construct mosques, something that invariably astonishes immigrant Muslims, who have no prior experience with such ecumenism.

The U.S. government has taken steps to recognize Islam. In 1990, President George Bush began the custom of congratulating American Muslims on the occasion of the Islamic holidays. A year later, Muslim men of religion began the practice of opening sessions of Congress with recitations from the Qur'an. The president, the first lady, and the secretary of state have all hosted Muslim delegations to celebrate the breaking of the Ramadan fast. In 1996, Vice President Al Gore became the highest-ranking American official to visit an American mosque. In 1997, the National Park Service installed a star and crescent in the Ellipse Park near the White House, along with the National Christmas Tree and a Hanukkah menorah. When the first Muslim ambassador was appointed in 1999 to represent the United States to Fiji, he took the oath of office by swearing on a Qur'an.

The U.S. military has been forthcoming to Muslims. In 1992 a military aircraft took seventy-five enlisted Muslim soldiers to Mecca for the pilgrimage. In 1993 a first Muslim chaplain was commissioned by the U.S. Army, and a second one in 1996—the first ever American chaplains to be not Christian or Jewish. The armed forces provide halal meals for Muslims and do not require daily physical training during Ramadan.

The Nation of Islam has similarly benefited from government sanction. Prison authorities long ago relented in their efforts to ban the group, to the point that they consider its members a very positive factor ("I have always held them in the highest regard," says the deputy director of the Washington, D.C., Department of Corrections).[20]

On the local level, too, Islam has made much progress. The District of Columbia has passed a Religious Accommodation Amendment Act that makes it simple for city employees to observe the Islamic festivals. The New Jersey state legislature became the first in the country to pass a Halal Food Consumer Protection Act, which ensures that anyone claiming to sell halal food actually does so.[21] New York City suspends the alternate-side-of-street parking rules during the two Eids—a matter of high policy in that town.

The media treat Islam and Muslims with a unique delicacy. The religion itself is portrayed only in positive terms (Ft. *Lauderdale Sun-*

Sentinel "Islamic faith anchors family in Boca Raton").[22] Other articles explain the appeal of Islam to converts (*Chicago Tribune*: "Searching Americans embrace the logic behind the teachings of Islam")[23] and its spiritual rewards (*Orange County Register*: "In the footsteps of the prophets: A pilgrimage to Mecca defines a couple's faith and marriage").[24] Ramadan inspires a series of articles; the *Los Angeles Times* ran no less than seven major stories in less than a month during the holiday season of December 1999 and January 2000, bearing headlines like "Muslim fast of Ramadan begins today: Local families celebrate the month long tradition, which focuses on cleansing and clarity" and "For many, Eid al-Fitr completes this holiday season: As Ramadan's month of fasting ends, growing numbers in the U.S. are learning to appreciate their Muslim neighbors"[25] Virtually every other Los Angeles media outlet had similar Ramadan stories, as CAIR itself noted in a proud press release ("Ramadan draws positive media coverage").[26]

Frequent articles show Muslims as good neighbors (*Newsday*: "Inside Islam: A visit with the Muslims of Long Island")[27] who hardly differ from everyone else (*The Washington Post*: "Muslim camps offer youths fun, religion)."[28] Story after story tells about a solitary Muslim turning up in some small town in America, suffering loneliness and isolation, organizing fellow Muslims to start a mosque, then the emergence of a substantial and prosperous community (*Wichita Eagle*: "Mosque's creation to fortify community: As the Muslim population in Wichita has grown, so has its need for a place to worship").[29] Muslims are shown as part of the fabric of society (*Christian Science Monitor*: "Muslims learn to pull political ropes in US),"[30] except that they have a rougher deal (*Atlanta Journal-Constitution*: "Muslims complain of increasing discrimination at metro businesses").[31]

Far from substantiating claims of media bias, this is some of the most favorable coverage anyone gets in the United States.

Public Expression of Islam

When observant Muslims seek to live by the precepts of their religion, especially in the workplace and in schools, the picture again is a positive one, judging by what one sees in connection with Islamic holidays and prayers, as well as men wearing beards and women head coverings.

Holidays. The Islamic holidays present two challenges: based on a lunar calendar, they move forward each solar year by about ten days, making it impossible to schedule an annual time for them; and while there are only a few main holidays, one of them (Ramadan) lasts a month, during which pious Muslims fast during the day and carouse at night—customs not exactly conducive to work. Several corporations—including Northrop—permit their Muslim staff to work a shortened day during Ramadan. Getting employers to permit several days off during two of the other holidays, called the Eids, has not always proven easy, but one American employer after another has acquiesced in this demand, including the Larus Corporation. Several school districts, such as New York City's, permit Muslim students to be absent on five Islamic holidays; Paterson, New Jersey, is unique in actually closing its schools for the two Eids. Some corporations—notably Northrop—allow Muslim employees to take off the several weeks or even months required to make the full-scale pilgrimage to Mecca.

Prayers. Muslims are required to pray at five designated but changing times through the day. Although it is permissible to make up the prayers at a later time, many pious Muslims insist on praying exactly on time. If they work or attend school, this means fulfilling two conditions: getting time off and finding a suitable venue. Remembering that there are millions of American Muslims, the problems are relatively few in number; they tend to involve factories, where it is difficult to let employees take off at times of their choosing.

Muslim plaintiffs at times win substantial settlements against employers for prayer-related issues. In Lincolnshire, Illinois, Mohammad Abdullah's habit of leaving his job at about noon on Fridays for prayers caused him to be fired, even though he arrived early to work or stayed late to compensate. After taking his case to the Equal Employment Opportunity Commission (EEOC), he won a $49,000 settlement in 1997. In Jacksonville, Florida, Fareed Ansari won $105,216 from Ray's Plumbing Contractors, his former employer, for firing him when he insisted on leaving work early on Fridays to attend the weekly prayer service.

With this as background, it is not surprising that Muslims usually prevail when they seek accommodations for prayer from such employers as American Industries, Inc., Cleo Inc., Larus Corporation, the Mark Hopkins Hotel in San Francisco, Minnesota Diversified Industries, Nu-kote International, the St. Paul, Minnesota, school district, and the Washington Metropolitan Area Transit Authority. Somali workers at National Electric Coil in Columbus, Ohio, convinced their employer to grant them permission to take off an hour and a half, triple the usual lunchtime, to attend Friday afternoon prayer services away from the factory. In Columbia, Missouri, a junior high school reached an agreement with the parents of fifteen Muslim students allowing the students to perform prayers during school hours.

Muslims have been known to pray in abandoned areas and even in restrooms. When they demand—sometimes on threat of quitting their jobs—a place for prayer, corporations (such as a meatpacking plant in Minneapolis and Mountain Air Express) sometimes set aside a storage area. Elsewhere, as at National Electric Coil, workers have won the right to roll out mats in a corner of the plant for prayers. At Seagate Technology, an incident in which a manager allegedly kicked a Muslim worshiper as he knelt in prayer led to a room being set aside for prayers and Muslim employees getting time off for praying. Thirty-three Somalis in Suwanee, Georgia, working the assembly line making cellular phones for Solectron walked off the job when offered two five-minute prayer breaks and working on a different shift—deemed insufficient by the Muslim employees. Some workers have won rights to a floating break period designed to coincide with the ever-changing times of prayers, restroom facilities with floor-level sink basins for prayer ablutions, and an on-site Qur'anic study group.

Beards. Wearing a beard has great symbolic importance for some Muslim men, being a way to emulate the Prophet Muhammad and signal membership in a pious community. This was the case, for example, for Pakistani-born Mohammad Sajid: "It was a big thing for me. I was afraid of a new society. It was just like [being in] a jungle."[32] But because, against corporate rules, he insisted on wearing a beard, he was briefly dismissed as a dishwasher at a fast-food eatery in Sacramento. Eventually, however, Sajid got his job back, as did Muslim males at such companies as Adirondack Transit Lines, Coca-Cola, Hilton Hotels, McDonald's, Safeway Inc, and Taco Bell.

When a Muslim goes to court over this issue, he invariably wins. The Minnesota Unemployment Appeals Court decided in favor of a fired Muslim who refused to shave his beard, ruling him entitled to receive unemployment benefits from his employer, Sims Security/Burns International Services. The EEOC found that United

Parcel Service discriminated against a beard-wearing Muslim in Illinois by refusing to promote him to a driver's position. A Federal Appeals Court backed a Muslim policeman in Newark, New Jersey, entitling him to wear a beard and receive $25,000 in back wages, finding that the police department's policy "violates the First Amendment."[33]

Modesty. The usual modesty issue concerns women wearing the *hijab*, a cowl-like headscarf that covers the hair. For Muslim women, this fabric serves as a sign of reserve and a means of self-identification. For American employers, it is occasionally perceived as mildly offensive or an impediment to customer relations. When they demand its removal, the Muslim women frequently protest or file discrimination law suits, again with considerable success. In March 1999, after apparently being fired from their jobs with Argenbright Security at Dulles International Airport screening passengers and baggage, five immigrant Muslim women filed a suit with the EEOC, claiming that having to remove their scarves violated the 1964 Civil Rights Act. The two sides settled out of court, with the women receiving written apologies, $750 in back pay, $2,500 in additional compensation, their jobs back, and the company promising to provide religious sensitivity training at all of its U.S. locations.[34]

Mindful of such precedents, a number of corporations—Bank of America, Bojangles' Restaurant, Boston Market, Cox Communications, Domino's Pizza, Kmart, Manpower Inc., McDonald's, Sheraton Hotels, the University of California at Berkeley, Taco Bell, and US Airways—have agreed to reconsider *hijab*-wearing female Muslim applicants or reinstate job holders. Some companies—such as Hudson Belk—also agreed to provide "diversity training" about Islamic clothing and customs to their staff. Hertz fired eleven Somali women at its car rental outlet in the Atlanta airport for wearing ankle-length dresses, then quickly reinstated them, despite its claims that the long dresses caused the women to trip while getting in and out of cars.

Modesty issues also arise in schools, where students dressing modestly occasionally—but only briefly—run afoul of dress codes. A Muslim girl attending high school in Fort Worth, Texas, won permission to wear a *hijab* while playing soccer.[35] High school students in Williamsport, Pennsylvania, won the right to have their mandatory swimming instruction in private. A Muslim boy at the Lincoln Middle School in

Gainesville, Florida, was sent home because he would not tuck in his shirt, as the school dress code demanded; when the student's parents argued that long, loose-fitting, and untucked shirts are more modest, the school permitted this exception. A female applicant to The University of Health Sciences in Kansas City, Missouri, requested not to be palpated (physically examined) by male colleagues; the school initially declined her application, but then reversed its decision and accepted her, although this meant disrupting the usual practice of having medical students learn from examining each other.[36]

Other accommodations occur here and there in the public square. Pennsylvania women may wear a headscarf for their driver's license pictures.[37] Muslim mothers in Alsip, Illinois, may wear a headscarf (and clothes) as they watch their children at the pool, on condition they stay six feet away from the water.[38] Female skaters wear headscarves at a private rink in Seabrook, Maryland.[39] Two Muslim women, Najla E. Doran and Sherma D. Humphrey, were briefly detained for wearing full-face veils on the street, violating an anti–Ku Klux Klan state law prohibiting the wearing of masks on the street.[40] But, unknown to the arresting officers, the law had been changed in 1991 to permit the Muslim covering. For this momentary mistake, the city of Portsmouth, Virginia, had to pay $100,000 to each woman. If the unscientific poll conducted by a local Web site can be relied on, this was a popular decision, with a 2-to-1 majority saying the women deserved compensation.[41]

Disrespect for Islam

Muslims are undoubtedly right when they say that Islam suffers from a poor reputation in the United States. But they cannot complain about receptivity to their complaints. Public figures who make statements perceived as inimical to Islam by Muslim groups usually apologize right away. Two days after Senator Joseph Biden, Jr. (Democrat of Delaware), worried on television that bombing Iraq might "embolden Islam to become more aggressive with the United States," he contradicted his words: "Islam is one of the world's great religions. It stands for peace, tolerance, and justice and it is responsible for many enlightening advances in human thought and practice over the centuries."[42]

When the media offends Muslims or makes a factual mistake, an apology or retraction follows with (uncharacteristic) speed. Jay Leno of

NBC's *Tonight Show* apologized for a seemingly inoffensive comedy sketch about an imaginary amusement park in Iran and promised to be "more diligent in the future."[43] Martin Goldsmith, host of National Public Radio's *Performance Today*, related a legend about the Prophet Muhammad relying on special coffee to "make love to forty women in one night" over forty nights. He soon offered "sincere apologies" for giving offense and thanked his listeners for making their concerns known.[44] After Paul Harvey, said to be the most listened to radio broadcaster in America, called Islam a "fraudulent religion," he quickly dubbed this an "unintentional slur" and duly apologized on air for having "understandably offended" Muslims.[45]

Jewish media do likewise. The *Jewish Journal* in Miami published a letter to the editor stating that "Muslims are killing non-Muslims worldwide. Israel is beset by these animals on all sides with no peace possible. . . . Adherents of Islam are indeed insane. There will never be peace on earth as long as they exist."[46] The editors then apologized to "our Islam brothers" for comments that "went beyond the limits of civilized discourse."[47]

Book publishers do more; they actually recall books, at considerable expense to themselves. Simon & Schuster withdrew a children's book, *Great Lives: World Religions* by William Jay Jacobs, when made aware of its treatment of the Prophet Muhammad ("He took pleasure in seeing the heads of his enemies torn from their bodies by the swords of his soldiers").[48] Books are also recalled when they contain nothing particularly egregious, only mistakes. That was the case with *Muslim Holidays* by Faith Winchester; the publisher, Capstone Press, called the book back because it showed pictures of Muhammad, transliterated a holiday in a nonstandard way, and repeated some odd folk tales.[49]

The Internet follows these same special rules for Muslims, who are protected from the sort of things routinely said about blacks or Jews. AT&T WorldNet Service removed a site that defamed the Prophet Muhammad as a "rapist" and found him worse than Adolf Hitler. GeoCities took down a Web site that called Islam "a threat to the whole world" and profaned the Prophet ("Mohammed The Playboy" and "Prophet Mohammed's Libido Exposed!"). America Online closed down a site that published pseudo-Qur'anic verses, on the grounds that it was "clearly designed to be hurtful and defamatory."[50] This is not prejudice but kid-glove treatment.

ン   The military is no less sensitive. When U.S. forces bombed Iraqi targets in late 1998, sailors on the USS *Enterprise* engaged in the time-hallowed practice of scribbling aggressive graffiti on a bomb; the Associated Press ran a picture showing an inscription: "Here's a Ramadan present from Chad Rickenberg." When a Muslim group protested this "bigoted sentiment," the Pentagon spokesman expressed distress at what it called "thoughtless graffiti" and dismissed the episode as "a rare exception that does not reflect American policy or values."[51]

As one might expect, schools are hypersensitive. A professor at Southern Connecticut State University allegedly gave an anti-Islamic tract to a student; the university responded by instituting educational seminars on Islam.[52] An assistant professor at Southeast Oklahoma State University, a convert to Islam, complained that colleagues continued to use his former name; in response, a representative of Oklahoma's coordinating board for higher education communicated his concerns "to the appropriate officials . . . to take appropriate action."[53] More drastic action is not uncommon. A high school teacher in Rochester, Minnesota, was reassigned for expressing dislike of Muslim modesty practices; and a school official warned that "One misstep and she's gone."[54] A New Jersey professor who said "God-damn Muslims" in front of a class was reportedly out of a job.

Advertisements that take the faith lightly are withdrawn with alacrity. Total Sports, Inc., canceled an ad showing a group of Muslims "praying" to a basketball.[55] Burger King pulled an ad in which a character bearing a Muslim name ("Rasheed") praises the restaurant chain's bacon-laden Whopper sandwich.[56] The Colorado Lottery pulled radio advertisements that began: "You've heard the old expression about the mountain coming to Mohammed?" on the grounds that Islam forbids gambling.[57] The *Los Angeles Times* dropped its ad campaign contrasting two types of readers—bikini-clad and chador-clad—because Muslims objected.[58] Many other companies—including Anheuser-Busch, DoubleTree Hotels, MasterCard International, Miller Brewing Company, Seagrams, and Timeslips Corporation—also withdrew ads after hearing Muslim complaints.

The use of Arabic for decorative purposes often arouses Muslim objections, due to its sacral associations, and corporations respond quickly. Warehouse One withdrew a women's shirt with Arabic script from the Qur'an on the front and the sleeves.[59] Liz Claiborne discontinued the use of Arabic lettering from the Qur'an on its clothes and issued an abject apology ("We are profoundly sorry that any of our products reflected insensitivity toward the Muslim faith, as this was certainly never our intent").[60] The willingness not to offend Muslim sensibility reached a climax when CAIR contended that the logo on a Nike basketball shoe could "be interpreted" as the word "Allah" (God) in Arabic script.[61] Though Nike denied any such intent (the logo was to look like flames, not Arabic letters), the threat of a worldwide boycott by Muslims prompted Nike to withdraw the shoe, investigate the incident, introduce changes in its design shop, learn about Islamic designs, and produce educational CDs and videos about Islam. Nor was that all; Nike also agreed to sponsor events in the Muslim community, donate Nike products to Islamic charitable groups, and pay for sports facilities at several Islamic schools (the first payment was $50,000 for the Dar Al-Hijrah Islamic Center in northern Virginia).[62]

Employees with grievances sometimes make out well in court. Lule Said, a Somali immigrant, was working in 1991 as a guard for Northeast Security of Brookline, Massachusetts, when a co-worker complained about his origins and faith, announced that he hated Muslims, wiped his feet on Said's prayer rug and kicked it aside, then threatened him. Said complained to his supervisor but was told to stop praying or he would lose his job. The Massachusetts Commission Against Discrimination awarded Said $300,000 (about a decade worth's of his salary) for these tribulations and chewed out Northeast Security: "This case uniquely demonstrates . . . the debilitating impact discrimination has on an individual's well-being."[63] Ahmad Abu-Aziz, an immigrant from Jordan, claimed that from the start of his employment for United Air Lines in California in 1994, he faced discrimination—being compared to a terrorist, his name ridiculed, derogatory comments about his religion and national origin, unfair work assignments. When Abu-Aziz complained to his supervisor, he was ignored, then terminated for supposed misconduct. He went to court and a jury awarded him $2.9 million in damages, a sum sustained by appellate court.[64]

In other words, just as American Muslims have benefited from multiculturalism, so they are benefiting from the government readiness to dictate workplace rules.

Recognizing Fortunate Circumstances

American Muslims fully recognize their fortunate circumstances. A mid-1980s survey found that "No Muslim interviewed reported that he or she had ever experienced any personal harassment in the workplace or knew of any experienced by a friend or associate as a result of being either Muslim or foreign-born. Nor did any of those interviewed report any problems in buying or renting homes or apartments as a result of perceived prejudice."[65] An early 1990s study into Muslim youth found that all the women interviewed "denied they were oppressed in any way in the United States."[66] In 2000, an AMC poll found 66.1 percent of Muslims agreeing with the assertion that "U.S. society currently shows a respect towards the Muslim faith."[67]

Individual Muslims concur. Fereydun Hoveyda, a former Iranian official now living in New York, finds that in the United States "there is no animosity at all to Islam.[68] Jeffrey Lang, the Christian-born professor of mathematics, writes of his conversion to Islam: "I do not believe it has greatly affected my career."[69] "Our life in this county has been terrific and we love it," an immigrant to Virginia named Hisham Elbasha tells *The Washington Post*.[70] Muslims also note that bias is diminishing; in 1999 a young Muslim in Washington said he witnessed "increased tolerance observing the month of Ramadan this year."[71]

Even those same Muslim organizations that complain about discrimination and "Islamophobia" sometimes admit that things are going well. Ibrahim Hooper of CAIR, one of the most vocal supporters of this position, acknowledges that "Domestic policy towards the Muslim community is quite good."[72] His boss, Nihad Awad, makes a similar point, that "here anti-Muslim feelings have no roots, unlike Europe."[73] Institutionally, CAIR finds that things are better in the United States than in some Muslim countries: "Muslims in America," it has said, "take for granted rights routinely denied to their co-religionists in Turkey."[74] Khaled Saffuri of the Islamic Institute goes further, conceding that in the United States, "there is relatively speaking a better degree of freedom compared to many Muslim countries."[75] It all sounds very good indeed.

All this is not to deny that some bias against Muslims does exist. But no immigrant group or non-Protestant religion is wholly free of this. Buddhists and Hindus, adherents of religions yet more alien to most Americans, also face prejudices and are subjected to ridicule. Their temples are on occasion vandalized with swastikas smeared on temple walls, with one attack specifically timed to take place on the anniversary of Kristallnacht, the Nazi rampage against Jews in 1938.[76] Buddhists and Hindus do not receive the favorable media treatment accorded Islam. Yet they hardly complain, much less do they have a protest industry.[77]

Further, what bias against Muslims does exist is contained, illegal, and of relatively little import. Linda S. Walbridge, an anthropologist who immersed herself in an American Muslim community, offers a useful comparison with anti-Catholic sentiment: the latter "has not disappeared from America, but it is at a low enough level that it certainly does not hinder Catholics from participating in all spheres of activity. There is no reason to think that Muslims . . . will experience anything much different."[78] Adjustment is needed, to be sure, to accommodate a new and still alien faith: employers have to learn about beards, headscarves, prayers, and fasts; advertisers will take a while to understand Muslim sensitivities. Nonetheless, the record shows an impressive flexibility on the part of American institutions, public and private, to acknowledge Islam and oblige Muslims. To help the process along, Muslims have considerable sway over the media and are in the process of building an impressive lobbying organization.

If one were to speculate about the reasons for this happy circumstance, two explanations spring to mind. One is American openness to the immigrant and the exotic, combined with a historic disposition to offer a level playing field to all. The other is a genuine multiculturalism—not the specious doctrine of racial and ethnic "diversity" imposed so successfully on American institutions but a sincere willingness to accept and learn from other civilizations. Other factors play a part as well, including the growth of the regulatory arm of government and especially its readiness to dictate workplace rules. American Muslims have been quick to avail themselves of these benefits, as is, of course, their right.

It is also the right of CAIR, AMC, and the Muslim Public Affairs Council to devote their resources to promoting the idea of Muslim victimization. They do so for the same reasons that some other ethnic and religious defense groups do—to pay the bills and fuel the grievances they hope to ride. But the reality is stubbornly otherwise: far from being victimized, the Muslim American community is robust and advancing steadily. For non-Muslim Americans, the lesson should be clear: even as they continue to welcome active Muslim participation in American life, there is no reason to fall for, let alone to endorse, spurious charges of "discrimination and harassment."

16

"HOW DARE YOU
DEFAME ISLAM"

The problem began to manifest itself clearly in January 1989, when Muslims living in Bradford, England, decided to show their anger about *The Satanic Verses*, a new novel by the writer Salman Rushdie, which contained elements making fun of the Prophet Muhammad. A group of mostly Pakistani immigrants purchased a copy of the novel, took it to a public square, attached it to a stake, and set it on fire. Television news showed this *auto da fé* in great detail, and pictures of the scene were splashed across the British media for days, making it a major topic of discussion throughout the country as well as in Pakistan.

After a month's buildup in anger, an unruly mob of some ten thousand persons took to the streets of Islamabad, the capital of Pakistan, to protest the novel. Symbolically, they marched to the American Cultural Center, even though Rushdie is not American, where they proceeded with great energy, but not much success, to set the heavily fortified building on fire. Six people died in the violence and many more were injured. These events caught the attention of Ayatollah

171

Khomeini, Iran's revolutionary ruler, who took prompt and drastic action. On February 14, 1989, he issued an edict calling on "all zealous Muslims quickly to execute" not just Rushdie but also "all those involved in its publication who were aware of its content."[1]

This edict led to two weeks of intense international debate about blasphemy and freedom of speech. When the dust settled, Khomeini had failed in his specific goal of eliminating Rushdie. Over a decade later, the author is in fine fettle, traveling about the world, accepting prizes and writing well-received books. But if Khomeini did not manage to harm Rushdie, he did accomplish something far more profound: he stirred something in the soul of many Muslims, reviving a sense of confidence about Islam and an impatience to abide criticism of their faith. His almost spontaneous edict against Rushdie had the effect of inspiring Islamists around the world to go on the offensive against anyone they perceived as defaming their Prophet, their faith, or even themselves.

Violence and Intimidation

Khomeini himself passed from the scene just weeks after issuing his edict, but the spirit it engendered very much lives on. During the decade since 1989, militant Islamic efforts to silence those who critique Islam or Muslims have had impressive results. Some of these acts of intimidation involved the Rushdie case itself, and most notably various translators of the book, who were stabbed and seriously injured in Norway and Italy, and murdered in Japan. In Turkey a fire set to a hotel did not kill the intended victim, another translator, but did kill thirty-seven others.

More impressive than these acts of terror, however, has been the way Islamists have changed the discussion of Islam around the world. In Muslim-majority countries, it has become virtually impossible to comment critically about Islam. By way of example, here are several celebrated cases from just one country, Egypt: A professor of literature, Nasr Hamid Abu Zayd, who wrote that certain references to supernatural phenomena in the Qur'an should be read as metaphors, found his marriage dissolved by a court—on the grounds that his writing proved him an apostate, and a Muslim woman may not be married to a non-Muslim. In another case, an author of a nonconformist essay on Islam named 'Ala' Hamid, his publisher, and the book's printer were all sentenced to eight years in jail on the charge of blasphemy. Naguib Mahfouz, the Arabic language's elderly and only Nobel Prize winner in literature, was seriously injured when an assailant knifed him in the neck in 1994, presumably for an allegorical novel he wrote in 1959. Farag Foda, an intellectual who poured scorn on the militant Islamic program, was shot and murdered.

Nor was the campaign of intimidation limited to the traditional Muslim countries; as Khomeini's edict against Rushdie, a London resident, implied, it also extended into the West. Still focusing on Egyptians, we find that one person, Makin Morcos, was killed in Australia for criticizing the Islamists' anti-Christian campaign in Egypt. Rashad Khalifa, an Egyptian-born biochemist living in Tucson, Arizona, was stabbed to death in 1990 to silence his heretical ideas; government records show that a member of the violent Al-Fuqra carried out the murder, assisted by a member of Al-Qaeda named Wadih El-Hage. These incidents sent a clear and chilling message: you can run but can't hide.

Nor is physical intimidation limited to immigrants; it can also involve non-Muslim Westerners. In some cases, personal issues are the cause: in one celebrated case in the United Kingdom, Jack Briggs has been on the lam for years, hiding with his wife from her Pakistani family who have vowed to kill both of them (even though they are properly married and he even converted to Islam to win their approval). In other cases, threats have a public quality: Steven Emerson had his life threatened for producing _Jihad in America_, an award-winning television documentary that drew on the Islamists' own commercial videos to show their anti-Semitic and anti-American views. Emerson related his story to a congressional committee in 1998; it bears quoting at length as an insight into what is happening under our very noses:

> Immediately following the release of "Jihad in America," I became the target of radical militant Islamic groups throughout the United States (and internationally) who fiercely denied the existence of "Islamic extremism" and accused me of engaging in an "attack against Islam." For this "transgression," my life has been permanently changed.
>
> Explaining the details of just one incident—to pick among a whole series—will help you understand the changes I have been

forced to endure. One morning, in late 1995, I was paged by a federal law enforcement official. When I returned the call, this official immediately instructed me to head downtown to his office and specifically directed me to take a taxi rather than my car. The urgency in this person's voice was palpable. When I arrived at the office, I was ushered into a room where a group of other law enforcement officials was waiting. Within minutes, I found out why I had been summoned: I was told a group of radical Islamic fundamentalists had been assigned to carry out an assassination of me. An actual hit team had been dispatched from another country to the United States. The squad, according to the available intelligence, was to rendezvous with its American based colleagues located in several U.S. cities. Compounding the jolt of being told about this threat was an additional piece of information: the assassination squad had been successfully able to elude law enforcement surveillance.

I was told that I had limited choices: since I was not a full-time government employee, I was not entitled to 24 hour a day police protection. However, I could probably get permission to enter the Witness Security Program under the right circumstances. But the prospect of being spirited away and given a new identity was not acceptable to me—especially since that would afford the terrorists a moral victory in having shut me down. Frankly, however, the alternative option was not that attractive either—being on my own and taking my own chances. And yet that for me was the only effective option.[2]

Emerson remains doggedly on the trail of Islamists, and especially the terrorist-supporting elements among them, yet he has for years been forced to live at a clandestine address, always watching his movements. His courage and his willingness to undergo so total a disruption of his life make this remarkable man that rarity in modern America, a hero.

Even in the United States, the Khalifa and Emerson cases suggest, the Constitution may guarantee freedom of religion and freedom of speech, but unapproved thinking about Islam can lead to personal danger or even death.

Nonviolence

In the West, however, violence can only achieve so much; were force the only tool in the militant Islamic war chest, their achievements would be limited. Contrary to their reputation, many Islamists are of the modern world, at home with computers, with K-Street lobbying techniques, and adept at the game of victimology. Energetic and goal-oriented, they have wielded these tools with skill. One of their most important goals in the West is to build an inviolate wall around Islam, giving the faith some resemblance of its privileged position in the traditionally Muslim countries.

A few examples illustrate what this means in practice. At the United Nations, such nondiplomatic terms as "blasphemy" and "defamation of Islam" have become part of that institution's normal discourse. This has served as a convenient way to shut off those, Muslim or not, who would speak out on such unpleasant matters as slavery in Sudan or Muslim anti-Semitism. In France, a very prominent and controversial Catholic bishop, Marcel Lefebvre, was fined nearly $1,000 for saying that when the Muslim presence becomes stronger, "it is your wives, your daughters, your children who will be kidnapped and dragged off to a certain kind of place as they exist in Casablanca [Morocco]." In Canada, a Christian activist handed out leaflets protesting Muslim persecution of Christians; in response, Muslim organizations accused him of "inciting hatred" and a court indeed found him guilty of breaking Canada's hate speech laws. It sentenced him to 340 hours of community service and six months of probation time in jail.[3] In Israel, a Jewish activist was sentenced to two years behind bars for putting up posters showing Muhammad as a pig.[4]

And the United States? Concepts of freedom of speech are far more resolute there than elsewhere; the First Amendment prevents the government from fining or jailing anyone for offensive speech. Islamists understand this but still seek to win what sanction they can to censor others. This explains their sponsorship of Senate Resolution 133, an innocent-appearing motion titled "Supporting religious tolerance toward Muslims." Its contents, though, are not so innocent. It states as a fact that "Muslims have been subjected, simply because of their faith, to acts of discrimination and harassment that all too often have led to hate-inspired violence" and concludes that any criticism of Islam, though legal, is morally reprehensible: "while the Senate respects and upholds the right of individuals to free speech, the Senate acknowledges that individuals and organizations that foster such intolerance create an atmosphere of hatred and fear that divides the Nation."[5]

The Council on American-Islamic Relations

At the end of the day, however, Senate resolutions are a weak tool for suppressing open discussion. To achieve this, Islamists must adapt to prevailing mores. Implementing Khomeini's edict of shutting down debate may be their goal, but they cannot use his blunt methods. Instead, they do so by conducting hostile campaigns against anyone who runs afoul of their views. Accordingly, while their efforts generally do not include overt threats of violence, they tend to be exceedingly unpleasant, with the effect that all but the most determined individuals decide to avoid these topics. Taken in the context of the worldwide use of violence against critics, militant Islamic efforts in the United States have an unmistakable stench of intimidation about them.

The leading instigator of this campaign, though by no means the only one, has been the Council on American-Islamic Relations, a Washington-based institution founded in 1994. CAIR presents itself as a standard-issue civil rights organization whose mission is to "promote interest and understanding among the general public and government officials with regards to Islam and Muslims in North America; and conduct educational services." Sometimes, CAIR does this. In 1997, for example, it protested when, at a Board of Education meeting in South Carolina, an official said, "Screw the Buddhists and kill the Muslims." At other times, it comes to the defense of women who lose their job because of wearing a headscarf, or of men who wear beards.

But these occasional good works serve to deflect attention from CAIR's primary goal, which appears to be twofold: help build Hamas against Israel and promote militant Islam's agenda in the United States. On the first score, Steve Pomerantz, a former chief of counterterrorism for the FBI, explains that "any objective assessment . . . leads to the conclusion that CAIR, its leaders, and its activities, effectively give aid to international terrorist groups. Unfortunately, CAIR is but one of a new generation of new groups in the United States that hide under a veneer of 'civil rights' or 'academic' status but in fact are tethered to a platform that supports terrorism."[6] Of course, the Hamas connection only increases the intimidation when CAIR sends out one of its hundreds of "action alerts" and thereby generates dozens or even hundreds of protests, many of them vulgar and aggressive.

The goal of helping Hamas explains why anyone who lauds or defends Steven Emerson's work uncovering Hamas and other terrorist networks in the United States must be ready for abuse from CAIR's activists. A. M. Rosenthal found this out after praising the documentary *Jihad in America* in his *New York Times* column.[7] When *Boston Globe* columnist Jeff Jacoby protested CAIR's getting National Public Radio to blacklist Emerson, CAIR created a letterwriting campaign ("Dear JEW . . . How dare you defame Islam. . . . There is enough muslim bashing going on, I am sure your resigning will not make a difference to our jewish media") and, in a bit of raw intimidation, threatened the *Globe* with legal action.[8]

CAIR's defense of militant Islamic violence takes other forms as well—picketing the *Dallas Morning News* for revealing the Hamas infrastructure in Texas[9] or launching a campaign against the *Tampa Tribune* for uncovering the Islamic Jihad network in Tampa.[10] And what is one to make of its attempt to censor a magazine for children, *The Weekly Reader's Current Events*, on account of its September 2, 1996, issue carrying an anodyne article on terrorism, even though it almost entirely avoids mentioning Islam?[11] CAIR also denounced *The Atlantic Monthly* for an article on militant Islamic violence in Sudan and a Senate Subcommittee for holding a hearing on "Foreign Terrorists in America: Five Years After the World Trade Center Bombing."[12]

Silencing Critics

As for the other goal, promoting militant Islam in the United States, CAIR forwards its program by focusing on one topic: silencing those who have anything negative to say about militant Islam. In this spirit, CAIR attacked the Wiesenthal Center for portraying Ayatollah Khomeini as a Hitler-like enemy of Jews.[13] Likewise, it went after *Reader's Digest* for documenting the repression of Christians in several Muslim countries.[14]

The CAIR approach tends to be bare-knuckled. When James Jatras, a Senate aide, published in his private capacity a critique of Islam ("Islam is a self-evident outgrowth not of the Old and New Covenants but of the darkness of heathen Araby"), CAIR took out a full-page newspaper ad in *The Washington Times* calling for his dismissal from his job. Father Richard Neuhaus, the distinguished author and editor of *First Things*, wrote in the October 1997 issue of his journal a decidedly negative review of historical Islam ("Islam's spectacular spread was brought about by brutal military conquest, rapine, spoliation, and slavery") and its culture (" 'Islamic civilization' was derived from the vanquished"). Moving to the present, he maintained that "the Islamic world stews in its resentments and suspicions, alternating with low-grade jihad in the form of the persecution of Christians, international terrorism, and dreams of driving Israel into the sea," and concluded that "The biggest problem in sight is Islam." In response, CAIR called on the Catholic Church "to investigate" Neuhaus,[15] and its followers sent a cascade of abusive mail to Neuhaus, accusing him of being "Obviously mentally ill" and "Doing the work of Adolf Hitler." Neuhaus noted that while the campaign against him "stopped short of issuing a fatwa . . . there was a little nervous joking around here about who would get to open the mail."[16]

Then, in mid-1999, CAIR turned its focus on this writer, sending out some nine attacks in just seven weeks. These were in response to articles in the *Los Angeles Times* and *National Post* (Toronto), both of which emphasized the distinction between pious, traditional Muslims on the one hand and Islamists on the other. CAIR compiled quotes of mine and unflattering appraisals about my work going back to 1983. In response to my article about the Treaty of Hudaybiya (in which, contrary to other American commentators, I found that "Muhammad was technically within his rights to abrogate the treaty"), it sent out a bulletin entitled "Daniel Pipes Smears Prophet Muhammad"—fighting words for many Muslims. CAIR then bought a Web site with my name (DanielPipes.com) in 2000 and for the next year posted these calumnies on it, compelling me to come up with a point-by-point refutation posted on my own Web site (DanielPipes.org).

These attacks reverberated through the Internet and were widely reprinted in Muslim publications, spurring dozens of letters, overwhelmingly negative, to the papers carrying my articles. One urged me to enroll in sensitivity training at CAIR. Others called me harsh names ("bigot and racist"), compared me to the Ku Klux Klan and neo-Nazis, and characterized my writing as an "atrocity" filled with "pure poison" and "outright lies." More alarming, the letters accused my writings of either prompting hate crimes against Muslims or in themselves constituting a hate crime. The letterwriters also issued a range of vague threats: "Is Pipes ready to answer the Creator for his hatred or is he a secular humanist? . . . He will soon find out." Or this: "I believe people who dis-inform and create fear and HATE among citizens should be held responsible for their action."[17]

Why It Matters

These activities of CAIR and other Islamists matter even to Americans not directly attacked. First, were Islamists to get their way, freedom of speech concerning Islam and militant Islam would shut down, leaving only Islamist representations. Richard Curtiss, a former American diplomat now closely aligned with the Islamists, explicitly wrote of his hope that critics of militant Islam will "lose their mainstream media access."[18] To a small extent, this has already happened; National Public Radio had blacklisted Emerson until the *Boston Globe* forced a retraction,[19] yet even after the retraction he remains strangely absent from its airwaves.[20]

Second, militant Islamic scare tactics render certain topics unfit for objective and scholarly treatment. Bernard Lewis notes with irony that an English-language biographer of Jesus has total freedom of speech, while his counterpart working on Muhammad feels compelled to follow the pious Muslim version. More broadly, as a letterwriter protesting my *National Post* article wrote, with idiosyncratic grammar: "It's is interesting to me as a Muslim American to hear you, a non Muslim, speaks about Islam as an expert without you first consulting with an American Muslim organization like CAIR for an example, to get their opinion about what you are about to print." I understand by this that I should write about Islam only after vetting the contents with Islamists.

Third, if CAIR et al. achieve their goal of silencing critics, a broad range of topics will gain a uniquely privileged status in the United States. Every other religion would have to cope with the slings and arrows of critics and malcontents, but Islam would be immune. Every other sensitive topic would remain open for debate—such as black genetic inferiority or Holocaust denial—but not the career of the Prophet Muhammad or the origins of the Qur'an. Nor is militant Islamic terrorism to be discussed, or "honor" killings of women, slavery in Sudan and Mauritania, or the repression of Middle Eastern Christians. Eventually, this could lead to a situation in which denying the prophecy of Muhammad amounts to a punishable infraction; and non-Muslims will find they do not talk publicly about Islam except in terms acceptable to Muslims (as, for example, is the case in Egypt).

Finally, this silencing has a larger implication: it means the United States has taken a first step toward the application of Islamic law, for it is a basic premise of that law that no one, and especially not non-Muslims, may openly discuss precisely those subjects that CAIR wishes to render taboo. To permit the Islamists to get their way on this matter signals that they can proceed on others too. Permitting the Shari'a to trump the Constitution in even one arena signals to Islamists that they have a chance to turn non-Muslims in the United States into a sort of *dhimmi* population, where *dhimmi*s (according to Islamic law) are non-Muslims who accept a range of Islamic restrictions in return for being left alone. However absurd it may appear that Muslims, who make up a tiny proportion of the U.S. population, can impose their will on the vast majority of Americans, it is a fact that willful minorities can get their way. And were this first step toward the *dhimmi* status to be put in place, others would likely follow.

17

LESSONS FROM THE PROPHET MUHAMMAD'S DIPLOMACY

O n May 10, 1994, Yasir Arafat gave what he thought was an off-the-record talk at a mosque while visiting Johannesburg, South Africa. But a South African journalist, Bruce Whitfield of 702 Talk Radio, found a way secretly to record his English-language remarks. The moment was an optimistic one for the Arab-Israeli peace process, Arafat having just six days earlier returned triumphantly to Gaza; it was widely thought that the conflict was winding down. In this context, Arafat's bellicose talk in Johannesburg about a "*jihad* to liberate Jerusalem" had a major impact on Israelis, beginning a process of disillusionment that has hardly abated in the intervening years.

No less damaging than his comments about Jerusalem was Arafat's cryptic allusion about his agreement with Israel. Criticized by Arabs and Muslims for having made concessions to Israel, he defended his actions by comparing them to those of the Prophet Muhammad in a similar circumstance: "I see this agreement as being no more than the agreement signed between our Prophet Muhammad and the Quraysh in Mecca." Arafat further drew out the comparison, noting that although Muhammad had been criticized for this diplomacy by one of his leading companions (and a future caliph), 'Umar ibn al-Khattab, the Prophet had been right to insist on the agreement, for it helped him defeat the Quraysh tribe and take over their city of Mecca. In a similar spirit, "we now accept the peace agreement, but [only in order] to continue on the road to Jerusalem."[1] In the years since he first alluded to Muhammad and the Quraysh, Arafat has frequently mentioned this as a model for his own diplomacy.[2]

Though this allusion to events in early Islamic history is completely obscure to most nonbelievers, many Muslims are familiar with the Prophet's agreement with the Quraysh. Mentioning it in Johannesburg and oftentimes since permits Arafat to send an almost clandestine message about his intentions toward Israel, one intelligible to Muslims but not to the rest of the world. What intentions did Arafat convey with his reference to the Prophet's biography? An answer requires a historical excursus to the original incident nearly fourteen centuries ago.

There is a second reason carefully to review Arafat's reference, for it set off an unsettling debate in the United States, one which provoked some threatening comments. These in turn raise freedom of speech issues when the topic concerns Islamic sensitivities.

Historiography

The Prophet Muhammad's life is by no means a conventional topic of research, and so requires a few words of introduction.

A century ago, the French critic Ernest Renan famously observed that Muhammad was the only religious leader who lived "in the full light of history." By this, he meant that the Arabic literary sources—religious texts, biographical accounts, chronicles, and much more—are replete with information about Muhammad's life. Beyond the impressive level of detail, they also provide plenty of evidence that can be interpreted as detrimental to the Prophet's reputation—which of course only adds to their credibility.

Nonetheless, the sources that seemed so solid in Renan's time soon came under a sustained critique from scholars who cast severe doubts on their accuracy. Starting with the publication in 1889–90 of *Muhammadan Studies* by the great Hungarian orientalist Ignaz Goldziher, orientalists such as the legal scholar Joseph Schacht and the religious historian John Wansborough have developed a complex theory about the origins of Islam. In very brief, they note that the conventional biography of Muhammad was only recorded in literary sources decades or even centuries after the events they described. The scholars theorize that the information about Muhammad was not (as Muslims hold) passed down from one generation to another via an oral tradition; instead, it was conjured up only much later as ammunition for heated arguments about the Islamic religion. To score points, Goldziher and others argue, the latter-day polemicists associated their own views to the life of Muhammad.

Scholars who accept this approach more or less ignore the standard Muslim account about early Islam and the life of the Prophet. In their new version of those events, Mecca, Muhammad, and the Qur'an are all quite transformed. In perhaps the most radical of these efforts, *Hagarism*, a 1977 study by Patricia Crone and Michael Cook, the authors completely exclude the Arabic literary sources and reconstruct the early history of Islam only from the information to be found in Arabic papyri, coins, and inscriptions, as well as non-Arabic literary sources in a wide array of languages (Aramaic, Armenian, Coptic, Greek, Hebrew, Latin, and Syriac). This approach leads Crone and Cook in significant new directions. In their account, Mecca's role was replaced by a city in northwestern Arabia and Muhammad was elevated "to the role of a scriptural prophet" only about A.D. 700, or seventy years after his death.[3] As for the Qur'an, it was compiled in Iraq at about that same late date.

While these ideas are fraught with implications for the Islamic religion, many of them potentially beneficial,[4] believing Muslims have for the most part studiously avoided paying any attention to this line of research. And so a strange—and ultimately unsustainable—duality now exists, with the scholars in the role of termites eating away at the magnificent traditional structure and the believers acting as though the beams and joints were as strong as ever.

Turning to the Treaty of Hudaybiya and the conquest of Mecca: every last detail about these subjects comes from the Arabic literary sources.[5] For the purposes of this discussion, which has to do with Arafat's statement and his audience's interpretation of it, the issue is not at all what happened in the seventh century, but what the Arabic

written sources tell about those events and how Muslims today understand them. In other words, we need only look at the literary sources—
which greatly simplifies matters, for all analysts work from precisely the
same texts.

The Event

The sources tell of tensions between Muhammad and the grandees of
the Quraysh tribe who controlled Mecca, his home city. The Quraysh
leaders viewed the upstart Prophet as a direct threat to their interests
because his monotheistic message undermined Mecca's status as a pilgrimage destination for followers of the polytheistic Arabian religions.
Tensions between Quraysh and the nascent Muslim community eventually forced Muhammad to flee the city in 622 C.E., when he found
refuge in Medina, a town to the north of Mecca. By 628, Muhammad
had built enough strength in Medina to challenge the Quraysh and
possibly to vanquish them and take their city; instead, he reached an
agreement with them. Named the Treaty of Hudaybiya after the town
where it was signed, this pact disappointed many of the Muslims, who
were spoiling for a fight. The treaty held that the two sides "agreed to
remove war from the people for ten years. During this time the people
are to be security and no one is to lay hands on another. . . . Between
us evil is to be abstained from, and there is to be no raiding or spoliation."[6]

In the twenty-two months after signing the treaty, Muhammad significantly built up his power base. He made new conquests and formed
alliances with powerful tribes, in particular with the Bani Khuza'a. As
a result, by 630 he was considerably stronger vis-à-vis the Quraysh
than at the time of the signing. Quraysh did less well in terms of making new alliances, but it did ally with another strong tribe, the Bani
Bakr.

At the time, the Bani Khuza'a and the Bani Bakr lived near each
other and had a long history of feuding—and feuding in Arabia, as in
Appalachia, was passed on from generation to generation. In December 629, some of the Bani Bakr, possibly with Quraysh help, took
vengeance on a party of the Bani Khuza'a, killing several of them.
Upon hearing this news, Muhammad instantly opted for the most drastic response: to attack Mecca. It appears that he had decided the time

had come to challenge the ultimate power base of Quraysh in their home city.

In response, Quraysh sent a delegation to Muhammad, petitioning him to maintain the treaty, and offering (as was the Arabian fashion) material compensation for the lives of the dead men. Muhammad, however, had no interest in a compromise and rejected all Quraysh entreaties. In an act of desperation, Abu Sufyan, leader of the Quraysh delegation, went to the mosque in Medina and proclaimed, "O people, I guarantee protection for all!" To this, Muhammad dryly replied, "You say this, O Abu Sufyan, not any one of us."

Muhammad had already made quiet preparations for an assault on the Quraysh. This meant once the desultory negotiations ended, he was ready in short order to advance with a huge force on Mecca. So impressive was his army that the Meccans made no effort to resist it. Instead, they surrendered their city without a fight in January 630. And so ended the Hudaybiya incident.

Assessments

Two points stand out from this sequence of events. First, Muhammad was technically within his rights to abrogate the treaty, for the Quraysh, or at least their allies, had broken its terms. Second, it is equally clear that his response was disproportionate to the infraction: a raid by an allied tribe, even possibly with Quraysh connivance, hardly warranted conquest of the enemy's entire territory.

Combining these points leads to this conclusion: If there is no basis to accuse the Muslims of breaching their promise, there is reason to wonder what validity the treaty had if the Muslim forces were at the ready, seemingly prepared to exploit any minor incident to destroy a rival. The issue here is not a legal one but a moral and political one.

Nearly all Western historians agree with this judgment. Here, in rough chronological order, is how a few authorities have assessed Muhammad's actions. Note that while the earlier writers used harsher language ("pretext," "*casus belli*"), the later authors do not disagree with them on the essentials:

William Muir, writing in 1861: "the alleged infraction . . . by the Coreish afforded Mahomet a fair pretext for the grand object of his ambition, the conquest of Mecca."[7]

Carl Brockelmann, 1939: Muhammad "was simply waiting for a pretext to settle accounts with [Quraysh] once and for all. A brawl between a Bedouin tribe converted to Islam and some partisans of Quraysh, in which some townsmen from Mecca itself are supposed to have taken part, presented a pretext for declaring the peace broken."[8]

Bernard Lewis, 1950: "the murder of a Muslim by a Meccan for what appears to have been a purely private difference of opinion served as *casus belli* for the final attack and the conquest of Mecca."[9]

Montgomery Watt, 1956: "In the year 628 at al-Hudaybiyah it had suited Muhammad to make peace and end the blockade, for he was then able to devote greater energy to the work among the nomadic tribes. In the twenty-two months following the treaty, however, his strength grew rapidly; and when his allies of Khuza'ah appealed for help he apparently felt that the moment had come for action."[10]

John Glubb, 1970: "It is possible that the Prophet himself was ill content at the prospect of having to wait ten years before he could march on Mecca, which now seemed as ready as a ripe plum to fall into his lap. He may consequently have welcomed the opportunity Beni Kinana had supplied, enabling him to break the truce."[11]

Marshall Hogdson, 1974: "Muhammad interpreted a skirmish between some Bedouin allies of the Quraysh and of the Muslims as a breach of the treaty by the Quraysh."[12]

Frank Peters, 1994: "The violation might have been settled in other ways—the Quraysh appeared willing to negotiate—but in January 630 A.D. Muhammad judged the occasion fit and the time appropriate for settling accounts with the polytheists in Mecca for once and for all."[13]

Given these opinions, what does the reference to Hudaybiya suggest about Arafat's future actions? It appears that he drew the comparison with the Prophet Muhammad to make several points to a Muslim audience about his own actions:

- He made unpopular concessions that will turn out well in the end.[14]
- He will achieve his goal—though what that goal is remains ambiguous: it might be just the city of Jerusalem (in parallel to the city of Mecca) or the whole of Israel (in parallel to the whole Quraysh dominion).

- He intends, at the right moment, to exploit a minor transgression to attack his enemy.

The third point is the operational one, permitting Arafat to imply not that he will break his agreements with Israel but that he will, when his circumstances change for the better, take advantage of some technicality to tear up existing accords and launch a military assault on Israel.

It bears noting how easily Arafat, or another future Palestinian leader, will find this to do—legally. Arafat has signed five complex agreements with Israel that include hundreds of pages of mind-numbing detail. The Oslo II agreement of September 28, 1995, for example, runs 314 pages without attachments and includes a myriad of specifics. To take just one clause: Israeli authorities have obligated themselves to help the Palestinian Authority maintain a statistical system by transferring the "estimation procedures, forms of questionnaires, manuals, coding manuals, procedures for and results of quality control measures and analysis of surveys."[15] The Hudaybiya precedent implies that Arafat can choose any lapse or transgression (say, not receiving the results of quality control measures) and turn this into a *casus belli* for an all-out attack on the Jewish state.

Muhammad as a Perfect Human

Arafat's Hudaybiya reference has reverberated for years, spurring debate about both the Hudaybiya episode itself and his intentions. Newspapers and magazines not usually in the business of opining on seventh-century events, much less dealing with the sacred history of Islam, find themselves thrust into a wholly unfamiliar (and thoroughly discomforting) subject area. Often they make mistakes. Whether they deal with this topic accurately or not, the response of American Muslim institutions bears close watching. In general, they respond to any criticism of Muhammad's actions with unvarnished rage and sometimes even with intimidation.

Before delving into the American scene, some background is again needed, this time on Muslim attitudes toward the Prophet Muhammad: Early Muslims saw Muhammad as an exemplary human but by no means a perfect one. Indeed, they dared not. The Qur'an itself refers to Muhammad as "erring" (93:7) and includes much information that reveals his foibles. Perhaps the most damning concerns the Satanic verses episode when, for evidently political reasons, Muhammad recognized the validity of pagan Meccan gods (53:19–21), thereby temporarily making Islam into a polytheistic religion (and appeasing his Quraysh critics).[16] Internal evidence suggests to Muhammad's leading modern Western biographer, Montgomery Watt, that the Satanic verses incident must be true: "It seems impossible that any Muslim could have invented this story."[17]

Then, over the centuries, Muhammad's blemishes faded. That is because, as Annemarie Schimmel explains in her study of the Prophet's place in the Islamic faith, "the personality of Muhammad is indeed, besides the Koran, the center of the Muslims' life."[18] The jurists, the mystics, and the pious turned Muhammad into a paragon of virtue, explaining away his apparent faults. Islamists took this process a step further; in their eyes, Muhammad has acquired a Jesus-like perfection. In the case of the Satanic verses episode, for example, an influential Egyptian intellectual simply dismissed information about it as "fabricated (even though it is in the Qur'an itself)." Indeed, he calls it nothing less than "a fable and a detestable lie."[19]

This Muslim attitude of protectiveness toward Muhammad also creates deep resentment of Western Christians, who have never been shy about expressing their own, rather less elevated views of Islam's Prophet. To get the tone of these it may suffice to note that one of Muhammad's medieval names, Mahound, is defined in the *Oxford English Dictionary* as meaning the false prophet Muhammad, any false god, a monster, or the devil. In modern times, too, disagreement on the matter of Muhammad remains widespread and intense. On occasion, it even has direct political consequences. Encountering the Christian hatred of Muhammad made the European imperialist venture that much more unacceptable to Muslims; for example, Schimmel argues that this "is one of the reasons for the aversion of at least the Indian Muslims to the British."[20]

The sanctity of the Prophet among the believers is such that Muslims resist any but a completely pious discussion of his character and actions—and all the more so coming from unbelievers. As Shabbir Akhtar puts it in his aptly titled book *Be Careful with Muhammad!*, "endorsement of Muhammad's prophethood was the distinguishing feature of the Muslim outlook. It was the responsibility of the Muslims, therefore, to guard the honor of *their* Prophet."[21] Even the allegation of Muhammad's faults is deemed an insult against Islam and in some places is legally punishable. Pakistani law mandates imprisonment or death for "willful defiling, damaging or desecration of the Holy Quran, and directly or indirectly, by words either spoken or written or by visible representation, or by an imputation, innuendo or insinuation defiling, the name of the Holy Prophet."[22] This law has been often implemented, with several Christians sentenced to death under the law (one specifically for telling a Muslim that Salman Rushdie depicted the Prophet Muhammad accurately),[23] though no capital sentences have yet been carried out. In addition, dozens of people are awaiting trial in Pakistan on blasphemy charges.

The sort of open-ended discussion that the West holds on virtually every topic is precisely what Muslims most do not wish to permit about their Prophet. Accordingly, Westerners doing what comes naturally to them, saying just what they think about Muhammad, find themselves under a barrage of bitter criticism from Islamists. The most celebrated case, Salman Rushdie's, happens to involve a Muslim who lives mainly in Great Britain, but the same sort of threat could befall a person of any religion living in any country (which explains, for example, why the author of *Why I Am Not a Muslim* felt constrained to write under a pseudonym).[24]

Controversy

This long legacy and vehement set of attitudes meant that when American journalists, scholars, and politicians gave their opinions about the Treaty of Hudaybiya, the Muslim institutional reaction was predictably hostile. The Washington-based Council on American-Islamic Relations, an organization credibly said to have a "close connection" to Hamas,[25] took the lead in trying to suppress critical discussion of Arafat's Hudaybiya reference. When a commentator or politician had the temerity to raise this subject, CAIR orchestrated an abusive Muslim response. The first instance occurred in an editorial in *U.S. News & World Report* on June 10, 1996, when the magazine's editor in chief, Mortimer B. Zuckerman, touched briefly on Hudaybiya:

> The Israelis have a historic question: Is Arafat a true peacemaker, or does he believe his own rhetoric when he echoes the doctrine of the

prophet Muhammad of making treaties with enemies while he is weak, violating them when he is strong?

In the next issue of *U.S. News & World Report*, dated June 17, the editors noted publicly in a "word to our readers" that "Many Muslim readers have called or written to complain that we spoke badly of the prophet Muhammad and his legacy"; privately, they told of feeling "under siege." In a lengthy and carefully worded retraction, the magazine made the following key points:

> Readers ought to be assured that no disrespect for Islam as a religion or for the prophet Muhammad was intended in any way. . . . The 10-year truce was broken two years later by the Meccans.

Still, the outraged messages kept coming in, for the magazine had not repudiated the notion that Muhammad had a "doctrine" of breaking his word. A week later, the editors addressed this point, and wrote what their Muslim critics insisted on hearing:

> We deeply regret any ambiguity in the language; Mr. Zuckerman meant no insult. He was referring to Mr. Arafat's reference to the Prophet and did not intend to state that this was the doctrine of the Prophet . . . it was the Meccans, not the prophet Muhammad, who broke the peace of Hudaybiah of 628.

This abject apology was sufficient, and the controversy came to a close.

In a second incident, Yehoshua Porath, a well-known professor of Middle Eastern history at the Hebrew University in Jerusalem, wrote in *The New Republic* of July 8, 1996:

> Arafat repeatedly equated the Oslo agreement with the Khudaybiya agreement, which the prophet Muhammad concluded during his wars with the Quraysh tribe. Muhammad broke the agreement eighteen months after its conclusion, when the balance of power changed in his favor, and it has become a guiding precedent in Islamic law for how to deal with non-Muslim powers.

Porath's credentials and stature perhaps explain why the reaction to this passage was particularly vehement. The *New Republic* editors explained in the July 15 issue:

> Within days of publication, TNR was the target of hundreds of abu-
> sive phone calls, letters and e-mail accusing us of defamation of the
> Prophet and worse. It turned out that CAIR had, through CAIR-
> NET, its Internet site, exhorted the faithful to tell us off, and they
> did.

Then follows a selection of foul, abusive, and threatening letters. A
typical one read:

> You guys had better watch out, ok? Because this is not going to go on
> further anymore, ok? You'd better watch out that f *ing Jew . . . tell
> him where he is coming from, ok? Because you know mother-f *er
> bastard, mother—his mom is a bastard. ok? He can't talk about Mus-
> lim shit and you get your act together . . . all of you. We don't want
> to hear anymore about this problem, ok? You got that right?

The final case involved a politician, Representative Jim Saxton, a
Republican of New Jersey. He wrote of Arafat in December 1998, "how
can anyone trust an agreement compared to the Treaty of Hudaibiya
enacted by the Prophet Muhammad, in which a treaty lasts as long as
political expediency dictates[?]"[26] CAIR had Saxton's office deluged
with aggressive but not threatening hate mail, making the congress-
man feel, in his words, "uncomfortable." He wrote CAIR a letter on
January 5, 1999, in which he quoted the U.S. News & World Report
editors' note cited above (that "The 10-year truce was broken two
years later by the Meccans"). CAIR issued a press release on January
11, 1999, quoting this phrase, then gilding the lily by adding five words
in parenthesis and ascribing them to Saxton:

> The 10-year truce (of Hudaibiya) was broken . . . by the Meccans
> (not by the Prophet Muhammad).

Reviewing these three cases suggests that Islamic organizations
like CAIR either do not fully understand or do not accept the First
Amendment and its strictures about freedom of speech. The rough-
and-tumble of American life does not allow for a taboo to descend on
certain subjects, no matter how holy they may be to a portion of the
population. Even the most delicate issues—Holocaust denial, Jesus
portrayed as a practicing homosexual, genetic black inferiority—get a

full and lively airing. Attempts by the Council on American-Islamic Relations and like-minded organizations to impose on Americans the Middle East's notions of sacredness, censorship, and privilege are doomed to fail.

Given the vigorous U.S. tradition of free speech—indeed, its near sanctity—American Muslims might be advised that they can best protect the Prophet Muhammad's reputation (as well as forward the other views of most concern to them) not by demanding silence, much less by threatening those who disagree, but by convincing the audience of their views. The sooner they accept this approach, the better they will represent their interests and the healthier the American body politic will be.

18

CHARLOTTE'S WEB:
HIZBULLAH'S CAREER
IN THE DEEP SOUTH

Mohamad Youssef Hammoud, an eighteen-year-old Shi'i Muslim from Lebanon, arrived at New York's Kennedy Airport on June 6, 1992. He had come, accompanied by two close male relatives, from Caracas, Venezuela, where each of them had paid $200 for a counterfeit U.S. visa. American border guards caught the fraud and the trio did not exactly begin their American careers with distinction; but they did begin them in character—with a crime. The U.S. government also responded in character, just as it would many times over the next eight years: it allowed them into the country.

Then followed a fairly typical sequence of events for illegal immigrants. In November 1992, Hammoud claimed political asylum on the grounds that Israel's Lebanese allies were out to get him, making this fear his justification for buying a fake U.S. visa. One whole year later, in December 1993, an immigration judge turned down this transparent action and ordered Hammoud deported. To no avail: Hammoud promptly appealed the decision, permitting him to stay longer. In December 1994, while still awaiting a verdict, he married an American named Sabina Edwards, and this gave him legal standing to apply for permanent residency. The Immigration and Naturalization Service (INS) did some sleuthing and found both the marriage certificate and her birth certificate fraudulent, so in August 1996 Hammoud was again ordered deported, this time within the month.

Nonetheless, Hammoud went underground and in May 1997 married a second American, Jessica Wedel. In September 1997, while still married to Wedel, he took a third wife, Angela Tsioumas. (That she was already married to another man perhaps evened the score.) The INS, not too adept at recordkeeping, mislaid its file on Hammoud's earlier marriage fraud and never noticed that both of the nuptial pair were married to others; so, on the basis of Hammoud's marriage to Tsioumas, it granted him conditional residency in July 1998. Only in October 1998 did Hammoud get around to divorcing Wedel.

To make matters even more complicated, the Hammoud-Tsioumas bond turns out to have been a complete fiction, just a way for him to acquire citizenship and for her to earn a few thousand dollars. Hammoud appears to have (truly) married a woman in Lebanon in 1999; Tsioumas brags that, as soon as Hammoud no longer needs her, she will marry other would-be Americans "for the right price."[1]

Audacious Fund-Raising Scheme

One might imagine that Hammoud's desperate efforts to remain in the United States signaled his affection for the land of the free; or at any rate, his longing to walk its streets paved with gold. But one would be wrong. Like so many other Shi'is from the shantytowns south of Beirut, this young man has adopted Ayatollah Khomeini's brand of extremist Islam and virulent anti-Americanism. As a member of Hizbullah, the main militant Islamic terrorist and political organization of Lebanon, Hammoud came to the United States not as an immigrant intent on becoming American but as a missionary bringing Hizbullah's message into enemy territory.

Information about Hammoud is available in a powerfully detailed 85-page federal affidavit dated July 20, 2000, and filed at U.S. District Court in Charlotte, North Carolina,[2] based on the reports of six cooperating witnesses and five secret informants, physical surveillance, financial records, and much else. Hammoud, it seems, received military training in Hizbullah camps in Lebanon and boasts of being "well-connected" to Hizbullah leaders. One informant calls Hammoud "100% Hizbullah." Another thinks him dangerous because he "would likely assist in carrying out any action against United States interests" if Hizbullah asked him to. A third says Hammoud "would not hesitate" to execute a terrorist act in the United States for Hizbullah.

He's hardly the first of this type, nor the most famous; that distinction probably belongs to New York's blind sheikh. In a bitter and ironic development little noted by Americans, many recent immigrants arrive, as Martin Peretz puts it, "not with the immigrant's psychological oneway ticket, not with the immigrant's love for America, but with a peculiar immigrant's hatred of America."[3] Islamists like Hammoud are perhaps the most significant of this breed, intensely hating the United States and all it represents, but savoring too the country's freedom of expression and of movement, its rule of law, its open institutions, its fine communications and transportation, and its superpower status. They also appreciate its affluence. As Iran, Saudi Arabia, Libya, and the other once-rich Middle East states curtail spending, militant Islamic groups like Hizbullah increasingly seek funding from coreligionists in the West.

Hammoud was active on behalf of Hizbullah since arriving in Charlotte. He organized his two brothers and three cousins, as well as other fellow Shi'is from his old neighborhood in Lebanon, into what one informant terms "an active group" of Hizbullah members. They arranged nocturnal meetings in each other's houses several times a week and engaged in morale-boosting activities. They sang rousing Hizbullah songs (downloaded by Hammoud from the Internet), heard inspiring speeches of Khomeini and Hizbullah's leader, watched videotapes of Hizbullah victories over Israel, and discussed Hizbullah "activities and operations." One person who attended these meetings—the last of which took place on July 13, 2000—calls their atmosphere "extremely anti-United States."[4]

Having heated their emotions, Hammoud solicited donations for Hizbullah from his group and worked with them on a simple but audacious fund-raising scheme for Hizbullah. It happened that these Muslims lived in North Carolina, home to the American tobacco industry and a state whose government adds a tax of just 5 cents per cigarette pack. Many of their Lebanese Shi'i associates live in the Detroit area, where the state of Michigan charges 75 cents per pack. All they had to do was drive a van the 680 miles from Charlotte to Detroit, a thirteen-hour trip, carrying 800–1,500 cartons of cigarettes, and they would net a profit of $5,000 to $10,000. The scam required no special skills and it made good use of existing pro-Hizbullah networks.

By early 1995, the smuggling operation was in place. The Hizbullahis bought tens of thousands of cigarette cartons at North Carolina's many tobacco outlets, loaded these into rental vans, made a quick round trip to Detroit, and returned the van, with no one the wiser but Hizbullah and they personally quite a bit richer. The sums were impressive: in the period 1996–99, Hammoud alone bought nearly $300,000 worth of cigarettes on ten charge cards. The smugglers spent some of the earnings on themselves; Hammoud lived in a middle-class neighborhood, another suspect bought himself two luxury cars, and yet others started what the affidavit terms "semi-legitimate" businesses: a tobacco shop to acquire cigarettes in bulk and a Lebanese restaurant to launder the resulting funds.

From 1996, they also smuggled large sums to Hizbullah. No estimate is available for the total amount transferred, but the affidavit charges Hammoud and four others with smuggling currency and indicates that just one suspect, Ali Hussein Darwiche, sent over $1 million. In addition, several of those arrested stand accused of sending technical materials such as digital photo equipment, computers, global positioning systems, and night vision goggles to Lebanon. One informant states that Hizbullah "sanctioned" the Charlotte group's criminal activities.[5]

The cigarette scam, however, became too obvious, especially as the smugglers kept getting arrested for driving offenses, then having large numbers of cigarettes (121,500, 436,500, 1,412,400) and dollars ($17,000, $45,922) confiscated. By 1996, the authorities finally figured out that an organized effort of Lebanese was engaged in systematically moving cigarettes. As a slew of local, state, and federal agents (FBI, INS, ATF) got involved, they learned of two unexpected developments.

First, cigarette running turned out to be just part of a larger pattern of criminal activity. Nearly all the Lebanese suspects reached the United States through deception, either visa forgery (like Hammoud) or bribery. This group lied about many things—claiming to speak English when they could not, creating children out of thin air, denying the existence of close relatives living in the United States. They nearly all contracted fake marriages, with one man arranging for himself, his brother, his sister, and her husband each to marry Americans. (Conveniently, he "married" the brother and brother-in-law to two female roommates who worked with him at Domino's Pizza). Curiously, the Lebanese men paid around $3,500 to the American females but a Lebanese woman paid just $1,500 to an American male.

Once settled, the Lebanese suspects began a minor crime wave. They relied on fraudulent Social Security numbers, passed bad checks, used stolen credit cards, passed stolen goods via mail drops, opened bank accounts under false pretenses, and engaged in forgery. One gang member, known for his ability to take on multiple identities, used so many false names (including those of his toddler kids) he had to pull a book out of a friend's safe and study it before going to the bank. He also became a specialist in "busting out" of credit cards—making a half million dollars from 1995 by getting a high credit limit, charging on it to the maximum, then disappearing without paying the debt off. Tax returns from gang members were virtuoso exercises in creative accounting: Hammoud and his fake wife Tsioumas made bank deposits in 1997 totaling $737,318 but reported total wages of just $24,693. The next year, another conspirator deposited $90,903 but listed no income at all. Hammoud's cousin owned a house-painting company; he employed illegal aliens to staff it, paid them under the table, and skipped on taxes. These are not just crooks, but a whole subculture steeped in criminality.[6]

Second, law enforcement observed a preparation for violence. Associates of the suspects built up a "virtual arsenal" of weapons, including a fully automatic AK-47-style assault rifle, with which they, along with Hammoud, regularly practiced—part of what was described as a "paramilitary-style training" in a remote range east of Charlotte.

Finally, on July 21, 2000, about 250 law enforcement officers swooped down on the group, arresting 17 individuals in the Charlotte area and 1 in Michigan. Eleven were Lebanese Muslims, seven were the American citizens who took money for pretend marriages. Charges included conspiracy to launder money, conspiracy to traffic in contraband cigarettes, immigration law violations, and attempted bribery. Pending the results of a search of businesses, cars, computers, and the like, other expected charges include RICO fraud and providing material support to Hizbullah, a designated foreign terrorist organization. These are serious charges. Cigarette smuggling carries a maximum sentence of five years in prison per charge and a $250,000 fine. Money laundering carries a maximum sentence of twenty years in prison per charge and a $500,000 fine.

The arrests were headline news in Lebanon, where Hizbullah predictably dismissed the charges: "Hizbullah does not have any organized group" in the United States, declared Na'im Qasim, its deputy leader. To account for the arrests, he added, "The U.S. authorities need to create an imaginary victory" to make up for their defeats.[7] Nonetheless, when the case finally reached the courts, Hammoud and three other defendants (Mohammed Atef Darwiche, Ali Hussein Darwiche, and Mehdi Hachem Moussaoui) pleaded guilty to racketeering conspiracy; also, all but Moussaoui pleaded guilty to money laundering. Moussaoui agreed to testify against the codefendants. In addition, the U.S. attorney indicated that three other defendants (Ali Fayez Darwiche, Angela Tsioumas, and Sam Chahrour) would plead guilty to racketeering.[8] The case took on extra importance when one defendant, Said Mohamad Harb, pleaded guilty to many charges, including material support to Hizbullah. With this, the Charlotte case became a test case of the 1996 law prohibiting material support to terrorist organizations.

Window on a Subculture

This case opens an important window on the small but worrisome subculture of militant Islamic immigrants who despise America even while living in it, who flaunt its laws and actively aid its enemies. The information from Charlotte prompts several reflections.

First, it confirms the inaccuracy of militant Islamic whining about American bias against Muslims. (One friend of the suspects told reporters, "The F.B.I. took the Koran from my home. It just shows the real reason they are doing this";[9] the American-Arab Anti-Discrimination Committee warned that their treatment "could lead to discrimination and hate crimes.")[10] Immigration and law enforcement authorities were mild to excess. Everyone cut the suspects a break and hoped for the best; note how Hammoud kept beating the system. Nonofficial Americans responded similarly. Scott Furr, who lived across the street from Hammoud, thought the nighttime meetings were a chance to "get together and have a good time." His girlfriend thought they were religious meetings.[11] Paul Booher, another neighbor, figured that this caring Lebanese housed fellow nationals until they found a place to live.[12] Dwayne Eldridge found Hammoud "strange" because he didn't wave or talk to anybody, "But that doesn't mean we thought they were helping terrorists or anything."[13] George Levkulich lived next door to another suspect, whom he called "a nice guy, a regular guy."[14] In other words, the neighbors assumed the most benign of intentions, whereas in fact criminality and perhaps terrorism were being plotted.

Second, the Charlotte case again shows that militant Islamic money flows from North America to the Middle East, not the other way around. Besides Hizbullah, other organizations funded from here include Hamas, Islamic Jihad, and the Algerian radicals. Middle Eastern governments note this pattern with alarm (Tunisia's president protests that the United States has become "the rearguard headquarters for fundamentalist terrorists"), but it has yet to be taken seriously by American leaders. How many more Charlotte-like webs are out there?

Third, the Lebanese suspects showed a contempt toward the United States that bordered on the bizarre. Though acting on behalf of an ostensibly devout Muslim organization, they felt entitled to break American laws at whim, without taking even elementary precautions. One defendant charged $45,677 to one credit card for cigarette purchases in a single calendar year; on trips to Detroit, the alleged smugglers paid for gasoline along the way with charge cards, not even trying to hide their movements. Even after arrest, they remained arrogantly unconcerned; according to the *Charlotte Observer*, at their court hearing the defendants "smiled, laughed and made jokes. They asked which of their homes, cars and bank accounts had been seized by the government."[15] This nihilism, quite common among uneducated militant Islamic immigrants, augurs trouble ahead.

Fourth, in this case, as in so many other instances of would-be terrorist violence, the authorities bungled things—and if it were not for alert local officers piecing suspicious activity together, the perps would still be at it. The INS showed itself to be hapless, not seeing through one fake marriage after another, losing records, and allowing deportees to disappear without a trace. The State Department proved susceptible to bribery. The FBI knew nothing until latterly brought into the case. Actually, this is frequently the pattern: in at least five cases over the past fifteen years, the local cop with eyes open was the key to stopping a major terrorist action. And while lucky breaks are very welcome, it is dismaying to see the inutility of national institutions.

It is even more dismaying to look at this bunch of criminal aliens and political extremists, many of whom have been expelled more than once from the United States, and to find them still there. The shock of September 2001's events may make some changes, but unless there is a major shift in mentality, it's a pretty safe bet that most of them will still be here another eight years from now, probably joined by an even larger number of fellow extremists and criminals.

19

AMERICA'S MUSLIMS VS.
AMERICA'S JEWS

On March 1, 1999, a Federal District Court in Brooklyn sentenced one Ghazi Ibrahim Abu Maizar, late of Hebron, to life imprisonment. He was found guilty of conspiring to use a weapon of mass destruction, threatening to do so, and carrying the actual device. Although Abu Maizar had not actually harmed anyone, when the police raided his apartment on July 31, 1997, they found plenty of evidence that the twenty-three-year-old was on the verge of setting off a pipe bomb later that very day.

Oddly, this verdict attracted almost no attention; *The New York Times* carried it below the fold on page B5. Editorials were not written. Politicians did not mention it. Jewish organizations did not take out ads about the incident. Attempted mass murder by an Arab in New York, it would seem, is not a noteworthy event.

Yet Mr. Abu Maizar's intended crime bears some attention, for it represents a larger phenomenon—that of Muslims ready to use violence, and even to give up their own lives, in the effort to kill American Jews. Here, complete with spelling and grammatical errors, are excerpts from the typewritten letter that police found in his apartment back in July 1997, captioned "In the name of the Gade [God]" and addressed to "the united states of america and U.S.A. citizens."

> no podey [nobody] can wein [win] the ware [war] against Islam and we are warring. . . . We are ready by our soul-blood boombes to deines [for whoever denies] our gouls [goals] . . . .we are going to buarn the ground under the america and Jewish stat[e]. . . . Our request shoud be done on our mujjahiddeenis [warriors] ready to hit every where by they [the] suuisid boomb.[1]

After his arrest, Abu Maizar told an FBI agent that he had decided to explode the pipe bomb on the B subway line (which runs from the northern tip of Manhattan to Coney Island at the very south of Brooklyn) "because there are a lot of Jews that ride that train."[2] At the trial itself, Abu Maizar told the court he had come to this country to do it harm as punishment for its Middle East policies: "because I feel that the United States is supporting the Jewish state and the United States should be punished for supporting Israel." He spoke openly of his plan for suicide bombings and his hopes to kill "as many [Jews] as I could take . . . I always dreamed to be a martyr."[3]

As these reference to God, *jihad*, and martyrdom suggest, Abu Maizar's virulent hatred of Jews derives directly from his outlook as an Islamist. In addition, Abu Maizar acknowledges supporting Hamas and his misspelled letter demanded the release of several Islamists imprisoned in the United States. When the verdict pronouncing him guilty was read, Abu Maizar leaped to his feet, held an open copy of the Qur'an over his head, and shouted: "Allahu Akbar!"[4]

Militant Islam

Jews are a central concern to Islamists when they, along with British and American "imperialists," are seen as the main obstacle to living by the law, which is often. In the view of militant Islam, Jews seek to dominate the world—including, of course, the Muslim countries. To weaken the Muslims, this view goes on, Jews do whatever they must, ruthlessly and efficiently, to keep them from living by the law, which means everything from unleashing Atatürk to Madonna, from Israel to CENTCOM. In response to this supposed assault, Islamists call for a no less ruthless war against the Jews. This attitude both explains the actions of someone like Abu Maizar and, recalling Hannah Arendt's thesis about their intrinsic anti-Semitism, confirms militant Islam's similarity with other totalitarianisms.

In one way, however, militant Islam has gone beyond its precursors: German Nazis and Soviet Communists never had the audacity to emigrate to the United States, much less did they hope to find a substantial base of support among sympathetic Americans. Yet that is precisely what militant Islam and its odd fellow traveler, the Nation of Islam (an amalgam of Islamic, black nationalist, and other elements), have done. The Brown Shirts and Communists of the 1930s never amounted to a significant force locally, but Muslims who hate the United States, and especially the Jews therein, are growing in numbers and reach.

Population figures are hard to come by; the best estimate of Muslims in the United States is between 2 and 3 million. Immigrants and their descendants (mostly from South Asia and the Middle East) make up something like two thirds to three quarters of this total, converts (mostly African-Americans) the remainder. Of the converts, only a very small number (perhaps 20,000) are members of the Nation of Islam (NoI), with the great majority adhering to a form of normative Islam as it is practiced in the traditional Muslim world. Despite its small membership, the Nation of Islam has great importance, for nearly all black converts to Islam have at some time had a connection to this organization or one of its many associated movements; it serves as the bridge between Christianity and Islam. Further, the NoI has a substantial following of sympathizers attracted to its teachings but not ready to take the huge step of converting out of Christianity.

Mainstream Muslims and NoI members differ so greatly in political outlook, socioeconomic status, ambitions, and relations with Jews that they need to be considered separately.

Normative Islam: Positive Relations

The basis for a positive Muslim bond with Jews does exist, for the two peoples bear many resemblances. Both faiths contain a sacred law; those who live by it lead similar lives, with pious Muslims and Orthodox Jews making their way through huge numbers of minute details.

Some of the laws are close (the ritual slaughter of animals), others nearly identical (male circumcision). The Islamic requirements for halal food resemble those of kosher food. Further, the two groups share much in the ways they dress, greet, speak, gesticulate, celebrate holidays, and the like. Put negatively, Sunday means nothing to either.

Jewish-Muslim reconciliation and cooperation does exist; the Detroit Round Table, a branch of the National Conference of Christians and Jews, actively brings Jews and Muslims together. A leading imam in Washington, D.C., joined with Christian and Jewish leaders in May 1980 to help defeat proposed legislation to legalize gambling. Muslims have also worked together with Jews on issues connected to welfare and children's education. A few brave voices also stand up to the Muslim attacks on Jews; most notably, W. Deen Mohammed (son of Elijah Muhammad), the leading figure among black converts to normative Islam, has at times adopted a stand against African-American attacks on Jews[5] and worked for interreligious harmony.

Jews and Muslims both profit by such connections. Jews gain a great number of allies; Muslims gain instant stature. Further, Jews have well-established and widely accepted institutions for combating prejudice, so joining forces with them offers a way for Muslims to win tolerance for their own customs. Indeed, some Muslims do raise the prospect of working with Jews. Robert Crane, a prominent American convert with close links to the Islamists, wants Muslims to establish coalitions with sympathetic Christians and Jews to battle "the chaos and evil" he believes is engulfing American society.[6] He foresees a great future for Muslims in America, and an epochal impact. "The destiny of Muslims in America is to work with like-minded traditionalists of America's other religions in a common strategy. . . . Together, the traditionalists of all religions can complete the American Revolution, because they are the only ones who can understand its meaning."[7]

Normative Islam: Negative Relations

But these positive attitudes are very much the exception among a barrage of bias, calumny, and conspiracy theory; nearly every Muslim organization and publication in the United States spews forth a blatant and vicious anti-Semitism, the sort that has otherwise disappeared from mainstream discourse. Talk of a bloody and decisive battle with

Jews is completely routine among both; openly extremist groups like the Islamic Association for Palestine and seemingly moderate ones like the Council on American-Islamic Relations (whose director has attended White House functions) have issued communiqués on behalf of Hamas in which they call for the killing of Jews.[8] These calls for murder are not just abstract notions, as shown by the fact that American Muslim groups have produced training videos for Hamas and recruited members on its behalf.

What accounts for such virulent sentiments toward Jews? Causes include the import of Middle East ideologies; anti-Zionist feeling about the American Jewish role in supporting Israel; and the militant Islamic hegemony over normative Islam.

Middle East ideologies. Some of this murderous invective is homegrown, but most of it comes straight out of the Middle East political swamp, where organizations like Hamas, Islamic Jihad, and Hizbullah speak freely about killing Jews, not Israelis, and openly celebrate acts of violence. Ironically, immigrants bring from the Middle East the hoary themes of Christian anti-Semitism, spreading medieval tales about the Jewish need for goy blood at Passover and the Torah being a forgery no less than nineteenth-century myths of Jewish attempts at world domination.[9] Even more alarming, the immigrants rely on a Nazi-like vocabulary of racism ("sons of monkeys and pigs and the worshippers of evil") and physical extermination ("O Muslim, servant of God, there is a Jew behind me, come and kill him").[10]

Leading Islamic groups in the United States keep in close contact with the Middle East, staying in regular touch with militant Islamic leaders, reprinting articles and books, and flying in their best spokesmen. These speakers then address huge conferences at downtown hotels in cities like Chicago and Oklahoma City. (The largest of them, the annual Islamic Society of North America Convention, attracts about fifteen thousand participants.) One of the most eminent Islamic theologians alive today, Qatar-based Yusuf al-Qaradawi, told an audience in Kansas City in 1989: "On the hour of judgment, Muslims will fight the Jews and kill them."[11] A leader of Islamic Jihad, 'Abd al-'Aziz 'Awda, told an audience at a meeting of the American Islamic Group in 1991 that Jews "understand only one language: The language of Jihad, and the language of confrontation, and the language of sacrifice."[12] A particularly hair-raising scene took place in December 1994, at the Chicago meeting of the Muslim Arab Youth Association, when Bassam Alamoush, a leading Jordanian Islamist, began his talk with an anecdote. From a videotape in his possession, Steven Emerson quotes Alamoush and describes what happened next:

> "Somebody approached me at the mosque [in Amman] and asked me, 'If I see a Jew in the street, should I kill him?' " After pausing a moment with a dumbfounded face, Alamoush answered the question to a laughing crowd: "Don't ask me. After you kill him, come and tell me. What do you want from me, a *fatwa* [legal ruling]? Really, a good deed does not require one." Later in the speech, Alamoush was interrupted by an aide with a note "Good news there has been a suicide operation in Jerusalem" killing three people. Thunderous applause followed his statement.[13]

This Middle Eastern poison has also affected American converts to Islam. Before his travels to Egypt, Saudi Arabia, and elsewhere, Malcolm X spoke of Zionism as a model for the black diaspora in relation to Africa; but after leaving the Nation in 1964, becoming a mainstream Muslim, and extensive travels in the Middle East, he portrayed Zionism as a conspiratorial force obstructing American blacks from learning about normative Islam. By the 1980s, vituperation against Jews had become a regular theme of mosque sermons, political analyses, and street rhetoric, often mixed with conspiracy theories and laced with highly charged invective.[14]

Anti-Zionism. In an moment of unusual candor, the late M. T. Mehdi, a New York–based Muslim leader, explained the need to destroy American Jews as part of the anti-Israel battle:

> the head of the snake is in America and the tail of the snake is in Palestine. The Arabs and Muslims for the last forty years have been fighting the tail of the snake and forgetting the head of the snake, which is America. Of course, it is not impossible to kill the snake by fighting the tail. I pleaded with all the Arab leaders, intellectuals, Kings, Queens, Presidents and Politicians, that the battleground for the liberation of Palestine is in America, even before being in Palestine.[15]

To "kill the snake," American Muslims focus on the need to match and overtake U.S. Jews in whatever ways count—population size, fund-raising capabilities, or clout in Washington. Institutionally, for example, the American Muslim Council sees itself in direct competition with the American Israel Public Affairs Committee. More generally, the Muslim intellectual Ali Mazrui wrote in 1997 about his hope that "By the next century, Muslims may be as influential as Jews in influencing policy."[16]

Militant Islamic hegemony. Like their coreligionists elsewhere, mainstream Muslims espouse a wide range of outlooks and one would expect these to be fully articulated in the Land of the Free. But no; Islamists control nearly every major American Muslim organization,[17] as well as a large and perhaps growing majority of mosques, weekly newspapers, and communal organizations. As a result, they dominate the discourse. In contrast to countries like Turkey and Egypt, where a lively debate takes place between moderates and Islamists, the former hardly have a voice in the United States. One of the few nonmilitant Islamic leaders in this country, Muhammad Hisham Kabbani, chairman of the Islamic Supreme Council of America, told the Department of State's Open Forum in early 1999 that extremism has "spread to 80 per cent of the Muslim population" in the United States.[18] As though to confirm his point, the Muslim response to his warning was heavyhanded and even threatening.

This near hegemony of Islamists has several causes. In part, it results from the funding and other support from the Middle Eastern governments, which goes almost exclusively to them. The Iranians, Saudis, and Libyans for years have helped the most aggressive militant Islamic groups; with a touch of hyperbole, Kabbani noted at the State Department that these regimes "have sponsored them with billions of dollars to be active in the United States." Also, whereas moderates tend to go out into the world and involve themselves in non-Islamic activities, Islamists are highly ideological and focused (think of them as the religious counterparts of union organizers). Finally, the United States has a perversely magnetic appeal to Islamists: hounded from their countries of origin, they disproportionately flee to a place with the rule of law, separation of church and state, wealth, excellent communications and transportation—and conspicuously little concern among law enforcement officials with their brand of ideology. What better place than Los Angeles to spread the faith, Chicago to make a fortune, or Jersey City to plot the overthrow of the home government?

Nation of Islam

The Nation of Islam is a separate phenomenon, a sect that began its existence isolated from the Middle East and its anti-Semitism. As contacts developed, however, through travels there and the immigration of Middle Eastern Muslims to the United States, anti-Semitism became a more central, and even an obsessive matter.

Relations with Jews were mixed during the long reign of Elijah Muhammad (1934–75). He hated whites but bore no particular grievance against Jews. Elijah Muhammad developed a highly original nutritional theory and praised Orthodox Jews for, of all things, their eating habits. Relations with Jews struck him as relatively unstrained: "Jews and Muslims have always been able to settle their differences between each other better than Christians and Muslims . . . the American Jew and the American Black Man may yet find some way of making a separate relationship out of the other world."[19] On occasion, Elijah Muhammad made Jews symbolic of his enemy, the Caucasians: Israel is "the whole of the white race," he said.[20] In all, if Jews were peripheral to the NoI, matters were already tense enough in 1959 that Senator Kenneth Keating of New York denounced the Nation for its "extreme anti-Semitism."[21]

After a short hiatus following Elijah Muhammad's death in 1975, Louis Farrakhan revived the Nation of Islam under his leadership; by 1984, he and his organization had become the most prominent propagator of anti-Semitism in the United States. Farrakhan, who regularly wins enormous media coverage and political attention, has made wild attacks on Jews his rhetorical hallmark. In turning his predecessors' mildly suspicious view of Jews into full-blown anti-Semitism, he has both repeated centuries-old themes and made up his own.

On the first score, the Nation of Islam purveys the *Protocols of the Elders of Zion*, a notorious anti-Semitic forgery, and Farrakhan expounds its themes when he holds Jews responsible for capitalism and communism, for the two world wars, controlling Hollywood, and causing the U.S. government to go into debt. He accuses them of dominating U.S. politics ("all presidents since 1932 are controlled by the Jews") and the media ("any newspaper that refused to acquiesce to controlled news was brought to its knees by withdrawing advertising.

Failing this, the Jews stop the supply of news print and ink").[22] Farrakhan calls Jews "the most organized, rich and powerful people, not only in America but in the world." In all, he asserts that "85 percent of the masses of the people of earth are victimized" by Jews.[23]

Farrakhan's lieutenants and acolytes endlessly repeat and embellish these calumnies. For example, in a speech that attracted wide attention after being reprinted by the Anti-Defamation League, Khalid Abdul Muhammad in 1993 told an audience at Kean College in New Jersey:

> I don't care who sits in the seat at the White House. You can believe that the Jews control that seat, that they sit in it from behind the scenes. They control the finance, and not only that, they influence the policymaking. We found out that the Federal Reserve isn't really owned by the Federal Government. The Federal Reserve is owned by the Jews.[24]

Vice President Al Gore blasted this speech as "the vilest kind of racism" and the Senate bestowed on it the rare distinction of voting 97–0 to condemn it as "false, anti-Semitic, racist, divisive, repugnant and a disservice to all Americans."[25]

If these are old tropes, Farrakhan also has the perverse imagination to conjure up novel assertions about Jews. His trademark invention is to accuse Jews of primarily carrying out the transatlantic slave trade that he claims killed 100 million Africans. His organization's "Historical Research Department" has even done some original pseudo-scholarship, publishing in 1991 a volume entitled *The Secret Relationship between Blacks and Jews*[26] that purports to prove how Jews took the lead in enslaving blacks, transporting them to America, and continuing their enslavement in the South. These ideas have become so influential in black circles, including some universities, that serious scholars have had to go to the trouble of producing book-length refutations.[27]

Turning to more recent times, Farrakhan blames Jewish "bloodsuckers" for blocking black advancement. He discredits active Jewish participation in black civil rights efforts by claiming this was part of a self-interested plot. By helping integrate blacks, he says, Jews destroyed the autonomous black economic institutions Jim Crow had spawned, then took over these businesses for themselves. Also, by encouraging blacks to work within the system rather than confront it, Jews prevented them from escaping the strictures of white supremacy. Of late, Jews injected the AIDS virus into black newborns and today are "plotting against us even as we speak."[28]

Farrakhan responds to these alleged plots as conspiracy theorists always do—with aggressive threats. He calls Judaism a "gutter religion"[29] and Adolf Hitler a "very great man."[30] Years ago he warned Jews: "If you harm Jesse Jackson, in the name of Allah, that will be the last one you harm,"[31] then used almost the same words to threaten Jews should they hurt himself: "if you rise up to kill me. . . . All of you will be killed outright."[32]

A Division of Labor

An effective division of labor exists in American Islam. While the Nation of Islam is the leading font of anti-Jewish ideology in the United States, mainstream Muslims have a near monopoly on violence against Jews. The Nation of Islam has far outpaced Christian rivals in the race for anti-Jewish influence. The Liberty Lobby cannot pack thousands into large arenas to hear its leader, much less hundreds of thousands on the Mall in Washington. The militiamen cannot organize full-time paramilitary forces in dozens of locations, much less win federal government grants to subsidize those forces, as the NoI does. (For-profit offshoots of the Fruit of Islam, the NoI's strong arm, have won contracts in several states to patrol high-crime areas.) The Ku Klux Klan leader cannot stand on a public stage literally hand-in-hand with the (Jewish) mayor of Philadelphia, as Farrakhan has in fact done. Posse Comitatus cannot find the resources to put together a "Historical Research Department" to produce a history of American tax codes. The Aryan Nation cannot find a foreign patron like Mu'ammar al-Qadhdhafi of Libya, who has offered NoI $1 billion.

And mainstream Muslims are the chief source of violence against Jews. Far right fanatics can only claim the June 1984 murder of Alan Berg, a Jewish talk-show host in Denver; in contrast, Muslim assaults on American Jews have included many lesser incidents (such as a series of attacks on Chicago-area synagogues) and a long list of major ones:

- March 1977: Hanafi Muslims, a group of black converts, seized three buildings in Washington (the District of Columbia building, the Islamic Center, and B'nai B'rith), holding hostages for thirty-nine hours, leading to one death and one severe injury.
- November 1990: El-Sayyid Nossair assassinated Rabbi Meir Kahane in a New York hotel.
- February 1993: The World Trade Center bombing was at least partially directed against Jews. Ramzi Yusuf, its mastermind, declared the towers not a civilian target but a military one—by virtue of the fact that they might house a "Zionist official."[33]
- June 1993: one of the gang planning the "day of terror" that was simultaneously to bomb the United Nations complex, the Lincoln and Holland tunnels, and other New York landmarks spoke of "Boom! Broken windows. Jews in the street."[34]
- March 1994: Rashid Baz, a Palestinian immigrant, opened fire on a van carrying Orthodox Jewish boys across the Brooklyn Bridge, killing sixteen-year-old Ari Halberstam.
- July 1997: Ali Hasan Abu Kamal, a sixty-nine-year-old Palestinian, shot seven tourists atop the Empire State Building, killing one and severely wounding another; his suicide note accused the United States of using Israel as "an instrument" against the Palestinians.[35]

It bears noting that the mainstream Muslim assault on American Jews fits into a larger pattern of violence. In Europe, too, they speak the language of overt anti-Semitism. For example, the broadcast of excerpts from Hitler's *Mein Kampf* on Radio Islam in Sweden has led to Ahmed Arami spending six months in a Swedish jail. According to *Anti-Semitism Worldwide*, an annual survey published by the Anti-Defamation League, while rightists harassed Jews and vandalized Jewish property in Europe in 1995–96, "violent attacks with the intent of causing bodily harm were perpetrated in most cases by Muslim extremists." Specifically, the only anti-Semitic terrorist act in Europe during 1995 was carried out not by skinheads but by an Algerian militant Islamic group (the attempted bombing of a Jewish school near Lyons, France).[36] The same problems exist elsewhere in the world, as indicated by the bombings of the Israeli Embassy and a Jewish community center in Argentina, as well as growing problems in South Africa.

Tomorrow's Problem

In all, while still potentially virulent, notably in Russia, Jew-haters of Christian origin are almost everywhere relegated to the fringes. Yes, anti-Semitism still exists in the Christian world, but it has declined in its reach and its ferocity. Cast out of the established churches and denounced by political leaders, Christian organizations are generally respectful of Jews and many, including the Christian Coalition, are enthusiastic about Israel. A figure like Pat Robertson constantly praises Jews and Israel.[37] Anti-Jewish sentiments, once commonplace, are now rare and fairly indirect. The raving anti-Semites constitute a tiny fringe virtually excluded from American public life. They cannot look to legitimate institutions for sympathy and support and so are denied the resources necessary to make real trouble. All signs point to Christian anti-Semites remaining marginalized.

If trends among Christians are positive, those among Muslim are not. If anti-Semitism lurks furtively in the Christian countries, in the Muslim world it proudly rules. In the former (again, with the exception of Russia), fringe groups keep this form of hatred alive; in the latter, it is common currency for heads of state, governing political parties, powerful opposition groups, mainstream newspapers, and leading intellectuals. In short, the historically Christian phenomenon of anti-Semitism is now primarily a Muslim phenomenon; Christians have passed the hate-filled baton to Muslims. The main locus of anti-Semitism has moved from the Christian countries to the Muslim world. Muslims, not Christians, now pose the greater danger to Jews. Christian anti-Semitism is yesterday's problem; Muslim anti-Semitism is tomorrow's.

Further, this pattern applies not just in the Middle East but in the United States and around the world. Recent immigrant Muslims from the Middle East appear to be the main carrier of the anti-Semitic virus. Before the current wave of immigration to the United States began in the late 1960s, American Muslims, whether mainstream or NoI, took little interest in Jews. The subsequent preoccupation with Jews echoes ideas, rhetoric, and methods that predominate in the Arab countries and Iran. It now appears that Muslims will with time potentially be in a position to challenge the political well-being and physical security of Jews in the United States.

This thought brings us back to where we began, for in the United States one would hardly know any of this from the response to Muslim anti-Semitism by the press, by most researchers, or even by the organized Jewish community. In *Looking for Farrakhan* (1997), a book-length effort to understand the Nation of Islam leader, Florence Hamlish Levinsohn explains his anti-Semitism exclusively in terms of his Christian background, saying not a word about its Islamic component.[38] The Anti-Defamation League, even while valiantly leading the fight against Farrakhan's anti-Jewish racism, sedulously avoids mentioning its religious context. Worst of all, many American Jewish organizations continue to devote considerable resources and energy to targeting the "Christian Right," while virtually ignoring the rise of Islamist fascism.

But whatever one thinks of the causes favored by the Christian Right—educational vouchers, school prayer, the display of religious symbols in public places, even the rollback of *Roe v. Wade*—they hardly constitute the most serious threat to the security of Jews in the United States today. The real and present danger is by no means the pro-Israel Christian Coalition but the rabidly anti-Semitic Muslim Arab Youth Association; not Jerry Falwell but Sheikh Omar Abdel Rahman; not those who wish, at the very worst, to convert Jews but those who, with every means at their disposal, intend to do them harm, who have already acted on those violent intentions, and who if unchecked will surely do so again.

20

MUSLIM SLAVES
IN AMERICAN HISTORY

S lowly, out of the surprisingly full records of slavery, an important
fact is coming to light: that Muslims constituted a significant per-
centage of the Africans brought to the Americas in servitude; and
that, as the most educated and resistant of the captive peoples, they
exerted a disproportionate influence on slave life in the Americas.
Groundbreaking studies by Allan D. Austin[1] and João José Reis[2]
showed what riches lie in store for those who study this topic; Sylviane
Diouf, a Ph.D. from the University of Paris now resident in New York,
has built on these and other studies, then done much research of her
own, and the result is a fascinating account, *Servants of Allah: African
Muslims Enslaved in the Americas* (1998). She takes up of the three
main topics: the background within Africa; the "difficult and sometimes astonishing steps" of Muslims to maintain their faith and traditions; and the legacy of this forgotten episode.[3]

It is sobering to realize that 2001 marks five centuries of "almost
uninterrupted" Islamic practices by people of African origin in the
western hemisphere. When the Spanish brought the very first Africans

to the New World in 1501, however, they sought to ensure that these were not Muslims but *ladinos*—that is to say, captives who had spent some time in Spain, where they had been forcibly converted to Christianity. As a royal Spanish order of 1543 explained, "in a new land like this one where [the Catholic] faith is only recently being sowed, it is necessary not to allow to spread there the sect of Mahomet or any other." The Spanish had a particular dread of the native Indians converting; among other reasons for this was the fact that if Africans, who knew about horses, converted the Indians and then taught them equine skills, much of the Spaniards' military advantage would have been lost. That the Spanish authorities went on to issue five pieces of legislation to keep Muslims out of the New World in the first fifty years of colonization suggests this effort was less than completely successful. That the Northern Europeans, less concerned with Islam, did not even attempt to maintain this ban meant that Islam was the second monotheism (after Catholicism, before Protestantism) in the Americas.

Maintaining an Islamic Way of Life

The heart of *Servants of Allah* consists of a detailed reconstruction of Muslim slave efforts in the United States to maintain, as much as possible, an Islamic way of life: their reluctance to convert to Christianity, or their pseudo-conversions; praying, giving alms, and fasting; keeping Muslim names, dietary restrictions, and sexual taboos; wearing beards, turbans, and even veils; and keeping apart from non-Muslims. In all, the author contends, the experience of slavery, "far from making the Africans' religious fervor disappear . . . deepened it."[4]

Diouf finds that Muslim slaves included a disproportionate number of the intellectual elite in West Africa, men far better prepared than the average farmer to sustain their faith. Being Muslim, in turn, helped them to do well in the horrifyingly difficult circumstances of American chattel slavery: "There is ample evidence that the Muslims actively used their cultural and social background and the formation they had received in Africa as tools to improve their condition in the Americas." The signs of this success were easy to see, even if slightly contradictory. On the one hand, Muslims rose to the top of the slave hierarchy (in at least one case, the slave kept his master's plantation records in Arabic), were manumitted more often, and returned to

Africa more frequently. On the other hand, Muslims had a disproportionately large role in establishing maroon communities and leading
slave rebellions, sometimes (most especially the great Bahia rebellion
of 1835 in Brazil) dominating their planning and leadership. "Islam
was an excellent organizing force," Diouf notes. In addition to the
communal solidarity it imbued in Muslims, knowledge of Arabic at
times served as a common and secret language for those planning
revolts.[5]

Some of this resulted from their sense of community and solidarity, which extended across linguistic boundaries to fellow Muslims in
bondage and also back to Africa; some from their resistance to being
dominated more than necessary by their Christian overlords; and
much of it resulted from their education. On this final point, Diouf
argues that "literacy became one of the most distinguishing marks of
the Muslims." She even claims, somewhat implausibly, that the literacy rate among Muslim slaves was "in all probability" higher than
among their masters. Islamic networks brought Arabic books produced
in Africa to Brazil. Qur'anic instruction reached as distant an outpost
as Lima, Peru.[6]

Unclear Legacy

The legacy of the Muslim slaves is somewhat controversial. It is common among African-American Muslims in the United States today to
call themselves not converts but *reverts*, alluding both to the fact that
Islam claims to be the natural and original religion of each person at
birth, and so turning to it later in life is a return; and to the fact that
some African slaves were Muslims, so they see themselves reverting to
that original faith, not converting to a new one. In this view, Christianity was enforced upon the slaves in America, not a faith they ever
truly accepted. According to C. Eric Lincoln, a scholar of the subject,
"The memory of Islam, however, tenuous, was never completely lost."[7]
Some analysts explicitly attribute Islam's success among blacks in the
twentieth century to their "Islamic roots."[8] Others go further and contend that "the religion of Islam is part of the genetic memory of
African-Americans."[9]

Diouf sharply rejects this romantic notion; instead, she flat out
declares that "Islam as brought by the African slaves has not survived."

To be more precise: "in the Americas and the Caribbean, not one community currently practices Islam as passed on by preceding African generations."[10] This discontinuity followed primarily from the Muslim slaves' inability to pass their religion on to their children, thanks to the gender disparities among slaves (far fewer women were imported), disrupted family lives, the absence of proper schools, and the pressure to convert to Christianity. So remote had Islam become that some grandchildren of enslaved Muslims did not even know their grandparents had been Muslims but remembered them as worshippers of the sun and moon (a wildly ignorant interpretation of their praying at dawn and dusk). As a result, the last Muslims of slave background died in the 1920s, though the last semi-Muslim (a person who outwardly accepted Christianity) was alive in Brazil as late as 1959.

If slave Islam as a faith died out completely, it nonetheless left many vestiges behind, some of them quite unexpected. Diouf catalogues Islamic influence "found in certain religions, traditions, and artistic creations" among peoples of African descent in the Americas. Most notably, it can be seen in the syncretic black religions of the Americas such as Candomble in Brazil, Santeria in Cuba, Voodoo in Haiti, and other cults. In Voodoo temples, for example, when a deity appears, the priest greets it with *Salam, Salam*, then goes on his knees and raises his arms, much as Muslims do when praying. Even some Christian rites—for instance, among the "Shouters," Trinidadian Baptists—have practices reminiscent of Islam (they move about in a circle, perhaps an echo of the circumambulation of the Ka'ba in Mecca).[11] African-style amulets are widespread.

Other, more subtle legacies also exist. Diouf notes a tradition among whites, going back fully two centuries, of finding the educated Muslims in their midst not to be African but rather "Moors" or "Arabs" or even "Turks." (Insisting that an educated African is not an African helped sustain the racist ideology that undergirded slavery.) This odd tradition lived on into the twentieth century and explains the confusing tendency of the new black converts to Islam repudiating their African heritage. The very first of these movements, founded in 1913, called itself the Moorish Science Temple of America and prominently claimed that blacks are in fact "Moors," "Moorish-Americans," or "Asiatics." This tradition continued in the Nation of Islam, with its leader Elijah Muhammad again and again telling his followers, "You are members of the Asiatic Nation, from the Tribe of Shaba. There is no such thing as a race of Negroes."[12] NoI members have a history of taking this idea very literally. Filling out a questionnaire from his draft board in 1953, Malcolm X filled in the blank for the question, "I am a citizen of ———," with the word "Asia."[13] The Five Percent Nation, an offshoot of the Nation of Islam, calls its membership the "Asiatic Black Man."

Islamic traces can be found in several kinds of music, such as the Arabic words found in songs off the Georgian and Peruvian coasts, in Cuba and Trinidad. More unexpected is the thesis, seemingly sound, that the "high lonesome complaint" so characteristic of blues music derives ultimately from recitations of the Qur'an by unhappy (but educated) slaves. One musicologist, John Storm Roberts, finds that the "long, blending and swooping notes" of the blues are "similar to the Islam-influenced styles of much of West Africa."[14] In some cases, whole songs (such as "Tangle Eyes") seem to have a Muslim African provenance.

Diouf speculates that the family name "Bailey" may in many cases derive from "Bilali," a common name for black-skinned Muslims. She suggests that some leading African-Americans of the post–Emancipation era (Frederick Douglass, Harriet Tubman) had Muslim ancestors. She traces the common habit of black American males of wearing handkerchiefs, rags, and bandannas around their heads to their Muslim slave ancestors' always wearing a turban or skullcap.

Diouf goes a bit far in her lyrical praise of Islam under slave conditions, at times idealizing it in inappropriate and even anachronistic ways; thus, she calls Islam "democratic and progressive in a society that was despotic, repressive, tyrannical, and racist." This may be connected to the paucity of sources and having to rely heavily on just four written slave narratives, all of them presumably recounting the highly unusual experiences of their authors. Despite this mild distortion, Diouf's account of Muslim life in the most horrific of circumstances is a truly moving one and at times an inspiring one: "The African Muslims may have been, in the Americas, the slaves of Christian masters, but their minds were free. They were the servants of Allah."[15]

21

THE RISE OF
ELIJAH MUHAMMAD

I n the early 1930s, when the Nation of Islam had just come into existence, its founder made the bold prediction that one day Islam
would replace Christianity as the primary faith of black Americans. At
the time, this assertion must have sounded incredible, if not slightly
mad; not only was the Islamic faith broadly despised in the United
States but only some dozens of African-Americans were at that time
Muslim. In 1959, however, a top leader of the Ku Klux Klan offered a
perverse endorsement of this claim when he wrote in a letter to the
New York City police commissioner: "If we fail to stop the Muslims
now, the 16,000,000 niggers of America will soon be Muslims and you
will never be able to stop them."[1]

By now, that long-ago prediction no longer seems inconceivable—
indeed, it has somewhat come true, with toward 1 million African-
Americans identifying as Muslims. An even brief visit to various black
neighborhoods quickly confirms that not only is an Islamic infrastructure a visible and important part of black life—mosques, Islamic
schools, female head coverings, and male skullcaps are very much in

evidence—but an active and ambitious drive to propagate Islam is underway. So vital is it, the director of a California-based church effort to stem the conversion of black Americans to Islam has made a memorable prediction: "If the conversion rate continues unchanged, Islam could become the dominant religion in Black urban areas by the year 2020."[2]

Which single person was most responsible for the remarkable career of Islam among African-Americans? There are five or so candidates, but undoubtedly the most common reply would be the man who was born as Malcolm Little and died as El-Hajj Malik El-Shabazz—and is best known as Malcolm X (1925–1965). Charismatic, eloquent, honest, a martyred seeker of true faith, Malcolm X did have a major impact on the spreading of Islam among blacks both in his day and ever since. His *Autobiography of Malcolm X*, with its powerful account of redemption through Islam, plus its hard edge of black nationalism, has had a very wide impact, and many blacks to this day cite it as a vital cause in their conversion to Islam.[3] And yet, for all his star qualities and impact, Malcolm X's Islamic career lasted not much over fifteen years. His influence seems outsized by virtue of his having joined the pantheon of American pop culture icons, his story captured on film by Spike Lee, baseball caps sporting an "X," T-shirts emblazoned with his face, rap musicians incorporating his voice in their songs, a U.S. postal stamp in his honor, and the 112 titles that amazon.com turns up when the name "Malcolm X" is entered as a subject.

In the final analysis, it was another man, Malcolm X's mentor, who actually had more impact on African-American Islam. That would be the uncharismatic, inarticulate, heterodox, long-lived Elijah Muhammad, with only eight titles at amazon.com, the man who dominated black Islam for over forty years, 1934–75.

The Early Years

During his lifetime, Muhammad was a mysterious figure, the subject of rumor and innuendo. He told contradictory stories about himself, avoided the press, surrounded himself with a wall of bodyguards, and punished those who revealed information about him. But recent scholarship has pieced his story together, mostly by relying on law enforcement records. It turns out that, starting in 1932 and continuing for over four decades, police agencies kept extremely close tabs on him, including (as part of the controversial COINTELPRO program) extensive FBI wiretaps and letter openings. The resulting reports, now available to researchers in all their immensity (the FBI's papers alone amount to well over 1 million pages), reveal the most intimate secrets of Elijah Muhammad's household, his power struggles, and his sexual escapades.

Two authors, an academic and a journalist, both black, have done yeoman's work culling these archives, as well as other documents (even including the owner's will bequeathing Muhammad's slave grandfather), producing impressively documented biographies of the man who liked to be called the Messenger of Allah. Claude Andrew Clegg III, then professor of history at North Carolina A&T State University, published *An Original Man: The Life and Times of Elijah Muhammad* in 1997.[4] Karl Evanzz of *The Washington Post* came out in late 1999 with *The Messenger: The Rise and Fall of Elijah Muhammad.*[5] The former is a well-rounded biography; the latter depends extremely heavily on the police documentation, thereby providing more new information but also a somewhat skewed picture (what the FBI did not concern itself with, such as theology, gets very short shrift). Clegg's study received almost no public attention and Evanzz's got a great deal; nonetheless, Clegg's is the superior book; indeed, it is perhaps the best book ever written on the Nation of Islam.

The two biographers disagree on a dismaying number of details, suggesting that much work on this topic remains to be done; but in the main, their accounts complement each other and make it possible, for the first time, to understand who exactly Elijah Muhammad was.

He was born Elija Pool in Sandersville, Georgia, in 1897, the seventh of thirteen children. Georgia at that time was an exceedingly racist, violent place and young Elija grew up with searing experiences of white scorn and brutality. The lynching of a friend in 1912 prompted him to flee his parents' house a year later. He met Clara Belle Evans in 1917 and married her in 1919; between 1921 and 1939, they had eight children. He fled Georgia for Detroit in 1923, then had the family follow him—the classic story of black migration to the North. In Detroit, Pool worked in several industrial plants before losing his job and joined a variety of organizations—notably Garvey's Universal Negro Improvement Association (UNIA), a proto-black nationalist movement, and the Black Shriners—but neither of these worked out for him. After an arrest for drunkenness in 1926, Elija Pool became Elijah Poole to symbolize his wish for a fresh start.

In a further effort to improve himself, Poole joined the Moorish Science Temple of America (MSTA) in 1928 and converted to its vaguely Islam-like religion, becoming intensely involved in the organization and in spreading its doctrines. This strangely named organization had little in common with the normative version of Islam coming from the Middle East, but it did establish a first connection in the twentieth century between African-Americans and Islam. Founded in 1913 by a Black Shriner named Timothy Drew (who renamed himself Noble Drew Ali), the MSTA had a mix of Islamic and non-Islamic qualities: it introduced Arabic personal names, the crescent and star motif, and the prohibition of pork; but it also predicted that all whites would be destroyed, promoted Drew as a prophet, and provided chairs in the place of worship. The MSTA went into steep decline with Drew's death in July 1929; Elijah Poole was among the many who quit the organization at that point. In the struggle for power that followed, three major factions emerged, all based in Chicago. One of the three leaders, a very recent MSTA convert named David Ford, moved to Detroit in November 1929. On arrival, he renamed both himself, as Wallace D. Fard, and his faction, as the Allah Temple of Islam (ATI). The new sect retained many of the MSTA's customs and ideas; Fard also introduced other elements, such as the whites-are-devils theme and paramilitary Fruit of Islam.

Fard began proselytizing among Detroit's blacks, now reeling from the depression, and met with some success. In early 1931, Elijah Poole met him and quickly became his enthusiastic disciple, becoming nearly inseparable from Fard and making himself indispensable. Fard recognized Poole's services by bestowing on him an "original" name, Elijah Karriem. In August 1932, Fard further rewarded Elijah by making him Supreme Master of the ATI and again changing his name: this third and final name change in six years was to Elijah Muhammad. Gradually, over the course of their three-year partnership, Fard and Elijah Muhammad bestowed a larger and larger theological role to Fard, who went from being Allah's messiah to being Allah. As that happened, Muhammad began to take over the Messenger of Allah role.

Nation of Islam

The ATI horrified the Detroit police, especially after one of its members ritualistically killed a man. The authorities made a deal with Fard, letting him out of a psychopathic ward on condition he shut down the ATI; Fard agreed to these terms. But he confused the police in January 1933 by changing the ATI's name to Nation of Islam (NoI) and kept it going. With the police searching for him, Fard had to leave Detroit; on his final departure in mid-1934, Muhammad made an attempt to take control of the NoI, but he met with considerable opposition. His more aggressive opponents sought to kill him, so Muhammad fled Detroit in September 1934, going first to Chicago, then spending a year in Milwaukee, before moving to Washington, D.C., where he lived until 1942. He took advantage of the capital to educate himself at the Library of Congress and travel throughout the eastern cities to spread his faith.

Elijah Muhammad, a light-skinned, diminutive man, won converts not through eloquence—nor even grammatical correctness—but through a soft, southern-accented intensity that his audience found somewhat reminiscent of a black Baptist preacher (which his father had been). Nonbelievers found it hard to understand how he roused his followers to standing ovations and utter devotion. Clegg explains that he had the exact measure of his audience: "Something ineffable about this 'squeaky, little man teaching hate' attracted African-Americans for an entire generation as few other leaders could."[6]

In very brief, Muhammad's message went as follows: Blacks came into existence 78 trillion years ago and lived an advanced and righteous life through the eons. This came to an end six thousand years ago when a deviant black savant named Mr. Yakub, known as "the big head scientist," rebelled against the black gods and created the white race with an eye to destroying the paradise blacks enjoyed. When blacks learned what Mr. Yakub was doing, they exiled him to an island in the Aegean Sea, where he continued his work. Six hundred years later, he had brought the white race into existence, with a mission to reign over blacks for six thousand years. That reign ended in 1914, though a seventy-year period of grace would extend it to 1984; W. D. Fard came to proclaim its end and show blacks how to reclaim their rightful place through the Nation of Islam—something they would definitely do by the year 2000. This imaginative schema explains white evil and black weakness, even as it inspires blacks to prepare themselves through discipline and hard work to seize power.

The NoI theology differs almost diametrically from core Islamic beliefs. In his worst nightmare, a Muslim could hardly imagine a religion more repugnant than one that identifies God with human beings, excludes most of humanity on racial grounds, believes in a post-Muhammadan prophet, and holds the Qur'an to be an imperfect, temporary document. Compared with these basic principles, the NoI's avoidance of pork, intermittent study of Arabic, and separation of the sexes are but minor details. Yes, NoI does incorporate a variety of Islamic details, but Christianity incorporates many Jewish details; that does not make them the same religion. The NoI is a folk religion with strong Christian overtones and hints of science fiction; it has little in common with normative Islam.

Success and Failure

Muhammad hated the United States and loved its enemies, especially non-Caucasian ones, so he rejoiced in the Japanese victory at Pearl Harbor in 1941 and not only refused to register for the draft but instructed his followers not to do so as well. Arrested for draft evasion in May 1942, he spent three years in jail on sedition charges, getting out only in August 1946. The Nation had barely been kept alive during those years by Clara, his wife, and some other faithful acolytes; on leaving prison, Muhammad found less than four hundred members. At this low point, Malcolm X turned up and, as Evanzz puts it, "gave new life to the Messenger." He joined the NoI in late 1948 and soon after his release from jail in 1952, devoted himself full time to building the organization, with great success. One notable newcomer, Louis Farrakhan, was recruited in 1955 by both Muhammad and Malcolm X.

Things began to happen. Members and money flowed in, new temples and schools opened, as did a range of small commercial enterprises (a bakery, grocery store, restaurant). The Nation bought real estate, both urban and rural. The money added up, making it the richest ever black organization in the United States.

The NoI's new wealth and stature had other beneficial consequences. It found access to meet foreign leaders and had direct contact
with such anti-American stars as Sukarno of Indonesia, Kwame
Nkrumah of Ghana, and Fidel Castro of Cuba. In 1959, Muhammad
confirmed these new relationships when he left on a triumphal tour of
the Middle East, Africa, and South Asia, including the minor pilgrimage to Mecca (which implied Saudi acceptance of his being a valid
Muslim). Many observers suspected the foreign governments of funding the NoI; thus did Thurgood Marshall dismiss the Nation as "a
bunch of thugs organized from prisons and jails, and financed, I am
sure, by [Egyptian president Gamal Abdel] Nasser or some Arab
group."[7] (In fact, serious amounts of foreign funding only arrived, from
Libya, Qatar, and Abu Dhabi, in the early 1970s.)

The Nation suddenly became a well-known institution in 1959,
when the national media discovered it. Mike Wallace's television
documentary, *The Hate That Hate Produced*, frightened many whites
but appealed to many blacks, thousands of whom joined up as new
members.

In spite of outward appearances, things began to deteriorate;
"rumors of oppressive disciplinary practices, deviations from the moral
code, and financial irregularities were seeping through the NoI's façade
of perfection," is how Evanzz describes it.[8] From the start, the NoI had
been steeped in violence; the first murder by a member took place in
1932, when it was still the Allah Temple of Islam: an acolyte took seriously the sect's demands for ritual sacrifice (later deemphasized) and
ceremonially killed his boarder. Through the decades, NoI members
who presumed to disagree with Muhammad were frequently injured or
killed, but this trend culminated after 1960 with the assassination of
Malcolm X (1965) and the 1973 murder of seven members of the
Khaalis family, a sect that broke away from NoI and attacked it ver-
bally. Nor were whites immune: the notorious "Zebra" murders that
left nine dead in Illinois (1972) and the Death Angels that killed fourteen in the San Francisco area (1973) were only the most spectacular
atrocities.

Lapses in prescribed behavior began in the late 1950s: Elijah
Muhammad's first known illegitimate child was born in January 1960,
the first of thirteen unrecognized children whom he fathered in a
seven-year period, 1960–67, by seven different mistresses, including

four children by one woman. The FBI, which was illegally taping him, recorded Muhammad telling each woman the same line about his sperm being "divine seed," then lying to them about his marital intentions; it also found that he had up to five affairs going at a single time and that he threatened violence against women who told of his paternity. To his wife's special shame, one of his relationships was not only incestuous but he took the girl's virginity. The charitable but inaccurate description of these women as Islamic-style wives fooled no one. Explaining how the Messenger violated the Nation's very strict moral code in this spectacular and blatant fashion, his son Wallace pointed out that Elijah Muhammad had "been worshipped as the final prophet of God for so long that he had convinced himself that it was true"[9]— and took the liberties that status seemed to confer. (Actually, he began to think of himself no longer as a prophet but as God.) It is hard to convey how shocking Muhammad's actions were in the context of the hugely moralistic mores of the NoI. They caused severe strains in the organization, putting its very existence in jeopardy; they were also perhaps the single most important reason for Muhammad's rift with the upright Malcolm X.

Newly affluent, Muhammad also lavished luxuries on himself and the "royal family," as it came to be known. He traveled in a Lockheed Jet Star Executive jet, wore a jewel-studded fez said to be worth $150,000, and let his family take hold of the NoI reins of power and bleed the organization for all it was worth. This focus on money had a deep, corrupting effect on Muhammad and his organization: it set the tone, Clegg points out, for the movement and "ultimately validated, by example, a trend toward materialism, even avarice, that would hamper the Nation as a religious organization."[10]

The greed also led to a change of policies, prompting Muhammad to adopt increasingly cautious and even reactionary policies. No matter how radical his rhetoric, by the 1960s he had become the captive of his own avarice, and this imposed an operational timidity quite at odds with his fire-breathing talk. He refused to sanction any response, for example, to police intrusions into NoI temples. He took part in discussions with Ku Klux Klan leaders to stay out of "non-Negro" areas in return for NoI members being left alone. The head of the American Nazi Party, George Lincoln Rockwell, spoke at the NoI's main annual event, which he used to praise Elijah Muhammad as the black's Adolf

Hitler (high praise in his view). On the more positive side, Muhammad in his final years sought U.S. government money to run antipoverty programs. Clegg concludes that by that time, "the Nation was more of a religious self-help organization than the vanguard of a coming revolution."[11]

These many strains led to Elijah Muhammad's near divorce from Clara, his throwing favorite-son Wallace out of the Nation, and his rupture with Malcolm X. The former two, both family members, he eventually made up with; not so with Malcolm X, whom his goons (apparently supervised by Louis Farrakhan) assassinated in 1965. Farrakhan then took Malcolm X's place as Muhammad's top lieutenant.

Wallace and Louis

Muhammad's slow physical deterioration also began about 1960, when he developed bronchitis, and this led to a protracted battle of succession. In the end, there were just two contestants, his son Wallace and his national spokesman Farrakhan. Each advanced his cause in imaginative ways—in early 1975, for example, Farrakhan married off two of his daughters to Muhammad's nephew and grandson. But when Elijah Muhammad died on February 25, 1975, Wallace moved faster and called a news conference at which he announced that his father had appointed him his sole successor. Beat to the punch, Farrakhan for a while went along with Wallace's radical purging of NoI's heterodox elements, making it almost overnight into a normative Islamic institution. Wallace also dismantled the Fruit of Islam, sold the commercial establishments, and spun off most of the infrastructure. Farrakhan seemingly endorsed the program, Arabizing his first name (to Abdul Halim), studying Arabic and the Qur'an, and growing a beard. In retrospect, it is clear he disagreed with the changes initiated by Wallace, but he did abide by them and even stumped the country promoting them. It took him several years to find the resolve to split with Wallace and start up his own revived NoI in competition, which he did in 1978.

For over two decades, Wallace—who now goes by the name W. Deen Mohammed—and Louis Farrakhan were bitter rivals. They make for an interesting contrast. Both born in 1933, they have known each other and disagreed about the nature of Islam and much else for over forty years. The two could hardly be more different in terms of personality. W. Deen Mohammed is moderate and scholarly, perhaps too intellectual for a mass following. A peacemaker who represents middle-class interests, he seems more interested in ethics than in politics, coming to life when he can talk about moral lessons in the Qur'an. Louis Farrakhan is an entertainer by training who became a brilliant orator and polemicist. He dominates his organization and thrives on controversy.

At base, they are fighting over the succession to Elijah Muhammad, each one claiming to be the true son. If W. Deen has an obvious biological advantage over Farrakhan, the latter married into the "royal family," won many of its members to his side, and remains far more faithful to Elijah Muhammad's message. Through two decades, each claimed to be the greater leader. The back cover of one of his books proclaims W. Deen Mohammed "the foremost leader of Muslims throughout America and in many other parts of the world."[12] In contrast, Louis Farrakhan had few Islamic aspirations and instead sought recognition as the most powerful leader of American blacks. Conversely, each side disparaged the other. A prominent NoI member described W. Deen's organization as faltering and seldom seen, "existing only in a few disconnected locations."[13] In turn, a partisan of W. Deen's asserted that his organization had "largely replaced" the NoI.[14]

The sterile rivalry went on, year after year, almost unchanged. Then, in February 2000, twenty-five years to the day after the death of Elijah Muhammad, W. Deen and Farrakhan suddenly stood on a public platform together, embraced, and proclaimed their intent to cooperate: "It's going to take all of us working together to establish Islam in America," Farrakhan told the cheering crowd.[15] The change was on Farrakhan's side; he somewhat ambiguously accepted the reforms that Wallace had initiated a quarter century earlier. He apparently renounced the NoI theology and accepted the seventh-century Muhammad ibn 'Abdullah as the seal of the prophets, though it remains to be seen what Farrakhan exactly had in mind when he announced that "Allah sent Muhammad with the final revelation to the world." (Which Allah, the omnipresent one or the human one? Which Muhammad, the Meccan or the Georgian?) Also, there are a profusion of other groups which continue to purvey the old NoI message of Fard and Elijah Muhammad.

Details aside, the larger trend is clear, and it points to the decreasing relevance of Elijah Muhammad's old organization, the Nation of Islam. It is close to having fulfilled its historical role of introducing African-Americans to Islam; when that is done, it will no longer be needed and will lapse into irrelevance. E. U. Essien-Udom, author of a book-length study on the NoI, noted as early as 1962 that "few join the nation and remain in it."[16] Some return to Christianity; more move on to normative Islam. This reflects the fact that the NoI, whatever its claims to legitimacy, in fact purveys a jumble of primitive and unsustainable myths with no connection to normative Islam. As new members join the NoI ranks, they inevitably come into closer contact with normative Islam and then feel its inexorable pull; how can a folk religion founded in Detroit in the 1930s stand up to a religion with nearly fourteen centuries of history, nearly a billion adherents, fifty state governments, and one of the world's great civilizations?

A second factor concerns the NoI's cultic nature. Its profusion of splinter groups are all centered on a dominant figure and all of them, Evanzz points out, even Farrakhan's organization, are "little more than a cult of personality. When their aging leaders are gone . . . all that will remain is a storefront temple here and there."[17]

A final point arguing for the NoI's expiration concerns its odd combination of bourgeois values and racial militancy Its emphasis on hard work, thrift, and the family inculcates exactly the sort of good habits that permit members to escape poverty, and many members do just that. But as they rise economically, they need a less angry and alienated faith. It is a decidedly odd mix that can be seen symbolically in the contrast between Farrakhan's bodyguards, who "project an air of militancy," whereas "his darks suits and bow tie are straight out of a chamber of commerce meeting."[18] By advocating contrary values— integration and militancy—the NoI confuses its members and undercuts its appeal. Many NoI members who moved ahead found normative Islam an attractive alternative. "The message of Elijah Muhammad did not fit the times," observes one member, and so the "transition to the Qur'an and the Prophet Muhammad under Wallace was a relief."[19]

Impact

For all his foibles and failures, Elijah Muhammad had a massive impact. To begin with, he altered the course of black culture and politics. As Clegg notes: "The Muslims were 'black' before it became fashionable to be labeled as such, and the Black Power Movement and all subsequent African-American protest styles, from the rhymes of the nationalistic rap group Public Enemy to the raison d'être of the Million Man March, are undeniably offshoots of the legacy of Elijah Muhammad."[20] But Muhammad's religious legacy is even more consequential. True, the wild notions of his own little religion are disappearing, but he is genuinely the patron of all African-American Muslims, not just NoI members; nearly every one of them has a direct connection to the NoI, personal or familial. Muhammad can claim to have spawned a substantial new Muslim community. Without his efforts, the hundreds of thousands of African-Americans who are now Muslims would presumably still be Christians.

One way to appreciate Muhammad's impact is statistically: African-Americans in the United States are two hundred times more likely to convert to Islam than whites. If Islam has only modest appeal to white Americans (who usually convert to marry a Muslim or for mystical reasons), it has become a powerful presence among the black population. Further enhancing Islam's importance in the United States is the fact that whites convert individually; blacks convert in a social way, giving them a greater political impact. Nor is it hard to imagine that conversions to Islam will begin to increase significantly among American blacks; this is an Islamic pattern that goes back over a millennium[21] and is likely to hold in the United States too. If that point is reached, Muslim blacks may outnumber Christian blacks.

Already, there are signs of such a momentum building up. The Arabic name Malik, for example, has been the single most popular given name for newborn black American boys. Islam reaches deep into the culture; according to one scholar, "all African-American youths have at least some familiarity with Islam, either through a personal encounter, a relative, a friend, a fashionable item of apparel, or, as is more frequently the case today, in the form of rap music poems."[22] Consider just the music: Ice Cube, King Sun, KMD, Movement X, Queen

Latifa, Poor Righteous Teachers, Prince Akeem, Sister Souljah, and Tribe Called Quest all support Farrakhan, sometimes by name in their music. The Five Percenters, a yet more aggressive NoI offshoot, claim the allegiance of Grand Puba, Big Daddy Kane, Lakim Shaba, and Eric B. and Rakim. In the view of Farrakhan's biographer, Mattias Gardell, the "hip-hop movement's role in popularizing the message of black militant Islam cannot be overestimated."[23]

Islam has established for itself an enviable reputation among non-Muslim blacks, in good part due to the discipline on young men it is thought to impose—thereby addressing what may be the community's number one problem. A Baptist woman whose son converted to Islam captures this favorable disposition: "This Islam sounds like true religion to me. They don't believe in smoking dope, drinking liquor and no adultery. I say we could use more teaching like that. . . . When my son reached over to be a Moslem, I was not going to fault him. I enjoy listening to him talk about it, and how it came out of Africa, and that sounds pretty good."[24] Another Christian mother actively hopes her son will join with Farrakhan: "I have to leave my son where he's going to get protection. Before I close my eyes in this world, he's going to be Farrakhan's."[25]

From a social point of view, the newfound sobriety and seriousness of African-American converts to Islam, whether to the NoI or the standard version, is all to the good. Though violence and recidivism remain very real problems—the conviction of Jamil Al-Amin on charges of having murdered a policeman being a case in point—the manly atmosphere of convert Islam has helped many ex-cons and others at the bottom of society to find the straight path and stick to it. From a political point of view, however, the situation is more worrisome, as black converts tend to adopt anti-American and extremist views. Those in the Nation become black nationalists, pumped up with incendiary antiwhite rhetoric, whereas many of those who join normative Islam become Islamists—admirers of such figures as Ayatollah Khomeini and Osama bin Laden. Whether followers of NoI or normative Islam, they tend to become vehemently anti-American, anti-Christian, and anti-Semitic.

It does not take much imagination to see that, should Islam in fact replace Christianity as the primary religion of African-Americans, this fact will have vast significance for all Americans, affecting everything from race relations to foreign policy, and from popular culture to the separation of religion and state. As C. Eric Lincoln, one of the leading authorities on African-American Islam, has written, the Nation of Islam "may well change the course of history in the West."[26] Should that come to pass, the credit, or blame, will belong above all to the "squeaky little man teaching hate," Elijah Muhammad.

22

THE CURIOUS CASE
OF JAMIL AL-AMIN

The man once known as H. Rap Brown, whose behavior in the 1960s earned him a reputation as "the violent left's least-thoughtful firebrand,"[1] found himself in 2002 in the dock for murdering a policeman in Atlanta, Georgia. Not only was this one of the year's most spectacular court cases, but because the defendant has become one of the American Muslim community's leading figures, it had shined the spotlight on a host of disturbing questions pertaining to that community.

A History of Violence

The origins of the case go back to May 1999, when a fifty-five-year-old African-American man named Jamil Abdullah Al-Amin was stopped in the outskirts of Atlanta for driving a stolen Ford Explorer. To avoid arrest, Al-Amin flashed a police badge from White Hall, a small town in Alabama. The ruse worked, and he was let off—but not for long. Police research into the case found that Al-Amin was in fact no police officer. This led to his being indicted in September on three charges: theft by receiving, impersonating an officer, and driving without proof of insurance, punishable by up to ten years in prison. He was assigned a court date in January 2000.

Al-Amin failed to appear at his hearing, so on January 28 a bench warrant for his arrest was issued. This was a low-priority matter, so it was not until about 10:00 P.M. on March 16, 2000, that two sheriff's deputies, both African-Americans, Aldranon English, twenty-eight, and Ricky Kinchen, thirty-five, finally rode over to Al-Amin's small grocery store in West End, one of Atlanta's poorer sections, to serve the warrant. The young officers were cautioned about "Aggravated assault, possibly armed,"[2] but that's all they knew about their suspect.

They had no idea that they were pursuing a famous black nationalist who claimed "rap" music was named after him and a man who had a violent history going back even before they were born:

- In 1963, as H. Rap Brown, he was a founder of the Student Non-Violent Coordinating Committee (SNCC), which, despite its name, was indeed very violent, and by 1967 he was chairman of SNCC.
- He was an outspoken advocate of black violence ("We built the country up and we will burn it down, honkies and all"), who in 1967 incited a mob to torch two city blocks in Cambridge, Maryland ("It's time for Cambridge to explode, baby").
- In 1968 became "Minister of Justice" for the Black Panther Party.
- In 1970 he was a fugitive from justice listed on the FBI's most-wanted list.
- In 1971 he led an attempted robbery of the Red Carpet Lounge, a bar on New York City's Upper West Side; the shootout that followed left him and two police officers injured.
- In 1971–76 he served time as an inmate in the New York correctional system.

After a quiet period, his violence resumed in Atlanta in the 1990s:

- Accused of carrying a concealed and unlicensed .45-caliber pistol at the time of a 1995 arrest for shooting a drug dealer four times in the leg. (It is a federal offense for convicted felons to possess firearms.)

- Organizer of a group of thugs charged with many violent crimes.
- Banned by the judge from appearing at the armed robbery trial of one of those thugs because his presence intimidated a witness.
- Investigated in connection with fourteen homicides that took place in 1990–96, which a police report ascribed to revenge, an attempt to block competition, and efforts to eliminate those who "knew too much."
- Headed a mosque whose members received the same training as did the suspects in the first attack on the World Trade Center in New York.
- Arrested for driving a stolen car and carrying a concealed weapon in 1999.

Finally, Al-Amin's record of nonviolent illegality was also unknown to the two arresting officers:

- He twice carried an unauthorized police badge when arrested.
- He three times filed for bankruptcy since 1998 to escape creditors seeking payment of tens of thousands of dollars. A judge labeled the third attempt "an abusive filing" and accused Al-Amin of undertaking it not in "good faith."[3]
- He maintained a bigamous relationship with two wives, Amira and Karima, in two households in two parts of town.[4] (The strain of paying for them both seems to have been his undoing financially and helps account for the bankruptcies and the criminal behavior.)

So, when the two deputies found Al-Amin standing in a black trench coat by a parked black Mercedes-Benz, they were not prepared for what came next. Noting that Al-Amin's hands were concealed, they followed standard procedure and ordered him to show his hands. "OK, here they are," he replied and pulled out two guns, firing at the officers one round of high-powered .223 bullets from an assault rifle, then switching to a 9mm revolver. He seriously wounded English in both legs, the left arm, and chest. He killed Kinchen with six bullets.

English the next day identified Al-Amin as the shooter out of a selection of mug shots.

Al-Amin fled to White Hall, Alabama, 160 miles southwest of Atlanta and, for the second time in his life, though briefly, made the FBI's most-wanted list. Four days later, on March 20, 2000, he was caught—this time by no less than one hundred well-armed police officers. At the time of his apprehension, Al-Amin wore body armor. The police also found in White Hall a great deal of incriminating evidence: the license plate of Al-Amin's black Mercedes, then the car itself (complete with a telltale bullet hole), two cartridge clips, and a .223-caliber rifle and a 9mm handgun. Ballistic tests showed the guns to be those used to shoot English and Kinchen.[5]

The Fulton County district attorney in May 2000 announced that the state would seek the death penalty for Al-Amin. In January 2001, Al-Amin declared himself not guilty of murdering Officer Kinchen. His case went to court in January 2002. After a brief trial, the jury quickly found him guilty and sentenced him to life in jail without parole.

Hate-America Sentiments

The trial attracted much media attention because of Al-Amin's sixties fame, reopening well-worn debates about that decade. It also prompted a debate about gun violence; the National Rifle Association blamed Kinchen's death on the casual way Al-Amin was released in 1995, arguing that a convicted violent felon carrying firearms "should have been in a Federal prison for up to 10 years."[6] The trial's real significance, however, lies elsewhere—in Al-Amin's Islamic connection.

He experienced a jailhouse conversion in 1971 at the hands of the Dar-ul-Islam movement, a Sunni organization of African-Americans. He took the name Jamil Abdullah Al-Amin and, on release in 1976, went on pilgrimage to Mecca. He then settled in Atlanta, where he soon founded the Community Mosque. By 1980, he had become spiritual leader of over thirty Islamic centers belonging to the Dar-ul-Islam's "National Community," though this number subsequently declined. Apparently some ten thousand Muslims, nearly all of them African-Americans, now belong to mosques spiritually associated with Al-Amin.

The Islam that Al-Amin adopted is the radical kind. For Al-Amin, militant Islam serves as a way to extend and deepen the hate-America sentiments of a black nationalist sort that he had espoused in the 1960s. He believes that America and Islam are by nature opposed to each other: "When we begin to look critically at the Constitution of the United States," he wrote in 1994 in his *Revolution by the Book (The Rap Is Live)*, "we see that in its main essence it is diametrically opposed to what Allah has commanded."[7]

In a similar spirit, he sometimes spells his country "amerikkka"[8] and chastises American blacks for being too integrated into their country's life: "The problem with African-Americans is that they are so American."[9] A clue to what he means by this comes from the men who belong to Al-Amin's mosque: they either wear Islamic-style skull-caps and long robes or they don black nationalist regalia (combat boots and fatigues)—anything but normal American clothing. Members of his mosque were convicted of illegally shipping more than nine hundred firearms to Detroit, Philadelphia, and a militant Islamic gang linked to Sheikh Omar Abdel Rahman.[10] One young convert from Christianity who attended Al-Amin's mosque subsequently went to Kashmir to join the militant Islamic terrorists in their *jihad* against the Indian government, and was killed there in an attack on an army post.

Bearing such hatred of the United States, Al-Amin falls into the usual trap of the extremist: he mirror-images. That is, he assumes that the U.S. government reciprocates with a hatred akin to his own and targets Islam as its enemy. This attitude emerges most clearly when Al-Amin finds himself in trouble with the law, offering as it does a useful explanation for his being under arrest. In 1995, he explained his travails in the very grandest and most conspiratorial of terms:

> Islam is under attack on a global scale by those who wish to control the world. . . . The charges leveled against me are in direct relationship to the success that Islam has experienced in our immediate area. My persecution by the U.S. government is nothing new.

He went on to call the United States a country "where Islam is under attack."[11] Similarly, his first words in an Alabama courtroom, accounting for his arrest in 2000, were: "It's a government conspiracy."[12] His habeas petition elaborated on this claim, stating that law enforcement authorities and organized crime "want him dead," and had joined forces to frame him for murdering a policeman.[13] A letter released to his followers built on these grandiose claims: "this matter is not just about me. It is about Islam and the entire Muslim Ummah [nation]. There is a pre-meditated conspiracy to destroy Islamic leadership. When the truth is being established, the disbelievers will start to do things."[14] In the same mode, Al-Amin proclaimed at his arraignment, "For more than 30 years, I have been tormented and persecuted by my enemies for reasons of race and belief."[15] On the eve of his trial, Al-Amin told a reporter, "They are trying to crush Islam before it realizes its own worth and strength," he said. "We are the biggest gang on the planet, and when you hear them talk about the 'crusade,' you know what they are talking about."[16]

Darling of the Islamic Establishment

One might think that, given his criminal record and radical views, Al-Amin would be shunned by the Islamic establishment in the United States. Just the opposite is the case, however: he is a giant in the world of American Islamic institutions and a man praised by the Council on American-Islamic Relations for, of all things, his "moral character."[17] In 1994, Steven Barboza described Al-Amin as "one of the nation's most influential Muslim leaders."[18] A coalition of Islamic organizations in 1995 called him one of American Islam's "leading figures."[19] Even as he sat in a Georgia jail, the American Muslim Council (AMC) hailed him as "a leader in the American Muslim community."[20]

So smitten are the Islamists, they have even endorsed Al-Amin's black nationalism (something they in principle should oppose). The American Muslim Alliance claims he was framed in the 1960s and the Muslim Student Association calls him a "hero" for his activities back then.[21]

Al-Amin was a much sought after speaker on the militant Islamic circuit, addressing such major organizations as CAIR, the Islamic Society of North America (ISNA), and the Islamic Committee for Palestine. He has held starring roles at large Muslim rallies, such as the Bosnia Task Force USA rally outside the United Nations in New York in October 1995, where an audience of eighteen thousand heard him condemn the world body for its "betrayal" of Muslims in Bosnia.[22] As an author, Al-Amin wins equal acclaim. His *Revolution by the Book* garnered rave reviews in the Islamic press. "Clear, sharp, focused, alert, lively, snappy; eminently reasonable and accessible to one and all," read one assessment, finding it "a classic of its genre."[23]

Appropriate to this lofty stature, three national organizations invited Al-Amin as an individual to join with them to form the Islamic Shura Council of North America, an institution that makes decisions about Muslim religious life in the United States, determining, for example, when precisely the month of Ramadan begins. He then served as president of this council for several years. He has also been acting president of the AMC, a Washington-based powerhouse. Al-Amin, in short, is the face of institutional Islam in the United States.

It is therefore not surprising that those institutions rally round to Al-Amin's defense whenever he finds himself in serious trouble. In 1995, the Islamic Circle of North America "expressed deep concern about his dubious arrest."[24] In 2000, four leading Muslim organizations (CAIR, ISNA, AMC, and the Muslim American Society) issued a joint statement maintaining that "The charges against Imam Jamil are especially troubling because they are inconsistent with what is known of his moral character and past behavior as a Muslim."[25] Nor was it just a handful of national organizations; mosques and mosque leaders, college groups and others rallied enthusiastically to Al-Amin's side. Louis Farrakhan visited Al-Amin in his jail cell, as did the executive director of CAIR.[26]

This institutional support sought to get Al-Amin exonerated of charges of cop-killing. The Jamaat al-Muslimeen of Baltimore set the target of a million signatures petitioning for his unconditional release from prison. Other groups sent observers to the trial. But fund-raising was the main activity. Various leading militant Islamic organizations joined together to raise $1.3 million for his legal expenses.[27] Mosques as far away as Connecticut, New York, and California held events to help pay Al-Amin's legal bills, ICNA sponsored events in several cities, and CAIR both held benefit dinners for him and publicly urged "generous donations" to his legal fund. The Southern California Association of Muslim Activists distributed a script to use for telephone fund-raising purposes. Such militant Islamic luminaries as Siraj Wahhaj, the New York mosque leader, went around the country raising money for him.[28] In addition, there has been a Hip Hop for Consciousness Benefit Concert for Jamil Al-Amin held in Los Angeles, with some notable musicians performing.

These efforts, however, apparently had limited success. Some members of Al-Amin's mosque gave up their campaign when they failed to raise enough to pay for the printing of fliers. Others raised money in a more unorthodox manner: Ishmael Abdullah and a partner robbed three banks in twenty-two days, yelling out as they escaped, "Free Al-Amin!" but their arrest in May 2000 brought their efforts to a quick end.[29]

Perhaps the most interesting response is that of Masjid Al-Islam, a mosque in Los Angeles. Calling Al-Amin "one of the pillars of our local Islamic communities," it portrayed his arrest as nothing less than a challenge to "establishing Islam in America." Indeed, the mosque claimed, somewhat hyperbolically, that how the trial comes out "may determine the future growth of Islam in America."[30]

It is not likely to do that, but this incident has a significance beyond the individuals personally involved, for the solidarity with Al-Amin reveals the true nature of the leading Muslim organizations—the very ones that are routinely invited to meet with the president and secretary of state, the ones sought out by the media for their opinions, and the ones invited to engage in interreligious dialogue. That nature shows when they praise Al-Amin's "moral character"—rather than condemn his thirty-five-year history of ideological extremism, political violence, and personal criminality. It shows when they collect money for his legal defense fund—and not for an educational fund to help pay expenses of the two young daughters left fatherless by Officer Kinchen's death. It shows when they sponsor a petition calling for Al-Amin's immediate release from prison—instead of renouncing his actions and calling for justice to be served.

Moreover, this fits into a larger pattern, where the militant Islamic organizations consistently come to the defense of Muslims engaged in criminal activities. When Ahmad Adnan Chaudhry was convicted of attempting to murder his roommate in San Bernardino, California, in 2000, CAIR scorned the court decision, deemed that he was found guilty of "a crime of which he is innocent," and set up a defense fund on his behalf.[31] Other groups have come to the aid of Mohammad Salah, who is accused of financing the terrorist activities of Hamas,[32] and of Mousa Mohamed Abu Marzook, detained on charges of murder and attempted murder on behalf of Hamas.[33]

Al-Qaeda's attack on the United states made Islam a central subject of American life, and this climate offered moderate Muslims a chance to give voice to the Islam that can be a positive force in American life. Among other steps, they should have publicly denounced the recidivist ex-con strongly suspected of killing a police officer in cold blood, as well as the organizations that so strongly identified with him. Unhappily, they missed this opportunity and militant Islam's hegemony remains in place, as strong as ever.

23

CONCLUSION:

WHO IS THE ENEMY?

Vagueness and Euphemism

With whom, or what, is the United States at war? The answer to this question has far-reaching implications for strategy, for public diplomacy, and for foreign and domestic policy alike. It may seem that the answer is obvious; but it is not.

In the first few weeks after September 11, 2001, whenever President George W. Bush referred to enemies, he insisted they were neither Afghans nor even Muslims but rather people, as I have noted earlier, whom he called "evildoers" or "the evil ones." This odd and somewhat theological-sounding phrasing seems to have been chosen deliberately so as not to offend anyone, or any group. It also permitted Bush to lump a variety of events under a single rubric even before it was known who was responsible for which of them. Thus, when mysterious anthrax letters began appearing, he again blamed these same amorphous "evildoers" for "continuing to try to harm America and Americans."[1]

What were the goals of these evildoers? Here, too, Bush was careful to speak in generalities. They were people "motivated by hate,"[2] or, somewhat more specifically, "people that [had] no country," or, on another occasion, "people that may try to take a country, parasites that may try to leech onto a host country."[3] When it came to what the United States was planning to do about them, the president was once more cautious to a fault, speaking mostly of "hunting down the evildoers and bringing them to justice."[4]

Not even after the war began in early October did Bush strive for greater precision, tending rather to refer to the hostilities as a "common effort to stamp out evil where we find it."[5] The one innovation was to introduce the concept of a "war on terrorism,"[6] sometimes modified as a "war on terrorism and evil."[7] But this made arguably even less sense. Terrorism is a military tactic employed by different groups and individuals around the world for different ends. To speak of a "war on terrorism" is a little like speaking about a war on weapons of mass destruction. One needs to know who owns or is deploying these weapons, and for what reason.

What about the objectives of the war? These were, and still are, equally murky. When Bush announced the initiation of military action on October 7, he defined the goal as "the disruption and . . . defeat of the global terror network," a neologism that once again begged the question. For what *is* the global terror network? Other than Al-Qaeda, what organizations belong to it? Does it include militant Islamic groups like Hizbullah and Hamas? Non-Muslim terrorist groups like the Irish Republican Army and the Tamil Tigers? States like Iraq?

Secretary of Defense Donald H. Rumsfeld, for one, seemed troubled by the vagueness of this dangerously ambitious goal. At one early point, he dismissed as unrealistic "the idea of eliminating [terrorism] from the face of the earth." But he proceeded to propose a no less elusive aim. Americans are a freedom-loving people, Rumsfeld said, so the definition of victory was an environment in which they could "in fact fulfill and live those freedoms," and in which others would be prevented "from adversely affecting our way of life."[8] This was admirable, especially the last part, though hardly an objective to hand to a general and say, "Accomplish this."

The actual unfolding of the "war on terrorism" has done little to dispel this lack of clarity. Initially, the declared purpose in Afghanistan was not to extirpate the Taliban regime but merely to compel it to hand over Osama bin Laden and his colleagues; only when the Taliban refused did the full force of the U.S. military descend on them. The same story may be repeating itself with respect to Iraq. In late November 2001, the president demanded that Saddam Husayn permit the resumption of weapons inspections or face the consequences. When asked at a press conference what those consequences might be, Bush cryptically replied: "He'll find out."

At least one well-informed observer understood this to mean that Bush did not know what he was going to do next.[9] Indeed, six months after September's events, it seemed safe to say that, beyond the fighting in Afghanistan, the U.S. government had not yet reached a decision on its future steps.

All this may be understandable enough. Conceptually, the conflict in which the United States is engaged is something new. It is being fought against shadows—no one, for instance, has yet made a completely forthcoming claim of responsibility for the atrocities of September 11—and this very fact has rendered meaningless such conventional war goals as defeating an army or seizing territory. Then, too, the United States was caught essentially unprepared on September 11. No matter how many times it had been hit by terrorists before—and there were many such occasions—Americans never expected to find themselves launching a full-scale war against this enemy.

Moreover, euphemisms in wartime can be beneficial, and all the more so when one is flying, so to speak, in the dark. Entering emergency mode on September 11, the government instinctively shied away from specifics lest they tie its hands. Targeting "evildoers" and "terrorism," mentioning no names beyond Osama bin Laden, offered maximum flexibility. By not insulting anyone in particular, Washington could more easily woo potential partners for the U.S.-led "coalition against terror."[10] By the same token, the administration could, at least theoretically, add or subtract targets as circumstances warranted; today's partner—Syria, for example—could become tomorrow's evildoer.

Nonetheless, vagueness also exacts costs. If politicians impart imprecise or contradictory goals to their military leaders, wrote Carl von Clausewitz in *On War* (1832), their efforts will almost certainly run up against major difficulties. The history of warfare throughout the ages confirms this iron rule, as Americans have had occasion to note in recent decades—from Eisenhower's not traversing Europe fast enough to fend off the Soviet advance in World War II to Norman Schwarzkopf's not eliminating Saddam Husayn's Republican Guard in Operation Desert Storm. Nor are generals the only ones who need to know whom they are fighting and what they are fighting for; so do others in government, so do foreign friends and enemies alike, and so, of course, do the American people.

Militant Islam

The message of September 11 was clear, allowing for no ambiguity about who is the enemy: it is militant Islam. No wonder, then, that even before knowing who exactly was responsible, the government has been reluctant to say so. In addition to the considerations I have already enumerated, there was the precedent of recent history to deter it.

In February 1995, at the peak of the horrific violence in Algeria that pitted armed and brutal Islamist groups against a repressive government, NATO secretary general Willy Claes declared that, since the end of the Cold War, "Islamic militancy has emerged as perhaps the single gravest threat to the NATO alliance and to Western security."[11] Indeed, Claes said, not only did militant Islam pose the same kind of threat to the West as communism before it,[12] but the scale of the danger was greater, for militant Islam encompassed elements of "terrorism, religious fanaticism, and the exploitation of social and economic injustice."[13]

Claes was absolutely correct. But his statements met with outrage from all over the Muslim world, and he was quickly forced to retract and to withdraw. "Religious fundamentalism," he explained lamely, "whether Islamic or of other varieties, is not a concern for NATO."[14]

In the wake of September 11, it may be somewhat easier to say what Claes was not allowed to say then; but only somewhat, and not for anyone in a position of authority. Certain it is that no one wants to have to retrace Claes's red-faced retreat. And yet, awkward as it may be to say, there is no getting around the fact.

At least since 1979, when Ayatollah Khomeini seized power in Iran with the war cry "Death to America," militant Islam has been the self-declared enemy of the United States. It has now become enemy number one. Whether it is the terrorist organizations and individuals Washington is targeting, the immigrants it is questioning, or the states it is holding under suspicion, all are Islamist or connected with Islamists. Washington may not speak its mind, but its actions express the real views.

To define militant Islam as the country's most worrisome, long-term opponent is hardly to deny the existence of other opponents. The United States has no dearth of non-Islamist adversaries: Communist tyrannies in North Korea and Cuba, secular Arab dictators in Iraq, Syria, and Libya, plus lesser foes around the world. But these adversaries, including even Saddam Husayn, lack several features that make militant Islam so threatening—its ideological fervency, its reach, its ambitiousness, and its staying power. Although the constituency of militant Islam is limited to Muslims, this constituency represents, in all, about a sixth of the human race, enjoys a very high birth rate, and is found in virtually every part of the world.

At a moment when the European-derived extremes of the Communist left and fascist right are tired and on the whole ineffectual, militant Islam has proved itself to be the only truly vital totalitarian movement in the world today. As one after another of its leaders has made clear, it regards itself as the sole rival, and the inevitable successor, to Western civilization. Although a number of (wrongheaded) Western observers have declared it to be a dying creed,[15] it is likely to remain a force to contend with for years if not for long decades to come.

Militant Islam's Supporters

Let me try to specify with greater exactness the constituency for militant Islam. It is divisible into three main elements.

The first is the inner core, made up of the likes of Osama bin Laden, the nineteen hijackers, other members of Al-Qaeda, leaders of the Taliban regime in Afghanistan, and the rest of the network of violent groups inspired by militant Islamic ideology. Such groups have mostly come into existence since 1970, becoming since then an ever more important force in the Muslim world. The network, dubbed the "Islamintern" by some Muslim critics, contains both Shi'ite and Sunni variants, appeals to rich and poor alike, and is active in such far-flung locations as Afghanistan, Algeria, and Argentina. In 1983, some of its members initiated a campaign of violence against the United States whose greatest triumph so far was the spectacular operation on September 11, 2001. In all, the network's adherents are as few as they are fanatical, numbering perhaps in the thousands.

The second ring comprises a much larger population of militants who are sympathetic to Al-Qaeda's radical utopian vision without themselves being a part of it. Their views were on display daily as soon as hostilities began in Afghanistan: protesters by the tens of thousands expressed a determined loathing of the United States and an enthusiasm for further acts of violence against it. Countries not normally heard from, and hardly hotbeds of radicalism, came to life to protest the U.S. campaign. The chants of these Islamists across the world bore a certain family resemblance:

> Indonesia: "U.S., go to hell!"
> Malaysia: "Go to hell, America" and "Destroy America."
> Bangladesh: "Death to America" and "Osama is our hero."
> India: "Death to America. Death to Israel. Taliban, Taliban, we
>   salute you."
> Sri Lanka: "Bin Laden, we are with you."
> Oman: "America is the enemy of God."
> Yemen: "America is a great Satan."
> Egypt: "U.S., go to hell, Afghans will prevail."
> Sudan: "Down, down USA!"
> Bosnia: "Long live bin Laden."
> United Kingdom: "Tony Blair, burn in hell."

As best I can estimate from election data, survey research, anecdotal evidence, and the opinions of informed observers, this Islamist element constitutes some 10 to 15 percent of the total Muslim world population of roughly 1 billion—that is, some 100 to 150 million persons worldwide.

The third ring consists of Muslims who do not accept the militant Islamic program in all its particulars but do concur with its rank anti-

Americanism. This sentiment is found at almost every point along the political spectrum. A secular fascist like Saddam Husayn shares a hatred of the United States with the far leftists of the PKK Kurdish group who in turn share it with an eccentric figure like Mu'ammar al-Qadhdhafi. Reliable statistics on opinion in the Muslim world do not exist, but my sense is that one half of the world's Muslims—or some 500 million persons—sympathize more with Osama bin Laden and the Taliban than with the United States. That such a vast multitude hates the United States is sobering indeed.

That is not to say, of course, that anti-Americanism is universal among Muslims, for important bastions of pro-American sentiment do exist. These include the officer corps of the Turkish military, who are the final arbiters of their country's destiny; several leaders of Muslim-majority states in the former Soviet Union; the emerging dissident element in the Islamic Republic of Iran; and, more generally, those Muslims who have experienced at firsthand the dominion of militant Islam.

These, however, constitute a minority. Elsewhere, and everywhere, anti-Americanism rears its head: among the sheltered females of the Saudi elite and the male denizens of Cairo's vast slums, among the aged in remote reaches of Pakistan and among the students at a Muslim school in the suburbs of Washington, D.C. Nor is hostility always limited to feelings. Since Vietnam, and even before September 11, more Americans died at the hands of Muslim radicals than from any other enemy.

Not a Clash of Civilizations

The situation, then, is grim. But it is not hopeless, any more than the situation at the height of the Cold War with the Soviet Union was hopeless. What is required, now as then, is not just precision and honesty in defining the enemy but conceptual clarity in confronting it. And perhaps the first step toward that end is to understand that, paradoxical as it may seem in the light of the statistics I have presented above, Americans are *not* involved in a battle royal between Islam and the West, or what has been called a "clash of civilizations."

This famous term was first given wide currency by Samuel Huntington. It has been seconded, in his own diabolical way, by Osama bin

Laden. The idea exercises an undoubted appeal, but it happens not to be accurate. True, many Islamist elements do seek such a confrontation, out of a conviction that Islam will prevail and go on to achieve global supremacy. But several facts militate against so sweeping a view of the objective situation.

For one thing, violence against Americans—and against Israelis, Westerners, and non-Muslims in general—is just part of the story; Islamist enmity toward Muslims who do not share the Islamist outlook is no less vicious. Did not the Taliban reign in Afghanistan make this clear? Their multiple atrocities and gratuitous acts of cruelty toward their fellow Muslims suggest an attitude that bordered on the genocidal; what it can feel like to be liberated from that repressive cruelty was well captured in a *New York Times* report from a town in Afghanistan on November 13, 2001:

> In the twelve hours since the Taliban soldiers left this town, a joyous mood has spread. The people of Taliqan, who lived for two years under the Taliban's oppressive Islamic rule, burst onto the streets to toss off the restrictions that had burrowed into the most intimate aspects of their lives. Men tossed their turbans into the gutters. Families dug up their long-hidden television sets. Restaurants blared music. Cigarettes flared, and young men talked of growing their hair long.[16]

Nor are the Taliban an exception: militant Islam has brutalized Muslims wherever it has achieved power, and wherever it has striven for power. I have already mentioned Algeria, a country that, as a result of a decade of barbarity by Islamists, and with something like 100,000 fatalities and counting, has become a byword for violence against fellow believers. But comparable if smaller-scale orgies of killing have taken place in Egypt, Lebanon, and Turkey. The largest Islamist bloodletting, however, was Iran's war on non-Islamist Iraq after 1982, leading to hundreds of thousands of Muslim dead. Militant Islam is an aggressive totalitarian ideology that ultimately discriminates barely if at all among those who stand in its path.

Another reason to question the notion of a clash of civilizations is that it inevitably leads one to ignore important and possibly crucial distinctions *within* civilizations. Such distinctions emerged with particular poignancy in 1989, when a significant minority of Muslims around the world denounced the death edict issued by Ayatollah Khomeini against the novelist Salman Rushdie—in Iran itself, 127 intellectuals signed a protest against the Khomeini edict[17]—even as more than a few prominent Westerners, secular and religious alike, were apologizing for it or finding some way to "understand" it. (In one typical statement, the president of the French bishops' conference explained that The Satanic Verses was an "insult to religion," as though this in some way accounted adequately for the threat on Rushdie's life.)[18]

Or take an example nearer to home and closer in time. After September 11, polls in Catholic Italy found a quarter of Italians holding the view that Americans had gotten what they deserved. Even some Americans sided with the attackers, or at least with their choice of target: "Anyone who can blow up the Pentagon has my vote," announced a professor of history at the University of New Mexico.[19] Does that make these people part of the Muslim world? And what about the tens and hundreds of millions of Muslims who were horrified by the suicide hijackings? Are they not part of the Muslim world?

This brings us to a large and closely related issue—namely, whether the "problem" is inherent to Islam itself. Like all great religions, Islam is subject to a number of interpretations, from the mystical to the militant, from the quietist to the revolutionary. Its most basic ideas have been susceptible of highly contrasting explications. At the same time, Islam differs from other religions in that it includes a large body of regulations about public life and relations with nonbelievers; these are quite at variance with modern sensibilities and have not yet been left behind. In short, the hard work of adjusting Islam to the contemporary world has yet really to begin—a fact that itself goes far to explain the attraction of militant Islamic ideology.

That ideology is not an entirely new phenomenon. Its roots go back in some form to the Wahhabi movement of the eighteenth century, to the writings of Ibn Taymiya in the thirteenth century, even to the Kharijites of the seventh century. But, as befits a modern-style ideology, today's version covers more aspects of life (including, for example, the economic dimension) than any premodern iteration. It has also enjoyed much greater political success. A radicalized understanding of Islam has taken hold, possibly over a wider swath than at any other time in the fourteen centuries of Muslim history, and it has driven out or silenced every serious rival.

This radicalism is today's enraged answer to the question that has bedeviled Muslims for two hundred years, as the power and wealth that once blessed the world of Islam ebbed away over the five centuries before 1800 and other peoples and nations surged ahead. Muslims asked themselves what went wrong. If Islam brings God's grace, as was widely assumed, why do Muslims fare so poorly? Muslims turned to a number of extremist ideologies in the modern period—from fascism and Marxism-Leninism to Pan-Arabism and Pan-Syrianism—all in an attempt to answer that question by almost any means other than introspection, moderation, and self-help. Militant Islam has turned out to be the most popular, the most deluded, and the most disastrous of these ideologies.

Yet the unprecedented nature of its dominance, ironically, offers hope. However ascendant the militant interpretation may be at present, it need not be so in the future. The terroristic *jihad* against the West is one reading of Islam, but it is not the eternal essence of Islam. Forty years ago, at the height of the Soviet Union's prestige, and during the heyday of Pan-Arab nationalism, militant Islam had scarcely any political influence. What then happened to bring it to the fore is itself a fascinating question, but the point for our purposes is that, just as militant Islam was not a powerful force a scant four decades ago, it is perfectly reasonable to expect that it may not be a powerful force four decades hence.

By contrast, if today's extremism were truly inextricable from Islam, then there would be no solution but to try to quarantine or convert one sixth of humanity. To say the least, neither of those prospects is realistic.

Moderate Muslims

If the earth-shaking clash of our time is not between two civilizations, it is and must be a clash among the members of *one* civilization—specifically, between Islamists and those who, for want of a better term, we may call moderate Muslims (understanding that "moderate" does not mean liberal or democratic but only anti-Islamist).[20] Just as the deviant Western ideologies of fascism and communism challenged and then had to be expelled from the West, so it is with militant Islam and the Muslim world. The battle for the soul of Islam will undoubtedly last many years and take many lives, and is likely to be the greatest ideological battle of the post–Cold War era.

Where, then, does that leave the United States, an overwhelmingly non-Muslim country? It obviously cannot fix the problems of the Muslim world. It can neither solve the trauma of modern Islam nor do a great deal even to reduce the anti-Americanism that is rife in the Muslim world. As the battle among Muslims unfolds, non-Muslims will mostly find themselves in the role of outsiders.

Nonetheless, outsiders, and the United States in particular, can critically help in precipitating the battle and in influencing its outcome. They can do so both by weakening the militant side and by helping the moderate one. The process has in fact already begun in the so-called war on terrorism, and in miniature the results have been dramatically on display in Afghanistan. So long as Washington stayed aloof, the Taliban held sway in that country and the Northern Alliance, a collection of anti-Taliban elements, appeared to be, and was, a hapless force. Once the U.S. military became involved, the Taliban crumbled and the Northern Alliance swept through the country in a few weeks. On the larger front the task is the same: weaken Islamists where they are in power, deter their expansion, and encourage and support moderate elements.

Weakening militant Islam will require an imaginative and assertive policy, one tailored to the needs of each country. Already the impress of American power has been felt in a number of places, from Afghanistan, where it toppled a government, to the Philippines, where $93 million in military and security aid, plus a contingent of advisers, is helping the government defeat a militant Islamic insurgency. In Pakistan, the FBI is training immigration officers to detect suspected terrorists infiltrating from Afghanistan. The anarchic areas of Somalia may be next on the list.

In some cases, change can be effected dramatically and swiftly; in others, the evolution will be long and slow. In Pakistan, the state must be forced to take control of the notorious *madrasas* (religious schools) that inculcate extremism and advocate violence. In Iran and Sudan, a far more vigorous and multipronged effort will be required to end the rule of militant Islam. In Qatar, the home of al-Jazeera television, pressure has to be put on the government to promote the teachings of a moderate sheikh rather than those of the entrenched extremist Yusuf al-Qaradawi.

↜   Saudi Arabia is a special case, being the home of Osama bin Laden himself and fifteen of the nineteen suicide hijackers, the seedbed of the ideas that stand at the heart of the Taliban, and the source of much of the funding of Islamist networks around the world. Although Saudi authorities have managed a working relationship with the West for decades, they have also permitted the kingdom's public discourse to be taken over by militant Islam. It must be urgently expunged from a school system in which, for example, tenth-grade textbooks warn students that "It is compulsory for the Muslims to be loyal to each other and to consider the infidels their enemy,"[21] and from the media ("God said to fight all the infidels"),[22] not to speak of other areas of public life.

On other fronts, money centers around the world, from the United Arab Emirates to Hong Kong, will have to be forced to crack down on the laundering of funds via "Islamic charities" to Al-Qaeda and other terrorist organizations. French president Jacques Chirac has acknowledged that "Europe has been a haven" for Islamic extremists; the problem has to be taken seriously, and acted upon.[23]

The war against militant Islam has domestic implications as well, for the danger within is no less ominous than the danger abroad. The goal is to prevent harm being done by radical anti-Westerners among us, and the means must include expelling, jailing, or otherwise restraining them.[24] This implies an active revision of immigration laws and in particular an end to the innocent assumption that all who intend to visit or immigrate to the United States wish the country well. It means adding an ideological filter to the admissions procedure and, in the president's words, "asking a lot of questions that heretofore have not been asked."[25] It means cracking down on Islamic "charitable" foundations that funnel money to militant Islamic groups. And it means military tribunals where needed; restrictions on lawyer-client privilege in certain cases; and, when appropriate, the serious use of "profiling" to uncover sleepers and other terrorists. Most obviously, it means that the president must stop meeting with and legitimizing militant Islamic leaders as he has done repeatedly both before and after September 11.

Let us not, however, delude ourselves. If the United States has over 100 million Islamist enemies, not to speak of an even larger number of Muslims who wish it ill on assorted other grounds, they cannot all be incapacitated. Instead, the goal must be to deter and contain them. Militant Islam is too popular and widespread to be destroyed militarily. It can only be fended off.

To adopt the phrasing of George Kennan in "The Sources of Soviet Conduct" (1947), his famous *Foreign Affairs* article about the threat of Soviet communism, the "main element of any United States policy toward [militant Islam] must be that of long-term, patient but firm and vigilant containment of [its] expansive tendencies." The goal must be to convince its adherents that the use of force against Americans is at best ineffectual and at worst counterproductive—that Algerians and Malaysians are entitled to their anti-American views, but they cannot act on them by harming Americans. The only way to achieve this goal is by scaring them. And that requires toughness and determination—and perseverance—of a sort that Americans have not mustered for a long time. It will also require allies.

Not an American Argument

That is where the moderate Muslims come in. If roughly half the population across the Muslim world hates America, the other half does not. Unfortunately, they are disarmed, in disarray, and nearly voiceless. But the United States does not need them for their power. It needs them for their ideas and for the legitimacy they confer, and in these respects their strengths exactly complement Washington's.

The U.S. government lacks any religious authority to speak about Islam, though it does not seem to realize this. Here is Osama bin Laden claiming that the world divides into good Muslims and evil non-Muslims, then calling for a *jihad* against the West; a secular and mostly Christian government cannot directly respond to this—although the administration has ineffectively tried to do just that.

Thus, on November 3, 2001, Christopher Ross, a former U.S. ambassador, spoke on behalf of the U.S. government in Arabic for fifteen minutes on al-Jazeera television. His task? Nothing less than to rebut Osama bin Laden's accusations that America is the enemy of

Islam. Ross also went on the offensive, telling his audience that the "perpetrators of these crimes have no regard for human life, even among Muslims,"[26] and that bin Laden was the real enemy of Islam.

Ross's appearance on al-Jazeera was just one of the many gambits developed by Charlotte Beers, the undersecretary of state charged with getting America's message out to the Muslim world. Beers, formerly the head of the J. Walter Thompson and Ogilvy & Mather advertising agencies and nicknamed the "queen of branding,"[27] is partly responsible for opening the Coalition Information Center (CIC), a public relations "war room." With two dozen staffers, it offers daily and weekly talking points for journalists and has developed a campaign to convince Muslims of the benign American attitude toward them and their faith. It made sure that more humanitarian supplies were dropped in Afghanistan as the holy month of Ramadan began, sent a "catalog of [Taliban] lies" to Pakistani newspapers, and arranged for journalists from Muslim-majority countries to meet with U.S. policymakers. It is also using popular culture to shift perceptions in the Muslim world, by, according to *Variety*, encouraging dialogue between young American and young Middle Eastern viewers of the music video channel MTV.[28]

With regard to Islam itself, CIC aims, in Beers's words, to make it "hard to miss" that Americans recognize and respect the religion.[29] This means having public officials talk about the compatibility of American and Islamic values, sending out tapes of a Muslim imam delivering the invocation to Congress, and printing posters depicting "Mosques of America." Of particular note was the president's invitation to fifty Muslim ambassadors to break the Ramadan fast in the White House, with Secretary of State Colin Powell and U.S. ambassadors around the world following suit. A senior State Department official explained the implausible goal of all this as demonstrating to the Muslim world that "Americans take [Islamic] holidays as seriously as they do Christian and Jewish holidays."[30] Plans for the future are far more ambitious, centering around a Middle East Radio Network that was scheduled to start transmission in February 2002 with a plan to program in twenty-six languages and an orientation toward Muslim youth.

These programs will not likely have the intended effect. Put aside the more absurdist aspects—using MTV to build civilizational bridges, establishing that Eid ul-Fitr is as precious to Americans as Christmas. Even the Christopher Ross episode bombed: "His performance was terrible. . . . He was like a robot who speaks Arabic," commented one Arab critic.[31] More profoundly, although the goal of CIC is a worthwhile one—this is, after all, a war of ideas—the premises of its campaign are deeply flawed. Someone other than Madison Avenue types, and other than Americans, will be needed to conceptualize and deliver the anti–bin Laden message, someone with the necessary Islamic credentials and deep understanding of the culture. That someone is the moderate Muslim, the Muslim who hates the prospect of living under the reign of militant Islam and can envisage something better.

Other Voices

When it comes to Islam, the U.S. role is less to offer its own views than to help those Muslims with compatible views, especially on such issues as relations with non-Muslims, modernization, and the rights of women and minorities. This means helping moderates get their ideas out on U.S.-funded radio stations such as the newly created Radio Free Afghanistan and, as Paula Dobriansky, the undersecretary of state for global affairs, has suggested, making sure that tolerant Islamic figures—scholars, imams, and others—are included in U.S.-funded academic and cultural exchange programs.

Anti-Islamists today are weak, divided, intimidated, and generally ineffectual. Indeed, the prospects for Muslim revitalization have rarely looked dimmer than at this moment of radicalism, *jihad*, extremist rhetoric, conspiratorial thinking, and the cult of death. Nonetheless, moderates do exist, and they have much to offer the United States in its own battle against militant Islam, not least their intimate knowledge of the phenomenon and of its potential weaknesses. In addition, the legitimacy they bring to any campaign against militant Islam, simply by rendering the charge of "Islamophobia" unsustainable, is invaluable.

In Afghanistan, the United States first crushed the Taliban regime, then turned the country over to the more moderate Northern Alliance; it is up to the Alliance to make something of the opportunity the United States created. The same holds with Islam writ large.

Washington can go only so far. Whether its military victories turn into political ones depends ultimately on Muslims. The fight against militant Islam will be won if America has the will and persistence to see it through, and the wit to understand that its message must be carried in the end by other voices than its own.

NOTES

INTRODUCTION

1. White House press release, 2 November 2001.
2. Radio Address by Laura Bush to the Nation, 17 November 2001.
3. Bernard Lewis, "The Roots of Muslim Rage," *The Atlantic Monthly* (September 1990).
4. "Symposium: Resurgent Islam in the Middle East," *Middle East Policy* (Fall 1994), p. 20.
5. Normative Islam means the religion commonly known as "Islam" whose key precepts—historically rejected by the Nation of Islam—include the seventh-century Muhammad ibn 'Abduallah being the final Prophet, the Qur'an being the literal word of God, and all humans being born Muslim.

PART I. MILITANT ISLAM

1. Is Islam a Threat?
1. Ayatollah Mohammad Emami-Kashani, Voice of the Islamic Republic of Iran, 12 August 1994.

2. Patricia Crone and Michael Cook, *Hagarism: The Making of the Islamic World* (Cambridge: Cambridge University Press, 1977), p. 147.

3. Martin Kramer, *The Jerusalem Post*, 31 December 1999.

4. Voice of the Islamic Republic of Iran, 26 August 1994.

5. Edward Shirley [pseudonym], *Know Thine Enemy: A Spy's Journey into Revolutionary Iran* (New York: Farrar, Straus & Giroux, 1997), p. 67.

6. This interpretation derives from Wilfred Cantwell Smith's brilliant *Islam in Modern History* (Princeton, NJ: Princeton University Press, 1957).

7. Anwar Ibrahim, *The Asian Renaissance* (Singapore: Times Books International, 1997), p. 120.

8. Quoted in Abbas and Magnum Photos, *Allah O Akbar: A Journey Through Militant Islam* (London: Phaidon Press, 1994), p. 288.

9. On which, see Asghar Schirazi, *The Constitution of Iran: Politics and the State in the Islamic Republic*, trans. John O'Kane (London: I. B. Tauris, 1997).

10. *Al-Ahram Weekly* (Cairo), 2–8 February 1995.

11. Simon Reeve, *The New Jackals: Ramzi Yousef, Osama bin Laden, and the Future of Terrorism* (Boston: Northeastern University Press, 1999), pp. 85, 125.

12. *Boston Herald*, 10 October 2001.

13. Radio Tehran, 8 January 1989.

14. Mohammad Javad Larijani, *Resalat* (Tehran), 28 June 1995.

15. François Burgat and William Dowell, *The Islamic Movement in North Africa* (Austin: Center for Middle Eastern Studies, University of Texas, 1993), p. 19.

16. Kuwaiti News Agency, 21 July 1995.

17. Fouad Salah, *Le Monde*, 4 April 1992.

18. H. C. ten Berge: "Notities te velde." *De Gids* (Hilversum, Holland), January 1994. Quoted in Koenraad Elst, "Postscript," in Daniel Pipes, *The Rushdie Affair: The Novel, the Ayatollah, and the West* (New Delhi: Voice of India, 1998), p. 310.

19. *The Wall Street Journal*, 9 October 1995.

20. *The New York Times*, 16 October 1994.

21. *The Philadelphia Inquirer*, 11 November 1993.

22. Agence France-Presse, 25 June 1998.

23. Associated Press, 25 June 1997.

2. The Imaginary Green Peril

1. *The New York Times*, 11 March 1990.

2. *Canberra Times*, 9 September 1984. Quoted in James P. Piscatori, *Islam in*

a World of Nation-States (Cambridge: Cambridge University Press, 1986), p. 2.

3. William S. Lind, "Western Reunion: Our Coming Alliance with Russia?," *Policy Review* (Summer 1989), p. 20.

4. Peter Jenkins, "A Russia with No Empire," *The Independent*, 25 January 1990. Actually, Europe's keeping Islam at bay began a lot earlier; Charles Martel's victory over the Arabs at Poitiers, not far from Paris, took place in A.D. 732.

5. Leonard Horwin, "The Thousand-Year War Still Rages," *The Wall Street Journal*, 5 February 1990.

6. *The Sunday Times* (London), 10 June 1990.

7. *Le Monde*, 4 July 1989.

8. *The Boston Globe*, 4 April 1990.

9. Radio Tehran, 6 April 1990.

10. *Jomhuri-ye Islami* (Tehran), 27 January 1990.

11. *Kayhan Hava'i* (Tehran), 7 March 1990.

12. *The Sunday Times*, 10 June 1990.

13. Lind, "Western Reunion," p. 20.

14. Walter A. McDougall, "Speculations on the Geopolitics of the Gorbachev Era," unpublished paper, April 1990, p. 62. The quotation comes from a letter written by Tsar Nicholas I in 1854 to Friedrich Wilhelm IV of Prussia, quoted by Nicholas V. Riasanovsky, *Nicholas I and Official Nationality in Russia, 1825–55* (Berkeley: University of California Press, 1959), p. 265.

15. David Pryce-Jones, *The Closed Circle: An Interpretation of the Arabs* (New York: Harper & Row, 1989), p. 16.

16. *The Independent*, 20 February 1989.

17. *Jeune Afrique* (Paris), 15 March 1989.

18. *Bild*, quoted in *Der Spiegel*, 13 February 1989.

19. Jean Raspail, *Le Camp des Saints* (Paris: Editions Robert Laffont, 1973).

20. *Jomhuri-ye Islami* (Tehran), 28 March 1990.

21. Islamic Revolution News Agency, 8 July 1989. See also *Tehran Times*, 8 July 1989.

22. Peregrine Worsthorne, "The Blooding of the Literati," *The Sunday Telegraph*, 19 February 1989.

23. *The New York Times*, 5 March 1989; *Le Monde*, 28 February 1989.

24. *The Independent*, 3 June 1989.

25. *The Guardian*, 27 February 1989.

26. John R. Weeks, *The Demography of Islamic Nations* (Washington, DC: Population Reference Bureau, 1988), p. 13.

27. Ann Sheehy, "Ethnic Muslims Account for Half Soviet Population Increase," *Report on the USSR* (Washington, DC), 19 January 1990, p. 15.

28. Patrick Buchanan, "Global Resurgence of Islam," *The Washington Times*, 21 August 1989.

29. Michael K. Roof and Kevin G. Kinsella, *Palestinian Population: 1950 to 1984* (Washington, DC: U.S. Bureau of the Census, Center for International Research, 1985), p. 140.

30. Durán Khálid, "Der Islam in der Diaspora: Europa und Amerika," in Werner Ende and Udo Steinbach, eds., *Der Islam in der Gegenwart* (Munich: Verlag C. H. Beck, 1984), pp. 459–62.

3. Battling for the Soul of Islam

1. Reinhold Loeffler, *Islam in Practice: Religious Beliefs in a Persian Village* (Albany, NY: State University of New York Press, 1988), p. 226.

2. IRIB Television (Tehran), 13 August 1994.

3. *Tawhid*, Shawwal-Dhu'l-Hijjah 1412, p. 154.

4. Samuel Huntington, "The Clash of Civilizations?" *Foreign Affairs* (Summer 1993), p. 32.

5. Amir Taheri, *Holy Terror: Inside the World of Islamic Terrorism* (Bethesda, MD: Adler & Adler, 1987), p. 232.

6. *Al-Jumhuriya* (Cairo), 23 February 1995.

7. Interview on 29 December 1978; text in Imam Khomeini, *Islam and Revolution*, trans. Hamid Algar (Berkeley: Mizan Press, 1981), p. 323.

8. *Hürriyet* (Istanbul), 28 March 1989.

9. *Asiaweek*, 24 February 1993.

10. Laurent Lamote, "Iran's Foreign Policy and Internal Crises," in Patrick Clawson, ed., *Iran's Strategic Intentions and Capabilities*, (Washington, DC: National Defense University, 1994), pp. 7–8.

11. Quoted in Edward G. Shirley [pseudonym], "Is Iran's Present Algeria's Future?," *Foreign Affairs* (May–June 1995), pp. 35–36.

12. *Turkish Daily News*, 23 November 1994.

13. *Milliyet* (Istanbul), 28 February 1995.

14. *Turkish Daily News*, 24 February 1995.

15. Zülfü Livaneli in *Milliyet*, 11 January 1995.

16. Quoted in Roger Savory, ed., *Introduction to Islamic Civilization* (New York: Cambridge University Press, 1976), p. 25.

17. *The Wall Street Journal*, 14 April 1994.

4. Do Moderate Islamists Exist?

1. *The Jerusalem Post*, 5 February 1995.

2. 'Abd al-Qadir 'Awda, *Al-Islam wa-Awda'una as-Siyasiya* (Cairo, 1951).

Quoted in Emmanuel Sivan, *Radical Islam: Medieval Theology and Modern Politics* (New Haven: Yale University Press, 1985), p. 65.

3. Ibrahim Ghawsha, *Keyhan* (Tehran), 31 October 1992.

4. *Ash-Sha'b* (Cairo), 3 June 1994.

5. Speech of 2 February 1979, in Ruhollah Khomeini, *Islam and Revolution: Writings and Declarations*, trans. and ed. Hamid Algar (Berkeley, CA: Mizan, 1981), p. 259.

6. For documentation, drawing on audiocassettes of some thirty major Muslim preachers, see Emmanuel Sivan, "Eavesdropping on Radical Islam," *Middle East Quarterly* (March 1995).

7. *The Wall Street Journal*, 4 November 1993.

8. Quoted in Abbas and Magnum Photos, *Allah O Akbar: A Journey Through Militant Islam*, p. 137.

9. Quoted by Saïd Sadi, *Le Point* (Paris), 6 August 1994.

10. Martin Kramer, "Is Islamism a Threat? A Debate," *Middle East Quarterly* (December 1999), p. 32.

11. Article 22, quoted in *Contemporary Mideast Backgrounder* (October 1988), pp. 8–9.

12. Quoted in Ze'ev Schiff and Ehud Ya'ari, *Intifada: The Inside Story of the Palestinian Uprising That Changed the Middle East Equation*, trans. Ina Friedman (New York: Simon & Schuster, 1989), p. 235.

13. Islamic Revolution News Agency, 9 August 1993.

14. *The Philadelphia Inquirer*, 13 February 1995.

15. Bernard Lewis, *The Shaping of the Modern Middle East* (New York: Oxford University Press, 1994), pp. 145–46.

16. Quoted in Shaul Bakhash, *The Reign of the Ayatollahs* (New York: Basic Books, 1984), p. 122.

17. *Ash-Sha'b* (Cairo), 22 July 1994.

18. *Tawhid*, Shawwal-Dhu'l-Hijjah 1412, pp. 154, 155.

19. Quoted in Sivan, "Eavesdropping on Radical Islam," p. 17.

20. *Ash-Sha'b*, 27 September 1994.

21. *Tawhid*, Shawwal-Dhu'l-Hijjah 1412, p. 152.

22. Ibid., p. 153.

23. *Resalat* (Tehran), 3 March 1993.

24. Assistant Secretary of State Robert H. Pelletreau, Jr., in "Symposium: Resurgent Islam in the Middle East," *Middle East Policy* (Fall 1994), p. 3.

25. Address by Anthony Lake, Washington Institute for Near East Policy, 17 May, 1994.

26. Quoted in Judith Miller, "Faces of Fundamentalism: Hassan al-Turabi and Muhammed Fadlallah," *Foreign Affairs*, (November/December 1994), p. 124.

27. Olivier Roy, *L'Echec de l'Islam politique* (Paris: Seuil, 1992), p. 10.
28. John L. Esposito, *The Islamic Threat: Myth or Reality?* (New York: Oxford University Press, 1992).
29. Leon T. Hadar, "What Green Peril?" *Foreign Affairs* (Spring 1993), running head.
30. *The Washington Post*, 13 January 1992.
31. Saad Eddin Ibrahim, "Civil Society and Prospects of Democratization in the Arab World," in Augustus Richard Norton, ed., *Civil Society in the Middle East*, vol. 1 (Leiden: E. J. Brill, 1995), p. 52.
32. *Le Point* (Paris), 6 August 1994.
33. *Le Figaro*, 2 August 1994.
34. *The Washington Post*, 1 April 1995.
35. *Middle East Quarterly* (September 1995), p. 77.
36. *Salam* (Tehran), 27 July 1994.
37. Voice of the Islamic Republic of Iran, 5 March 1993.
38. Quoted in Martine Gozlan, *L'Islam et la Republique: Des musulmans de France contre l'intégrisme* (Paris: Belfond, 1994), pp. 41–42.
39. *The Jerusalem Post*, 4 December 1994.
40. The only exception is Turkey. Should fundamentalists be voted into office there, we should accept that outcome. Turkey being a full democracy, the only one in the Muslim world, the fundamentalists will probably leave office; the military stands in the wings ready to force them out.
41. *Corriere della Sera* (Milan), 20 November 1994.
42. Edward G. Shirley [pseudonym], "Is Iran's Present Algeria's Future?," *Foreign Affairs* (May–June 1995), p. 44.
43. France-2 Television, 20 September 1994.
44. *The New Yorker*, 30 January 1995.
45. Judith Miller, "The Challenge of Radical Islam," *Foreign Affairs* (Spring 1993), p. 53.

5. Does Poverty Cause Militant Islam?

1. *The New York Times*, 14 October 2001.
2. *The Washington Post*, 15 September 2001.
3. Muhammad 'Abd al-Maqsud, *The New Yorker*, 12 April 1993.
4. *L'Unita* (Rome), 28 December 1994.
5. Hilal Khashan, "The Developmental Programs of Islamic Fundamentalist Groups in Lebanon as a Source of Popular Legitimation," *Hamdard Islamicus*, 18 (1995), pp. 51–71, demonstrates the success of these efforts.
6. For one example of this literature, see the discussion of Samih 'atef El-Zein, *Islam and Human Ideology*, trans. Elsayed M. H. Omran (New York: Kegan Paul International, 1996), in chapter 6.

7. *Novoye Vremya* (Yerevan, Armenia), 29 September 1992. Demirel was at that time prime minister.

8. *The Wall Street Journal*, 14 April 1994.

9. Tahsin Shardum, in *Yedi'ot Aharonot* (Tel Aviv), 25 November 1994.

10. Quoted in Geraldine Brooks, *Nine Parts of Desire: The Hidden World of Islamic Women* (New York: Anchor Books, 1995), p. 163.

11. Hooshang Amirahmadi, "Terrorist Nation or Scapegoat?," *Middle East Insight* (September–October 1995), p. 26.

12. "President Clinton Addresses Joint Session of Jordanian Parliament," *Federal News Service*, 26 October 1994.

13. *Hearings Before the Subcommittee on Africa of the Committee of Foreign Affairs*, U.S. House of Representatives, p. 97. Quoted in Fawaz A. Gerges, *America and Political Islam; Clash of Cultures or Clash of Interests?* (New York: Cambridge University Press, 1999), p. 106.

14. Comments at an American Enterprise Institute conference, 3 November 1993.

15. *Der Spiegel*, 2 January 1995.

16. Europe No. 1 Radio (Paris), 24 October 1994.

17. *Il Sole-24 Ore* (Milan), 16 July 1995.

18. *El Mundo* (Madrid), 30 November 1994.

19. *Middle East Quarterly* (March 1995), p. 78.

20. Reuters, 3 July 2001.

21. Michael Field, *Inside the Arab World* (Cambridge, MA: Harvard University Press, 1994), p. 17.

22. Ervand Abrahamian, *Khomeinism: Essays on the Islamic Republic* (Berkeley: University of California Press, 1993), p. 4.

23. Jeffrey Goldberg, "The Martyr Strategy," *The New Yorker*, 9 July 2001.

24. Saad Eddin Ibrahim, "Anatomy of Egypt's Militant Islamic Groups," *International Journal of Middle East Studies* (December 1980), p. 440.

25. Saad Eddin Ibrahim, "Egypt's Islamic Militants," in Nicholas Hopkins and Saad Eddin Ibrahim, eds., *Arab Society, Social Science Perspectives* (Cairo: American University of Beirut Press, 1987).

26. *The National Post*, 28 August 2001.

27. Galal A. Amin, *Egypt's Economic Predicament: A Study in the Interaction of External Pressure, Political Folly and Social Tension in Egypt, 1960–1990* (Leiden: E. J. Brill, 1995), p. 136.

28. Brooks, *Nine Parts of Desire*, pp. 7–8.

29. Associated Press, 28 September 2001.

30. Brooks, *Nine Parts of Desire*, p. 164.

31. *The Jerusalem Report*, 8 October 2001, p. 20.

32. *The Weekly Standard*, 29 October 2001.

33. *Die Tageszeitung* (Berlin), 25 July 1995.

34. Khalid M. Amayreh, "Reality Behind the Image," *The Jerusalem Post*, 24 February 1995.

35. Roy, *L'Echec de l'Islam politique*, pp. 50, 72.

36. Amayreh, "Reality Behind the Image."

37. Personal letter to the author, 2 August 2001.

38. Khalid Durán, "How CAIR Put My Life in Peril," *Middle East Quarterly* (Winter 2002), p. 43.

39. Shirley, "Is Iran's Present Algeria's Future?," p. 40.

40. Abbas Alnasrawi, *The Economy of Iraq: Oil, Wars, Destruction of Development and Prospects, 1950–2010* (Westport, CT: Greenwood Press, 1994), p. 151.

41. *Le Soir* (Brussels), 7 February 1995.

42. Amayreh, "Reality Behind the Image."

43. Serge Schmemann, "The Enemy of My Enemy . . . ," *The New York Times*, 23 August 1995.

44. Meron Benvenisti, *Intimate Enemies: Jews and Arabs in a Shared Land* (Berkeley: University of California Press, 1995), pp. 145–46.

45. *The Jerusalem Post*, 21 September 1994.

46. *The Jerusalem Post*, 20 August 2001.

47. On this phenomenon, see chapter 7.

48. Birthe Hansen, *Unipolarity and the Middle East* (New York: St. Martin's Press, 2001), p. 92.

49. Oğuzhan Asıltürk, secretary general of the Refah Partisi in Turkey, *Turkish Daily News*, 23 November 1994.

50. Amin, *Egypt's Economic Predicament*, p. 138.

51. *Tempo* (Istanbul), 29 March 1995.

52. As shown by the fact that a half century earlier, American analysts like Dean Rusk argued that communism owed its appeal to poverty.

53. David Wurmser, "The Rise and Fall of the Arab World," *Strategic Review* (Summer 1993), p. 43.

54. Associated Press, 28 September 2001.

55. Wajdi Ghunayim, *Suluk al-Khatib*; idem, *Hijab al-Mar'a al-Muslima*; Hasan Ayyub, *Fi-l Mar'a*; Yusuf al-Qardawi, *Khutba fi-l Mar'a*. All quoted in Sivan, "Eavesdropping on Radical Islam," p. 17.

56. *Keyhan Hava'i* (Tehran), 7 March 1990.

57. *Ash-Sha'b* (Cairo), 11 October 1994.

58. Quoted in Burgat and Dowell, *The Islamic Movement in North Africa*, p. 21.

59. *The New York Times*, 13 March 1995.

6. The Glory of Islamic Economics

1. Samih 'atef El-Zein, *Islam and Human Ideology*, trans. Elsayed M. H. Omran (New York: Kegan Paul International, 1996). All quotations are taken from this edition.

2. *Al-Islam wa Aydiyulujiyat al-Insan* (Beirut: Dar al-Kitab al-Lubnani, 1989).

3. For more original and consequential, but less pointed, versions of these ideas, see two studies by the Iraqi scholar Muhammad Baqir as-Sadr (1935–1980), *Lamha Fiqhiya Tamhidiya 'an Mashru' Dustur al-Jumhuriya al-Islamiya fi Iran* (Beirut: Dar at-Ta'awun li'l-Matbu'at, 1979), and *Iqtisaduna*, 2 vols. (Najaf: Matabi' an-Nu'man, 1961–64). On Sadr's writings, see Chibli Mallat, *The Renewal of Islamic Law: Muhammad Baqer as-Sadr, Najaf, and the Shi'i International* (Cambridge: Cambridge University Press, 1993).

7. The Western Mind of Militant Islam

1. *Ash-Sharq al-Awsat* (London), 17 March 1995.

2. *The New York Times*, 4 August 1995.

3. *The New York Times*, 5 August 1995.

4. Radio Monte Carlo, 3 August 1995.

5. *Le Figaro*, 15 April 1995. Turabi is right that fundamentalist leaders take pride in their knowledge of the West—with the great exception of Ayatollah Khomeini. Symbolic of this lack of curiosity, he spent almost four months in a suburb of Paris and not once set foot in the French capital.

6. *The New York Times*, 28 July 1995. There he was an active member of the Hamas-backed organization, the United Association for Studies and Research.

7. Hamid Dabashi, *Theology of Discontent: The Ideological Foundations of the Islamic Revolution in Iran* (New York: New York University Press, 1993), p. 326.

8. Olivier Roy, *Islam and Resistance in Afghanistan*, trans. by First Edition (Cambridge: Cambridge University Press, 1986), p. 68

9. Ronald L. Nettler, *Past Trials and Present Tribulations: A Muslim Fundamentalist's View of the Jews* (Oxford: Pergamon Press, 1987), p. 26.

10. Mary Anne Weaver, "Children of the Jihad," *The New Yorker*, 12 June 1995. Yusuf acknowledged this technical competence in *Al-Hayat*, 12 April 1995, and *Al-Majalla*, 28 May 1995.

11. Untitled paper issued by Ramzi in April 1995, starting: "My name is ABDUL-BASIT BALOCHI. . . ."

12. Weaver, "Children of the Jihad." Weaver also reports that Ramzi Yusuf's maternal uncle, who is being sought by the Pakistani police for his

involvement in fundamentalist violence, served as a regional manager for the Swiss-based charity Mercy International.

13. *Le Figaro*, 15 April 1995.

14. Martin Kramer, "The Jihad Against the Jews," *Commentary* (October 1994), p. 39.

15. *The Wall Street Journal*, 22 June 1995.

16. Seyyed Vali Reza Nasr, *The Vanguard of the Islamic Revolution: The Jama 'at-i Islami of Pakistan* (Berkeley: University of California Press, 1994), pp. 7–8. For a detailed exposition of Mawdudi's Western orientation, see Seyyed Vali Reza Nasr, *Mawdudi and the Making of Islamic Revivalism* (New York: Oxford University Press, 1996).

17. Shahed Amanullah, *The Minaret* (Los Angeles) (July–August 1994).

18. Voice of the Islamic Republic of Iran, 4 June 1994.

19. Quoted in Burgat and Dowell, *The Islamic Movement in North Africa*, p. 9.

20. *Shahid*, Farvardin 1369/1990.

21. W. Montgomery Watt, *Islamic Fundamentalism and Modernity* (London: Routledge, 1988), p. 3.

22. Walid Mahmoud Abdelnasser, *The Islamic Movement in Egypt: Perceptions of International Relations, 1967–81* (London: Kegan Paul International, 1994), p. 173.

23. Detlev H. Khalid [Khalid Durán], "The Phenomenon of Re-Islamization," *Aussenpolitik*, 29 (1978), pp. 448–49.

24. Shahrough Akhavi, "'Ulama': Shi'i 'Ulama,'" in John L. Esposito, ed., *Oxford Encyclopedia of the Modern Islamic World* (New York: Oxford University Press, 1995), vol. 4, p. 263.

25. S. D. Goitein, *Studies in Islamic History and Institutions* (Leiden: E. J. Brill, 1968), p. 111, n. 1.

26. Occasionally, a Muslim does recognize this distortion. Here is Omar Bakri Muhammad, qadi of the so-called Shari'ah Court of the United Kingdom: "Unfortunately, some Muslims have become consumers of the western culture to the extent that many Muslims celebrate and wrongly take the day of Friday as a weekly holiday in contrast to Saturday of the Jews and Sunday of the Christians. Whereas the idea of a holiday does not exist in Islam and contradicts with the Islamic culture" (decision dated 20 December 1999).

27. *Ma'ariv* (Tel Aviv), 3 February 1995.

28. *Le Figaro*, 15 April 1995.

29. *An-Nahar* (Beirut), 15 July 1995.

30. *Corriere della Sera*, 29 August 1994.

31. Valerie J. Hoffman-Ladd, "Women and Islam: Women's Religious Observances," in *Oxford Encyclopedia of the Modern Islamic World*, vol. 4, p. 330.

32. *Le Figaro*, 15 April 1995.

33. "An Interview with Iranian President Khatami," *Middle East Insight* (November–December 1997), p. 31.

34. Mohammad Javad Larijani, *Resalat* (Tehran), 28 June 1995.

35. Associated Press, 30 March 1997.

36. Shabbir Akhtar, *Be Careful with Muhammad! The Salman Rushdie Affair* (London: Bellew Publishing, 1989), p. 100.

37. Burgat and Dowell, *The Islamic Movement in North Africa*, p. 21.

38. Voice of the Islamic Republic of Iran, 7 June 1995.

39. Usama al-Baz, *The Washington Times National Weekly Edition*, 24–30 April 1995.

40. Roy, *Islam and Resistance in Afghanistan*, p. 80.

41. *The New York Times*, 28 March 1980.

42. *La Vanguardia* (Barcelona), 16 July 1995.

43. Joseph Schacht, *An Introduction to Islamic Law* (Oxford: Clarendon Press, 1964), p. 53. Those "administrative regulations" in fact amounted to a great deal of law.

44. Quoted in Milton Viorst, "Sudan's Islamic Experiment," *Foreign Affairs* (May–June 1995), p. 53.

45. Ann Mayer, "The Shari'ah: A Methodology or a Body of Substantive Rules?", in Nicholas Heer, ed., *Islamic Law and Jurisprudence* (Seattle: University of Washington Press, 1990), p. 182. This discussion relies heavily on Mayer's account.

46. *Kayhan Hava'i* (Tehran), 8 January 1988. Iran Liberation, 27 February 1988. Nor was this Khomeini's only pronouncement along these lines. For example, shortly after coming to power, he announced that "to serve the nation is to serve God" (Radio Tehran, 3 November 1979).

47. See Sayyed Ruhollah Mousavi Khomeini and Risalat Tawzih al-Masa'il, *A Clarification of Questions*, trans. J. Borujerdi (Boulder, CO: Westview, 1984).

48. Quoted in Miller, "Faces of Fundamentalism: Hassan al-Turabi and Muhammed Fadlallah," p. 132.

49. Mayer, "The Shari'ah," p. 193.

50. *The New Yorker*, 12 April 1993.

51. Minister of State Ghazi Salah ad-Din al-Atabani, quoted in Viorst, "Sudan's Islamic Experiment," p. 51.

8. Echoes of the Cold War Debate

1. Acting Assistant Secretary of State Mark R. Parris, testimony before the House of Representatives, 22 March 1994. Text in *Middle East Policy*, (Fall 1994), p. 188.

2. Jonathan Power, "Algeria Is a Fundamentalist Volcano Ready to Erupt," *Philadelphia Inquirer,* 27 August 1994.
3. Arnold Beichman, *The Washington Times,* 28 August 1994.
4. Assistant Secretary of State Robert H. Pelletreau, Jr., in "Symposium: Resurgent Islam in the Middle East," *Middle East Policy* (Fall 1994), p. 3.
5. Gerhard Jasper, "Christen und Muslime muessen den Weg zueinander finden," *CIBEDO—Beitraege zum Gespraech zwischen Christen und Muslimen,* 5 (1991), pp. 73–79.
6. Agence France-Presse, 10 August 1994.
7. France-Inter Radio, 15 August 1994.
8. John Esposito, *The Islamic Threat: Myth or Reality?* (New York: Oxford University Press, 1992).
9. Walter A. McDougall, "Speculations on the Geopolitics of the Gorbachev Era," unpublished paper, April 1990, p. 62.

9. The U.S. Government, Patron of Islam?

1. On 16 August 1998.
2. "Albright Offers Traditional Iftaar Dinner," United States Information Agency (USIA), 20 December 2000, at http://pdq.state.gov/scripts/ cqcgi.exe/@pdqtest1.env?CQ_SESSION_KEY=XOPAFQDKTJXD&CQ _QUERY_HANDLE=124357&CQ_CUR_DOCUMENT=1&CQ_PD Q_DOCUMENT_VIEW=1&CQSUBMIT=View&CQRETURN=&C QPAGE=1.
3. Deputy Assistant Secretary Ronald E. Neumann, "No Inherent Conflict Between Islam and West," Georgetown University, 23 September 1999, at http://usinfo.state.gov/regional/nea/gulfsec/neum0923.htm.
4. Samuel P. Huntington, "The Clash of Civilizations?", at www.cc. colorado.edu/dept/PS/Finley/PS425/reading/Huntington1.html.
5. Remarks to the 53d Session of the United Nations General Assembly, New York City, 21 September 1998.
6. Madeleine Albright, "Learning More About Islam," *State Magazine* (September 2000), at http://usinfo.state.gov/usa/islam/s090600.htm.
7. "Remarks Before the American-Iranian Council, Washington, D.C.," 17 March 2000, at http://secretary.state.gov/www/statements/2000/000317. html.
8. "Remarks Before the American Muslim Council," 7 May 1999, at http://usinfo.state.gov/usa/islam/s050799.htm.
9. Neumann, "No Inherent Conflict Between Islam and West."
10. Speech at the University of World Economy and Diplomacy, Tashkent, 8 February 2000, at www.usembassy.ro/USIS/Washington-File/200/ 00-02-08/ eur215.htm.

11. Department of State, "Fact Sheet: U.S. Government Views on Terrorism," 7 December 1999, at http://usinfo.state.gov/topical/pol/terror/99120704.htm.

12. Bruce Riedel, "The Pentagon Looks at Islam," *Middle East Quarterly* (September 1996), pp. 87–89, at www.meforum.org/meq/sept96/riedel.shtml.

13. R. James Woolsey, "Challenges to Peace in the Middle East," address to the Washington Institute for Near East Policy, Washington, DC, 23 September 1994, at www.washingtoninstitute.org/pubs/woolsey.htm.

14. "The U.S., Islam and the Middle East in a Changing World," address at Meridian House International, Washington, DC, 2 June 1992, quoted in Gerges, *America and Political Islam*, p. 80.

15. Comments at an American Enterprise Institute conference, Washington, DC, 3 November 1993.

16. "Deputy Secretary Wolfowitz with the German Foreign Minister," Bureau of Public Affairs, U.S. Department of State, 19 September 2001, at www.defenselink.mil/news/Sep2001/t09202001_t919wolf.html.

17. Remarks at a Democratic National Committee dinner, 21 October 1993, U.S. Government Printing Office, at www.gpo.gov.

18. News conference, Jakarta, 15 November 1994, U.S. Government Printing Office, at www.gpo.gov.

19. "Fact Sheet: U.S. Government Views on Terrorism."

20. Philip Wilcox, Jr., "Terrorism Remains a Global Issue," *United States Information Agency Electronic Journal* (February 1997), at http://usinfo.state.gov/journals/itgic/0297/ijge/gj-1.htm.

21. "Address of President Clinton to the Jordanian Parliament," 26 October 1994, at http://usinfo.state.gov/regional/nea/peace/clint94.htm.

22. "Clinton Oval Office Remarks on Anti-Terrorist Attacks," 21 August 1998, at http://usinfo.state.gov/topical/pol/terror/98082002.htm.

23. Anthony Lake, "From Containment to Enlargement," at www.uiowa.edu/~c030162/Common/Handouts/Other/Lake.htm.

24. Robert Pelletreau, Jr., "U.S. Policy toward North Africa; Statement before the Subcommittee on Africa of the House Foreign Affairs Committee," *U.S. Department of State Dispatch*, 28 September 1994, at http://dosfan.lib.uic.edu/ERC/briefing/dispatch/1994/html/Dispatchv5no40.html.

25. R. James Woolsey, testimony before U.S. House of Representatives, Committee on National Security, 12 February 1998, at www.loyola.edu/dept/politics/intel/19980212woolsey.html.

26. "Statement for the Record," House International Relations Committee, 12 July 2000, at http://usinfo.state.gov/topical/pol/terror/00071702.htm.

27. Speech, Tashkent, 8 February 2000, at www.usembassy.ro/USIS/ Washington-File/200/00-02-08/eur215.htm.
28. Wilcox, "Terrorism Remains a Global Issue."
29. Deputy Secretary Wolfowitz interview with PBS *The NewsHour with Jim Lehrer*, 14 September 2001, at www.pbs.org/newshour/bb/terrorism/ july-dec01/wolfowitz-9-14.html.
30. Speech to Congress, 20 September 2001, at www.nationalreview.com/ document/document092101.shtml.
31. Remarks by the president, Islamic Center of Washington, DC, 17 September 2001, at www.whitehouse.gov/news/releases/2001/09/20010917-11. html.
32. Press briefing by Ari Fleischer, 17 September 2001, at www.whitehouse. gov/news/releases/2001/09/20010917-8.html.
33. Interview on NBC's *Dateline*, 12 September 2001, at www.state.gov/ secretary/rm/2001/index.cfm?docid=4883.
34. White House, 19 September 2001, at www.whitehouse.gov/news/ releases/2001/09/20010919-8.html.
35. Interview on *The NewsHour with Jim Lehrer*, 13 September 2001, at www. state.gov/secretary/rm/2001/index.cfm?docid=4914.
36. Daily press briefing, 18 September 2001, at www.state.gov/r/pa/ prs/dpb/2001/index.cfm?docid=4940.
37. "Deputy Secretary Wolfowitz with the German Foreign Minister," at www.defenselink.mil/news/Sep2001/t09202001_t919wolf.html.
38. Quoted in Reeve, *The New Jackals: Ramzi Yousef, Osama bin Laden, and the Future of Terrorism*, p. 242. Judge Duffy accused Yusuf of merely pretending to be a pious Muslim; in reality, he "cared little or nothing for Islam." John Keenan, the judge in the "Millennium" bombing case, also held this sort of assumption; see Associated Press, 5 July 2001.
39. Speech, Tashkent, 8 February 2000, at www.usembassy.ro/USIS/ Washington-File/200/00-02-08/eur215.htm.
40. Remarks at the Anchorage Museum of Art and History, 11 November 1994, U.S. Government Printing Office, at www.gpo.gov.
41. News conference with King Hassan II of Morocco, 15 March 1995, U.S. Government Printing Office, at www.gpo.gov.
42. Speech, Tashkent, 8 February 2000, at www.usembassy.ro/USIS/ Washington-File/200/00-02-08/eur215.htm.
43. "Fact Sheet: U.S. Government Views on Terrorism."
44. "Pentagon Iftar Dinner for Muslim Servicemen," USIA, 19 January 1999, at http://usinfo.state.gov/regional/nea/gulfsec/pent0119.htm.
45. "The U.S., Islam and the Middle East in a Changing World," address,

Meridian House International, Washington, DC, 2 June 1992. Quoted in Gerges, *America and Political Islam*, p. 80.

46. Robert H. Pelletreau, Jr., "Symposium: Resurgent Islam."
47. USIA, 27 November 2000, at http://pdq.state.gov.
48. USIA, 22 December 2000, at http://pdq.state.gov.
49. Albright, "Learning More about Islam."
50. "First Lady Hosts Third Annual Eid Celebration," USIA, 22 January 1999, at http://usinfo.state.gov/usa/islam/a012299.htm.
51. Department of Defense news briefing, 22 January 1998, at www.defenselink.mil/news/Jan1998/t01261998_t122iftr.html.
52. Remarks to the 53d Session of the United Nations General Assembly, New York City, 21 September 1998, at www.un.int/usa/98_154.htm.
53. News conference with King Hassan II of Morocco.
54. "Islam and America: Changing Perceptions," American Studies Conference, Islamabad, 5 November 1999, USIA, at http://pdq.state.gov/scripts/cqcgi.exe/@pdqtest1.env?CQ_SESSION_KEY=VNRDNVEKTJXD&CQ_QUERY_HA NDLE=124385&CQ_CUR_DOCUMENT=12&CQ_PDQ_DOCUMENT_VIEW=1&CQSUB MIT=View&CQRETURN=&CQPAGE=1.
55. "The U.S. Is Against Terrorism, Not Islam," English Speaking Union of Lahore, 2 December 1999, at http://usinfo.state.gov/regional/nea/gulfsec/milam209.htm.
56. "Albright Hosts Iftar Dinner with American Muslim Leaders."
57. Hillary Clinton, "Islam in America," *Chicago Sun-Times*, 25 February 1996.
58. USIA, 30 June 1999, at http://usinfo.state.gov/usa/islam/a063099.htm.
59. USIA, Worldnet "Global Exchange," 3 March 1999, at http://usinfo.state.gov/usa/islam/a030399.htm.
60. "Fact Sheet: U.S. Government Views on Terrorism."
61. Clinton, "Islam in America."
62. "Albright Hosts Iftar Dinner with American Muslim Leaders."
63. "Remarks Before American Muslim Council," Washington, DC, 7 May 1999, at http://usinfo.state.gov/usa/islam/s050799.htm.
64. "The U.S. Is Against Terrorism, Not Islam," English Speaking Union of Lahore.
65. "Fact Sheet: U.S. Government Views on Terrorism."
66. Albright, "Learning More about Islam."
67. USIA, 30 June 1999, at http://pdq.state.gov.
68. USIA, Worldnet "Global Exchange."
69. "Fact Sheet: U.S. Government Views on Terrorism."
70. U.S. Government Printing Office, 27 November 2000, at www.gpo.gov.

71. Eid al-Adha greetings from President Bush, 6 March 2001, at www.whitehouse.gov/news/releases/2001/03/20010307-1.html.

72. "Fact Sheet: U.S. Government Views on Terrorism."

73. Napoleon's Proclamation to the Egyptians, July 2, 1798. Text in J. C Hurewitz, *The Middle East and North Africa in World Politics*, vol. 1, *European Expansion, 1535–1914* (New Haven: Yale University Press, 1975), p. 116.

74. Martin Kramer, *Islam Assembled* (New York: Columbia University Press, 1986), pp. 152–53.

10. A Monument of Apologetics

1. Ed. John L. Esposito, 4 vols. (New York: Oxford University Press, 1995). All quotations are taken from this edition.

PART II. ISLAM REACHES AMERICA

11. "We Are Going to Conquer America"

1. Remarks by the President at Islamic Center of Washington, DC, 17 September 2001.

2. Remarks by the President at Photo Opportunity with House and Senate Leadership, 19 September 2001, at www.whitehouse.gov/news/releases/2001/09/20010919-8.html.

3. Ibrahim Hooper, "CAIR Responds to Daniel Pipes' Anti-Muslim Hysteria," *The Muslim Observer*, 27 August–3 September 1999. Reuters news agency describes Wahhaj as "a respected scholar and leader of the Muslim community in Brooklyn," 24 April 2001.

4. *Congressional Record*—House, 25 June 1991.

5. Siraj Wahhaj, *Muslim Community Building in America*, undated videotape distributed by Islamic Educational Video Series of the International Institute of Islamic Research, Burlington, NJ.

6. *The Imam* (Midwinter 1998).

7. Letter from Mary Jo White, U.S. Attorney for New York, to Federal Judge Michael Mukasey, 2 February 1995.

8. For another example, see Daniel Pipes, "Islam's American Lobby," *The Jerusalem Post*, 20 September 2001.

9. Quoted in Andrew T. Hoffert, "The Moslem Movement in America," *The Moslem World*, 20 (1930), p. 309.

10. *Syracuse Sunday Herald*, 25 June 1922. Quoted in Richard Brent Turner, *Islam in the African-American Experience* (Bloomington: Indiana University Press, 1997), p. 122.

11. John L. Esposito, "Ismail Ragi al-Faruqi," in John L. Esposito and John O.

Voll, eds., *Makers of Contemporary Islam* (New York: Oxford University Press, 2001), p. 23.

12. Isma'il R. Al-Faruqi, "Islamic Ideals in North America," in Earle H. Waugh, Baha Abu-Laban, and Regula B. Qureshi, eds., *The Muslim Community in North America* (Edmonton, Canada: University of Alberta Press, 1983), p. 269.

13. *The Role of Muslims in the American Political Process*, videotape distributed by the International Institute of Islamic Research, Burlington, NJ, 1992.

14. Lecture (in Arabic) at a MAYA convention in Kansas City in 1989, available on commercial videotape entitled *Shaikh Ahmad Naufal, Rabita, Kansas City 1989*.

15. Masudul Alam Choudhury, "Perspectives in Islamization of the Labour Market: The Occupational Composition of Canadian Muslims," in Amber Haque, ed., *Muslims and Islamization in North America: Problems and Prospects* (Beltsville, MD: Amana and A.S. Noordeen, 1999), p. 87.

16. Shamim A. Siddiqi, "Islamic Movement in America—Why?," in Haque, ed., *Muslims and Islamization in North America: Problems and Prospects*, p. 361.

17. See, for example, www.islambook.com/dawah.htm and www.halalco.com/dawah.html.

18. Shamim A. Siddiqi, *Methodology of Dawah Ilallah in American Perspective* (Brooklyn, NY: The Forum for Islamic Work, 1989), pp. ix–x.

19. Ibid., p. 68.

20. Siddiqi, "Islamic Movement in America—Why?," p. 358.

21. Ibid., p. 355.

22. Siddiqi, *Methodology of Dawah Ilallah*, p. 69.

23. Ibid., pp. xii–xiii.

24. Ibid., pp. viii–ix.

25. *Christian Science Monitor*, 5 February 1997.

26. Weaver, "Children of the Jihad."

27. Detroit, 1991. Quoted in PBS documentary, *Jihad in America*, 21 November 1994.

28. Words found in a notebook kept by El-Sayyid Nossair, the Egyptian immigrant who assassinated Rabbi Meir Kahane in a New York hotel in November 1990.

29. Abu Muhammad, *Al-Bunyan 'al-Marsus* (July 1989).

30. Jeffrey Lang, *Even Angels Ask: A Journey to Islam in America* (Beltsville, MD: Amana, 1997), p. 117.

31. Syed Manzoor Naqi Rizvi, interviewed in Elias D. Mallon, *Neighbors: Muslims in North America* (New York: Friendship, 1989), p. 60.

32. *The New York Times*, 13 November 1990.

33. Mohammad O. Farooq, "Muslim American Dream," *The Minaret* (Los Angeles) (August 1995).

34. Isma'il R. Al-Faruqi, "Islamic Ideals in North America," in Waugh, Abu-Laban, and Qureshi, eds., *The Muslim Community in North America*, p. 269.

35. Wahhaj, *Muslim Community Building in America* (videotape).

36. Al-Faruqi, "Islamic Ideals in North America," p. 268.

37. Siddiqi, *Methodology of Dawah Ilallah*, p. 64.

38. Ibid., p. 76.

39. Speech in Dallas to the Islamic Association of Northern Texas, 15 November 1991.

40. Siddiqi, "Islamic Movement in America—Why?," p. 358.

41. Abul Hasan Ali Nadwi, "Message for Muslims in the West," 1992, at www.jamiat.org.za/isinfo/mwest.html.

42. For example, *The Autobiography of Malcolm X* (New York: Grove Press, 1964), with its moving account of redemption through Islam, has had a wide impact on American blacks (and even some whites, causing a substantial number of them to convert.

43. Larry Poston, *Islamic Da'wah in the West: Muslim Missionary Activity and the Dynamics of Conversion to Islam* (New York: Oxford University Press, 1992), p. 173.

44. Anayat Durrani, "Islam Growing Fast in America," *Arabia on Line*, 10 March 2000.

45. Muzaffar Haleem and Betty Bowman, *The Sun Is Rising in the West: New Muslims Tell About Their Journey to Islam* (Beltsville, MD: Amana, 1999), p. 8.

46. Siddiqi, *Methodology of Dawah Ilallah*, p. 61.

47. Siddiqi, "Islamic Movement in America—Why?," p. 360.

48. Siddiqi, *Methodology of Dawah Ilallah*, p. 66.

49. Ibid., p. 61.

50. Ibid., p. 63.

51. Ibid., p. 67.

52. Ibid., p. 66.

53. Siraj Wahhaj, *Islamic Voice* (August 2000).

54. Siddiqi, *Methodology of Dawah Ilallah*, p. 69.

55. Speaking at the Department of State's Open Forum, 7 January 1998; a transcript of the talk is available at www.islamicsupremecouncil.org.

56. Muhammad Hisham Kabbani, "The Muslim Experience in America Is Unprecedented," *Middle East Quarterly* (June 2000), p. 62.

57. www.amconline.org.

58. www.cair-net.org.

59. http://ampcc.net/mission/mpac.shtml.

12. Conversion and Anti-Americanism

1. Associated Press, 12 March 1996.

2. *The New York Times*, 15 March 1996.

3. Interview in *India Today*, 1–15 February 1980.

4. Quoted in Pete Hamill, "The Education of Mike Tyson," *Esquire* (March 1994).

5. Robert Dickson Crane, *Shaping the Future: Challenge and Response* (Acton, MA: Tapestry, 1997), pp. xix, 59–60.

6. Elijah Muhammad, *Message to the Blackman* (Atlanta: Messenger Elijah Muhammad Propagation Society, 1997), p. 130.

7. Malcolm X, with the assistance of Alex Haley, *The Autobiography of Malcolm X* (New York: Grove Press, 1964), p. 325.

8. *The New York Times*, 22 April 1984.

9. *The Final Call*, 15 April 1988.

10. *Kayhan* (Tehran) (February 1996); Reuters, 14 February 1996. Farrakhan later denied making this statement.

11. Cleveland, 3 April 1964. George Breitman, *Malcolm X Speaks: Selected Speeches and Statements* (New York: Grove Press, 1965), p. 26.

12. Jamil Al-Amin, *Revolution by the Book (The Rap Is Live)* (Beltsville, MD: Writers' Inc.-International, 1994), p. 126.

13. Quoted in Steve A. Johnson, "Political Activities of Muslims in America," in Yvonne Yazbeck Haddad, ed., *The Muslims of America* (New York: Oxford University Press, 1991), p. 115.

14. *The Guardian*, 17 January 1999. See also *Los Angeles Times*, 5 August 1996.

15. Jeffrey Lang, *Struggling to Surrender: Some Impressions of an American Convert to Islam*, 2d rev. ed. (Beltsville, MD: Amana, 1995), p. 119.

16. Maryam Jameelah, *Islam versus the West*, 6th ed. (Lahore: Muhammad Yusuf Khan & Sons, 1984), p. 125.

17. Spoken to an Islamic Committee for Palestine conference, Chicago, 1990; broadcast on the PBS documentary *Jihad in America*, 21 November 1994.

18. Khalid M. Alkhazraji, *Immigrants and Cultural Adaptation in the American Workplace: A Study of Muslim Employees* (New York: Garland, 1997), pp. 46, 63, 73, 66, 106, 95.

19. Lang, *Even Angels Ask: A Journey to Islam in America*, p. 200.

13. Fighting Militant Islam, Without Bias

1. *The Washington Post*, 21 September 2001.
2. *Los Angeles Times*, 24 September 2001.
3. Wirthlin Worldwide, "Survey Shows Surprising Support Among Americans for Tightened U.S. Immigration Laws Governing Muslims; Wirthlin Worldwide Survey Also Shows Americans' Disapproval of Vandalism, Threats Against Arabs," 26 September 2001.
4. Associated Press, 24 September 2001.
5. CNN–Time Magazine Poll, reported by Wolf Blitzer on Cable News Network, 28 September 2001.
6. *El Mundo* (Madrid), 24 July 1995.
7. *The New York Times*, 16 October 1994.
8. *Al-Musawwar* (Cairo), 21 October 1994.
9. *The Philadelphia Inquirer*, 20 October 1994
10. *The Wall Street Journal*, 22 June 1995.
11. *Corriere della Sera*, 9 June 1995.
12. William Langewiesche, "The Crash of Egyptair 990," *The Atlantic Monthly*, November 2001.
13. It bears noting that this analysis focuses only on Muslims, not Arabs or another nationality. Two comments: Most Americans of an Arabic-speaking background are Christian, and so cannot be Islamists; while Arabs have had a predominant role in anti-American violence until now, many other ethnicities have been involved, including African-Americans, Iranians, and Pakistanis.
14. Letter from Mary Jo White to Devorah Halberstam, 5 December 2000, p. 3.
15. Associated Press, 25 February 1997.
16. Steven Emerson, "Foreign Terrorists in America: Five Years After the World Trade Center Bombing," Senate Judiciary Subcommittee on Terrorism, Technology and Government Information, 24 February 1998.
17. Associated Press, 22 February 1997.
18. Associated Press, 25 February 1997.
19. United States Department of Transportation, "USDOT Issues Caution on Airline Discrimination," 21 September 2001.
20. Delta Airlines claims that "Safety is our first priority at Delta," but it also admonishes its staff not to let the events of September 11 "change you into someone suspicious of people just because of the way they look—if you do that, then the terrorists will have won." Memo from Fred Reid, President and Chief Operating Officer to All Delta Employees Worldwide on "Tolerance," 21 September 2001.
21. Associated Press, 18 September 2001.

22. *The Wall Street Journal*, 14 September 2001.

23. Uriel Heilman, "Murder on the Brooklyn Bridge," *Middle East Quarterly* (Summer 2001), pp. 34, 33.

24. *The Wall Street Journal*, 7 May 2001.

14. Catching Some Sleepers

1. White House, "The President's State of the Union Address," 29 January 2002.

2. Associated Press, 31 January 2002.

3. *Wolf Blitzer Reports*, Cable News Network, 14 December 2001.

4. *The Washington Post*, 5 November 2001.

5. *Mail on Sunday* (London), 14 October 2001.

6. *Sacramento Bee*, 30 September 2001.

7. Cable News Network, 12 January 2002.

8. *Middle East Newsline*, 4 January 2002.

9. NBC's *Meet the Press*, quoted in *The New York Times*, 15 October 2001.

10. Cable News Network, 12 January 2002.

11. Judge Leonard B. Sand, Federal District Court in Manhattan, 20 October 2000.

12. Cable News Network, 12 January 2002.

13. *The New York Times*, 22 December 2000.

14. *The Wall Street Journal*, 26 November 2001.

15. Reuters, 7 January 2002.

16. Cable Network News, 12 January 2002.

17. Department of Transportation press release, "USDOT Issues Caution on Airline Discrimination," 21 September 2001.

18. NBC's *Meet the Press*, quoted in *The New York Times*, 15 October 2001.

19. *Bergen Record*, 11 November 2001.

20. Assistant U.S. Attorney Kenneth Karas in *United States of America v. Usama bin Laden et al.* trial in the Southern District of New York, transcripts available at http://cryptome.org/usa-v-ubl-dt.htm; *Tampa Tribune*, 10 June 2001; *The Jerusalem Post*, 20 June 2001.

21. *Star Tribune* (Minneapolis), 21 December 2001.

22. *The Washington Post*, 25 August 1996.

23. *Le Nouvel Observateur*, 18 October 2001.

24. *Los Angeles Times*, 20 September 2001.

25. *The New York Times*, 22 December 2000. "*Military Studies in the Jihad Against the Tyrants* permits everything except wine and fornication," *The New York Times*, 5 April 2001.

26. *The Washington Post*, 9 December 2001.

27. *The New York Times*, 28 October 2001.

28. *Mail on Sunday* (London), 14 October 2001.
29. *Sydney Morning Herald*, 10 December 2001.
30. *The Washington Post*, 5 November 2001
31. Hassam Abukar, a past president of the Islamic Center of San Diego, quoted in Associated Press, 14 October 2001.
32. *The New York Times*, 4 December 2001.
33. *Star Tribune*, 21 December 2001.
34. *The Times* (London), 29 December 2001.
35. *Miami Herald*, 16 September 2001.

15. Are Americans Muslims the Victims of Bias?

1. White House, "Remarks by the President at Event Commemorating End of Ramadan," 10 January 2000.
2. Senate Resolution 133, 20 July 2000.
3. American Muslim Council, "Hatemongers Greet Ramadan with a Swastika," 30 December 1997.
4. Council on American-Islamic Relations, "Study Shows Marked Increase in Reports of Anti-Muslim Discrimination," 15 July 1998.
5. Council on American-Islamic Relations, "Fla. Jewish Newspaper Apologizes for Anti-Muslim Letter," 4 March 1998.
6. Council on American-Islamic Relations, "Report Outlines Political Attitudes of American Muslims 96 Percent Believe Muslims Should Get Involved in Local and National Politics," 22 December 1999.
7. And 35 percent students; *Muslim World League Journal* (November 1978), p. 30.
8. Arif Ghayur, "Ethnic Distribution of American Muslims and Selected Socio-Economic Characteristics," *Journal Institute of Muslim Minority Affairs* (January 1984), p. 49.
9. And 20 percent other professions, 6 percent laborers, and 35 percent students; Asad Husain and Harold Vogelaar, "Activities of the Immigrant Muslim Communities in Chicago," in Yvonne Yazbeck Haddad and Jane Idleman Smith, eds., *Muslim Communities in North America* (Albany: State University of New York Press, 1994), p. 235.
10. And 11 percent business owners, 9 percent teaching, and 5 percent blue collar; Brad Edmondson, unpublished paper, 1997, cited in Abdulkader Thomas, "Islamic Banking in North America: Growth and Obstacles," in Haque, ed., *Muslims and Islamization in North America*, p. 101.
11. Ibid.
12. Council on American-Islamic Relations, "Report Outlines Political Attitudes of American Muslims 96 Percent Believe Muslims Should Get Involved in Local and National Politics," 22 December 1999.

13. *The Washington Times*, 11 July 2000.

14. Thomas, "Islamic Banking in North America: Growth and Obstacles," p. 111.

15. Muqtedar Khan, "The Missing Dimension," *The Message* (December 1995).

16. *Los Angeles Times*, 21 June 2000. On Al-Marayati, see *Forward*, 16 July 1999.

17. Rabbi Gilbert Kollin: "no one has a right to suggest that he is an apologist for terrorism," JTA, 26 June 2000.

18. The Becket Fund for Religious Liberty, "Becket Fund to Defend Muslim Police Officers' Right to Wear Beards," 22 June 1998.

19. David Meadows, *Baltimore Sun*, 25 August 2000.

20. Walter Ridley quoted in *The Washington Times*, 25 April 1988.

21. Located at www.njleg.state.nj.us/2000/Bills/a2000/1919_il.htm.

22. *Ft. Lauderdale Sun Sentinel*, 13 August 2000.

23. *Chicago Tribune*, 8 September 1999. Also: "Finding a Home in Islam," *Orange County Register*, 9 December 1999,

24. *Orange County Register*, 16 March 2000. Also: "Muslim women say they find liberation in modest attire," *Columbus Dispatch*, 19 May 2000.

25. "Recognition for Ramadan: Muslims Aim to Bring Islamic Holiday Out of Christmas' Shadow"; "Adapting Old Ways [i.e., Ramadan] to a New Land"; "Muslims Seek Ramadan Site: Leaders hope Tustin or El Toro Marine base can be opened for Jan. 8 gathering to celebrate end of the holy month"; "A Ramadan Tradition: The Adaya family discovers the fulfillment of coming together to celebrate the Muslim holy month, drawing friends and neighbors into their prayers"; "Muslims search for Ramadan site: Lacking a venue large enough for 15,000 people, Orange County Fairgrounds is second choice"; *Los Angeles Times*, 9, 11, 11, 12, 22, and 26 December 1999, 6 January 2000.

26. Council on American-Islam's Relations, September 1999. The media coverage included: *Orange County Register*, *Santa Barbara News Press*, (L.A.) *Independent*, *L.A. Daily News*, *Daily Breeze*, *Glendale News*, *San Diego Union-Tribune*, O.C. News Channel TV, and KFWB Radio. Also on Ramadan: "Reflecting On Ramadan: Group raises awareness of Muslim observance," *San Francisco Chronicle*, 6 December 1999; "The Rhythms of Ramadan: During the holy month, Muslims try to transcend (Silicon) Valley's ambitions," *San Jose Mercury News*, 1 January 2000; "Bay Area's Muslims Feast, Rejoice," *San Jose Mercury News*, 9 January 2000.

27. *Newsday*, 22 March 1993.

28. *The Washington Post*, 16 August 2000.

29. *Wichita Eagle*, 17 August 2000. Also: "Maine Muslims: 'We are one voice,'" *Portland Press Herald*, 6 July 1999.

30. *Christian Science Monitor*, 5 February 1997. Also: "Matching Faith And Finances: Alternatives to Loans Cater to Area Muslims," *The Washington Post*, 28 October 1999.

31. *Atlanta Journal-Constitution*, 1 August 2000.

32. *Sacramento Bee*, 16 July 1998.

33. First Amendment Center press release, "Federal appeals panel sides with Muslims in suit against police department," 4 March 1999.

34. Associated Press, 28 April 1999.

35. *Fort Worth Star-Telegram*, 10 February 2000.

36. Council on American-Islamic Relations, "Missouri Med School Reverses Decision on Muslim Applicant," 28 July 1999.

37. Council on American-Islamic Relations, "Good News—Hijab Accepted on Penn. Licenses," 15 May 2000.

38. Council on American-Islamic Relations, "American Muslims Win Accommodation for Religious Practices," 29 September 1998.

39. Ibid.

40. Associated Press, 7 April 2000.

41. www.gohamptonroads.com/news/1999/09/29/muslim.html.

42. Council on American-Islamic Relations, "Sen. Biden Regrets CNN Remarks on Islam," 19 February 1998.

43. Council on American-Islamic Relations, *Spring 1999 Newsletter*.

44. Council on American-Islamic Relations, "Good News—National Public Radio (NPR) Host Apologizes for Offensive Remarks," 25 January 1999.

45. Council on American-Islamic Relations, "Paul Harvey Apologizes On-Air for Offensive Remarks," 27 January 1999.

46. *Jewish Journal*, 6 January 1998.

47. Council on American-Islamic Relations, "Fla. Jewish Newspaper Apologizes for Anti-Muslim Letter," 4 March 1998.

48. Council on American-Islamic Relations, "Publisher Recalls Book—Offers Apology for Inaccurate Information about Prophet Muhammad," 2 May 1997.

49. Council on American-Islamic Relations, "Minnesota Publisher Recalls Children's Book on Islam," 18 August 1997.

50. Council on American-Islamic Relations, "AOL Removes Web Site Attempting to Imitate Quran," 25 June 1998. For a full discussion, with links, see http://dspace.dial.pipex.com/suralikeit/.

51. Council on American-Islamic Relations, "Pentagon 'Distressed' by Desert Fox Bomb Graffiti," 22 December 1998.

52. Council on American-Islamic Relations, "Conn. University to Hold Seminars on Islam," Spring 1999.

53. Council on American-Islamic Relations, "American Muslims Challenge Discrimination," 30 June 1998.

54. Council on American-Islamic Relations, "Minn. Teacher Reassigned after Offending Muslim Students," 9 February 1999; St. Paul (MN) *Pioneer Planet*, 10 February 1999.

55. Council on American-Islamic Relations, "Sports Company Withdraws Ad Showing Muslims 'Praying' to Basketball," 22 February 2000.

56. Council on American-Islamic Relations, "Burger King Pulls Offensive Radio Commercial," 14 March 2000.

57. Council on American-Islamic Relations, *CAIR News* (Spring 1998).

58. Council on American-Islamic Relations, "LA Times Agrees to Remove Image of Muslim Women from Multi-Million Dollar Ad Campaign," 20 April 2000.

59. Council on American-Islamic Relations, "Canadian Retailer Withdraws Inappropriate T-Shirt," 15 December 1999.

60. Council on American-Islamic Relations, "Liz Claiborne Recalls Jeans with Verses from Quran on Back Pocket," 16 August 2000.

61. Nike press release, 24 June 1997.

62. Council on American-Islamic Relations, "Nike and Islamic Advocacy Group Hold Play Area Groundbreaking," 21 November 1998.

63. *The Boston Globe*, 22 August 2000.

64. Council on American-Islamic Relations, "Court Upholds $2.9 Million Judgement in United Air Lines Discrimination Case," 22 April 1999.

65. Yvonne Yazbeck Haddad and Adair T. Lummis, *Islamic Values in the United States* (New York: Oxford University Press, 1987), p. 77.

66. Richard Wormser, *American Islam: Growing Up Muslim in America* (New York: Walker, 1994), p. 50.

67. American Muslim Council, "AMC Press Conference Launches Recent Poll on American Muslims," 28 August 2000.

68. National Committee on American Foreign Policy, New York, 28 September 1999.

69. Lang, *Even Angels Ask: A Journey to Islam in America*, p. 97.

70. *The Washington Post*, 29 August 2000.

71. United States Information Agency, 22 January 1999.

72. *Financial Times*, 29 August 2000.

73. *Al-Liwa'*, 30 August 2000.

74. Council on American-Islamic Relations, "American Muslims Discuss Religious Rights in Turkey with State Department Officials," 15 March 1999.

75. Khaled Saffuri, "Worldnet 'Global Exchange' on Islam in America," Washington, DC, 25 March 1999.

76. *Far Eastern Economic Review*, 23 June 1994.
77. For a classic of the protest genre, see Robert Marquand, "Media Still Portray Muslims As Terrorists," *Christian Science Monitor*, 22 January 1996.
78. Linda S. Walbridge, *Without Forgetting the Imam: Lebanese Shi'ism in an American Community* (Detroit: Wayne State University Press, 1997), p. 209.

16. "How Dare You Defame Islam"

1. Kayhan Hava'i, 22 February 1989.
2. Steven Emerson, "Foreign Terrorists in America: Five Years After the World Trade Center Bombing," Senate Judiciary Subcommittee on Terrorism, Technology and Government Information, February 24, 1998.
3. *The Lawyers Weekly*, 2 March 2001.
4. *Forward*, 25 July 1999.
5. Resolution 133, 1 July 1999.
6. "Counterterrorism in a Free Society," *Journal of Counterterrorism & Security International*, Spring 1998.
7. *The New York Times*, 11 February 1996.
8. E-mail communications from Jeff Jacoby to the author.
9. http://web.archive.org/web/20010412184614/www.dallasnotnews.com/supporters.shtml and http://web.archive.org/web/20000511014956/www.dallasnotnews.com/index.shtml.
10. Council on American-Islamic Relations, "The Tampa Tribune and Steven Emerson," 15 April 1998.
11. Council on American-Islamic Relations, "Educational Publication Says Muslims Set Pattern for Terrorism," 5 September 1996.
12. Letters to the Editor, *The Atlantic Monthly*, September 1994; Council on American-Islamic Relations, "Senate Hearing on 'Foreign Terrorists in America," 20 January 1998.
13. Council on American-Islamic Relations, "American Muslims Say Museum Associated with Wiesenthal Center Promotes Intolerance toward Islam." 3 December 1997.
14. Council on American-Islamic Relations, " 'Global War on Christians' Smears Islam: Muslims Asked to Challenge One-Sided *Reader's Digest* Article," 24 July 1997.
15. Council on American-Islamic Relations, "*First Things* Journal Editor Defames Islam," 16 October 1997.
16. Richard John Neuhaus, "Islamic Encounters," *First Things*, February 1998.
17. From email communications to the author.
18. Richard Curtiss, review of *The Agent*, in *Washington Review of Middle East Affairs*, September 1999, p. 140.
19. Jeff Jacoby, "Tale of a Blacklist: 'It Is NPR Policy,' " *The Boston Globe*, 31 August 1998.

20. Jeff Jacoby, "Steven Emerson and the NPR Blacklist," *The Boston Globe*, 7 February 2002.

17. Lessons from the Prophet Muhammad's Diplomacy

1. Natasha Singer, "Arafat Text Raises Ire," *Forward*, 27 May 1994.
2. See, for example, his interviews on Palestinian television, 1 January 1995, and in *Al-Quds* (Jerusalem), 10 May 1998.
3. Crone and Cook, *Hagarism: The Making of the Islamic World*, pp. 18, 29.
4. As Toby Lester explains in "What Is the Koran?," *The Atlantic Monthly* (January 1999): "there are scholars, Muslims among them, who feel that [the mainly secular effort to reinterpret the Koran], which amounts essentially to placing the Koran in history, will provide fuel for an Islamic revival of sorts—a reappropriation of tradition, a going forward by looking back."
5. Andreas Görke in "Die frühislamische Geschichtsüberlieferung zu Hudaibiya," *Der Islam*, 1997, has shown that the earliest accounts of this episode go back to 'Urwa ibn az-Zubayr, who died in A.D. 712.
6. Text translated in W. Montgomery Watt, *Muhammad at Medina* (Oxford: Clarendon Press, 1956), pp. 47–48.
7. William Muir, *The Life of Mahomet from Original Sources*, new ed. (London: Smith Elder, 1878), p. 414.
8. Carl Brockelmann, *Geschichte der Islamischen Völker und Staaten* (Munich: R. Oldenbourg, 1939); trans. Joel Carmichael and Moshe Perlmann as *History of the Islamic Peoples* (New York: Capricorn, 1973), pp. 30–31.
9. Bernard Lewis, *The Arabs in History*, 4th ed. (London: Hutchinson University Library, 1966), p. 46.
10. Watt, *Muhammad at Medina*, p. 65.
11. John Glubb, *The Life and Times of Muhammad* (New York: Stein & Day, 1970), p. 303.
12. Marshall G. S. Hodgson, *The Venture of Islam*, vol. 1, *The Classical Age of Islam* (Chicago: University of Chicago Press, 1974), p. 194.
13. F. E. Peters, *Muhammad and the Origins of Islam* (Albany: State University of New York Press, 1994), p. 235.
14. This is the point that Arafat's flacks zeroed in on. His aide Ibrahim Kar'in, for instance, explained that his boss "merely wished to convey the fact that the Oslo agreement contained painful concessions that he accepted only because he thought these would lead to the restoration of Arab rule in Jerusalem." Quoted in *Forward*, 27 May 1994.
15. *Israeli-Palestinian Interim Agreement on the West Bank and the Gaza Strip* (Jerusalem: Ministry of Foreign Affairs, 1995), p. 166.

16. This episode became famous in 1988–89 when it provided the title of Salman Rushdie's magical-realist novel whose criticism of Muhammad and Islam ended up getting him condemned to death by Ayatollah Khomeini.

17. W. Montgomery Watt, *Islamic Fundamentalism and Modernity* (London: Routledge, 1988), p. 18.

18. Annemarie Schimmel, *And Muhammad Is His Messenger: The Veneration of the Prophet in Islamic Piety* (Chapel Hill: University of North Carolina Press, 1985), p. 8.

19. Muhammad Husayn Haykal, *Hayat Muhammad*, 9th ed. (Cairo: Maktabat an-Nahda al-Misriya, 1965), pp. 164, 167.

20. Schimmel, *And Muhammad Is His Messenger*, p. 5.

21. Akhtar, *Be Careful with Muhammad! The Salman Rushdie Affair*, p. 1.

22. Article 295(B) and (C) of the Pakistan Penal Code (PPC). These sections were added to the PPC through amendments in 1982 and 1986, respectively. Article 288(A) of the PPC protects all family members of the Prophet and the first four caliphs—*The Hindustan Times*, 24 May 1998.

23. *The Daily Telegraph*, 8 May 1998.

24. Ibn Warraq [pseudonym], *Why I Am Not a Muslim* (Amherst, NY: Prometheus, 1995).

25. Emerson, "Foreign Terrorists in America." Emerson establishes CAIR's ties to Hamas-connected organizations and individuals in his *American Jihad: The Terrorists Living Among Us* (New York: Free Press, 2002), pp. 201–02.

26. Originally posted on *Israeli and Global News* at www.cmep.com.

18. Charlotte's Web: Hizbullah's Career in the Deep South

1. Federal affidavit dated 20 July, 2000, filed at U.S. District Court in Charlotte, North Carolina, p. 17.

2. United States District Court, Western District of North Carolina, Affidavit in Support of Warrants for Arrests, Searches, and Seizures, unsealed 21 July, 2000, signed by Kent J. Hallsten, David D. Howell, and Richard D. Schwein, Jr., and subscribed before Chief United States District Judge Graham C. Mullen.

3. "Symposium: Is There a Cure for Anti-Semitism?," *Partisan Review* 61 (1994), pp. 429–30.

4. Federal affidavit, p. 35.

5. Ibid., p. 33.

6. Ibid., p. 74.

7. Reuters, 22 July 2000.

8. Associated Press, 11 March 2002.

9. *The New York Times*, 24 July 2000.
10. Associated Press, 27 July 2000.
11. *The New York Times*, 24 July 2000.
12. *Charlotte Observer*, 23 July 2000
13. *The New York Times*, 24 July 2000.
14. *The New York Times*, 22 July 2000
15. *Charlotte Observer*, 22 July 2000.

19. America's Muslims vs. America's Jews

1. *Newsday*, 7 July 1998.
2. *The New York Times*, 2 March 1999.
3. *The Jerusalem Post*, 24 July 1998.
4. *The Jerusalem Post*, 24 July 1998.
5. "Muslims Condemn Synagogue Attack," *Muslim Journal*, 3 October 1986.
6. Crane, *Shaping the Future: Challenge and Response*, p. 111.
7. Ibid., pp. xix, xxx.
8. Emerson, "Foreign Terrorists in America."
9. In the true tradition of anti-Semitism, this hatred also has its trivial side: "Don't eat that bagel!" a staffer at the American-Arab Anti-Discrimination Committee once screamed at a secretary. "It's Jewish food." Omar Qourah, "Palestinian American Speaks Up: Three Months at the ADC," *Mid-East Realities*, 10 June 1998.
10. Both quoted in Emerson, "Foreign Terrorists in America."
11. PBS documentary *Jihad in America*, 21 November 1994.
12. Emerson, "Foreign Terrorists in America."
13. Ibid.
14. For examples, see below, pp. 208–10.
15. Interview in *Inquiry*, the journal of the Islamic Committee for Palestine.
16. Ali Mazrui, interviewed in *Middle East Affairs Journal* (Winter–Spring 1997), p. 178.
17. Such as the American Muslim Council, the Islamic Association for Palestine, the Islamic Circle of North America, the Islamic Committee for Palestine, the Islamic Society for North America, the Muslim Arab Youth Association, the Muslim Public Affairs Council, the Muslim Students Association, and the United Association for Studies and Research.
18. Transcript of the 7 January 1998 talk available at www.islamic supremecouncil.org.
19. Elijah Muhammad, *How to Eat to Live* (Atlanta: Messenger Elijah Muhammad Propagation Society, 1967–72), vol. 2, p. 89.
20. Elijah Muhammad, *History of the Nation of Islam* (Atlanta: Secretarius MEMPS, 1994), p. 56.

21. Quoted in E. U. Essien-Udom, *Black Nationalism: A Search for an Identity in America* (Chicago: University of Chicago Press, 1962), p. 282.

22. Tynetta Muhammad, "$4.4 Billion Dollars Is Not Enough!," *The Final Call*, 17 December 1996. Tynetta Muhammad was one of Elijah Muhammad's mistresses and later became a Nation of Islam theologian.

23. *The Washington Post*, 1 March 1990.

24. Anti-Defamation League ad, *The New York Times*, 29 November 1993.

25. *The Washington Times*, 2 and 3 February 1994.

26. The Historical Research Department, *The Secret Relationship between Blacks and Jews* (Boston: Nation of Islam, 1991), vol. 1. The same Historical Research Department also publishes a newsletter, *Blacks and Jews News*.

27. Notably, Marc Caplan, *Jew-Hatred as History: An Analysis of the Nation of Islam's "The Secret Relationship between Blacks and Jews"* (New York: Anti-Defamation League, 1993), and Saul S. Friedman, *Jews and the American Slave Trade* (New Brunswick, NJ: Transaction, 1998).

28. Speech, 24 January 1994.

29. *The New York Times*, 29 June 1984.

30. Radio broadcast, 11 March 1984: "The Jews don't like Farrakhan, so they call me Hitler. Well, that's a good name. Hitler was a very great man."

31. *The New York Times*, 27 February 1984.

32. *The Jerusalem Post International Edition*, 11 January 1986.

33. *Al-Majalla* (London), 28 May 1995.

34. Associated Press, 29 June 1993.

35. Associated Press, 25 July 1997.

36. Dina Porat, et al., eds., *Anti-Semitism Worldwide, 1995/6* (Tel Aviv: Anti-Defamation League, 1996).

37. See, for example, Pat Robertson, *The New World Order* (Dallas: Word, 1991), pp. 74, 208, 243, 256–57.

38. Florence Hamlish Levinsohn, *Looking for Farrakhan* (Chicago: Ivan R. Dee, 1997), pp. 163–67.

20. Muslims Slaves in America History

1. Allan D. Austin, *African Muslims in Antebellum America: A Sourcebook* (New York: Garland, 1984).

2. João José Reis, *Rebelião escrava no Brasil: A história do leviante dos males 1835* (São Paulo: Editora Brasiliense, 1986).

3. Sylviane A. Diouf, *Servants of Allah: African Muslims Enslaved in the Americas* (New York: New York University Press, 1998), p. 69.

4. Ibid.

5. Ibid., p. 129.
6. Ibid., p. 121.
7. C. Eric Lincoln, "The American Muslim Mission in the Context of American Social History," in Waugh, Abu-Laban, and Qureshi, eds., *The Muslim Community in North America*, p. 219.
8. Umar A. Hassan, "African-American Muslims and the Islamic Revival," in Cyriac K. Pullapilly, ed., *Islam in the Contemporary World* (Notre Dame, IN: Cross Roads, 1980), p. 284.
9. Sabir Muhammad, quoted in the *Wall Street Journal*, 5 October 1990.
10. Diouf, *Servants of Allah*, pp. 2 and 179.
11. Ibid., pp. 68–69.
12. Atlanta Speech of 1961, quoted in Louis E. Lomax, *When the Word is Given . . . : A Report on Elijah Muhammad, Malcolm X, and the Black Muslim World* (Cleveland: World, 1963), p. 115. To make matters yet more confusing, Elijah Muhammad sometimes referred to Africa as "South Asia."
13. Quoted in Louis A. DeCaro, Jr., *On the Side of My People: A Religious Life of Malcolm X* (New York: New York University Press, 1996), p. 97.
14. Diouf, *Servants of Allah*, p. 197.
15. Ibid., p. 210.

21. The Rise of Elijah Muhammad

1. Karl Evanzz, *The Messenger: The Rise and Fall of Elijah Muhammad* (New York: Pantheon, 1999), p. 207.
2. Mike Wilson, quoted in Andrés Tapia, "Churches Wary of Inner-City Islamic Inroads," *Christianity Today*, 10 January 1994.
3. *Autobiograhy of Malcolm X* (New York: Grove, 1964).
4. Claude Andrew Clegg III, *An Original Man: The Life and Times of Elijah Muhammad* (New York: St. Martin's Press, 1997).
5. Evanzz, *The Messenger*.
6. Clegg, *An Original Man*, p. 118.
7. Ibid., p. 129.
8. Evanzz, *The Messenger*, p. 229.
9. Ibid., p. 262.
10. Clegg, *An Original Man*, p. 113.
11. Ibid., p. 272.
12. W. Deen Mohammed, *Islam's Climate for Business Success* (Chicago: The Sense Maker, 1995).
13. Shahrazad Ali, *The Blackwoman's Guide to Understanding the Blackman* (Philadelphia: Civilized Publications, 1992), p. 226.

14. Aminah Beverly McCloud, "This Is a Muslim Home," in Barbara Daly Metcalf, ed., *Making Muslim Space in North America and Europe* (Berkeley: University of California Press, 1996), p. 67.

15. Reuters, 26 February 2000.

16. E. U. Essien-Udom, *Black Nationalism: A Search for an Identity in America*, p. 182.

17. Evanzz, *The Messenger*, p. 438.

18. *The New York Times*, 3 March 1994.

19. Evelyn Akbar, quoted in Lawrence H. Mamiya, "Minister Louis Farrakhan and the Final Call," in Waugh, Abu-Laban, and Qureshi, eds., *The Muslim Community in North America*, pp. 249–50.

20. Clegg, *An Original Man*, p. 282.

21. Richard Bulliet establishes this for the early period of Islam in *Conversion to Islam: An Essay in Quantitative History* (Cambridge, MA: Harvard University Press, 1979), esp. chapter 3.

22. Robert Dannin, "Island in a Sea of Ignorance," in Metcalf, ed., *Making Muslim Space in North America and Europe*, p. 142.

23. Mattias Gardell, *In the Name of Elijah Muhammad: Louis Farrakhan and the Nation of Islam* (Durham, NC: Duke University Press, 1996), p. 295.

24. Louise Blake quoted in *The Washington Post Magazine*, 3 April 1983. Islam, it bears noting, did not "come out of Africa."

25. *The New York Times*, 5 March 1994.

26. C. Eric Lincoln, "The American Muslim Mission in the Context of American Social History," in Waugh, Abu-Laban, and Qureshi, eds., *The Muslim Community in North America*, pp. 221, 224.

22. The Curious Case of Jamil Al-Amin

1. Tony Norman, "The Return of H. Rap Brown," *Pittsburgh Post-Gazette*, 21 March 2000.

2. *Atlanta Journal-Constitution*, 1 April 2000.

3. *Atlanta Journal-Constitution*, 23, 26, and 31 March 2000.

4. *Atlanta Journal-Constitution*, 26 and 31 March 2000.

5. *Atlanta Journal-Constitution*, 3 May 2000.

6. Cable News Network, 19 March 2000.

7. Al-Amin, *Revolution by the Book (The Rap Is Live)*, p. 126.

8. Jamil Al-Amin, "I am a Political Prisoner, a Black Man in America." Letter to the UN Commission on Human Rights, 21 May 2001.

9. Al-Amin, *Revolution by the Book (The Rap Is Live)*, p. 130.

10. *The Washington Post*, 25 March 2000.

11. *The Minaret* (Los Angeles), 11 August 1995.

12. *Atlanta Journal-Constitution*, 21 March 2000.

13. *Legal News Network*, 13 April 2000.

14. "Letter of Invitation from Imam Jamil—To: Imams, Amirs, Alims," 29 June 2000.

15. "The Statement of Innocence of IMAM JAMIL ABDULLAH AL-AMIN," 19 January 2001.

16. *The New York Times*, 6 January 2002.

17. Council on American-Islamic Relations, "Muslim Groups to Monitor Trial of Imam Jamil Al-Amin," 21 March 2000.

18. Steven Barboza, *American Jihad: Islam After Malcolm X* (New York: Doubleday, 1994), p. 48.

19. Islamic Society of North America, "American Muslim Organizations Call for Justice Department Investigation of Muslim Leader's Arrest," 28 August 1995.

20. American Muslim Council, "New Website for Imam Jamil Al-Amin," 3 May 2001. The Peace and Justice Foundation called him "one of the most respected leaders in the U.S." "Background on Imam Jamil Al-Amin," undated press release (about 27 March 2000).

21. Student Alliance for Imam Jamil, "Who is Imam Jamil?," at www.msa-national.org/SAIJ/.

22. *Arab American News*, 6 October 1995.

23. *The Message* (September 1995).

24. Ibid.

25. American Muslim Council, "Muslim Groups to Monitor Trial of Imam Jamil Al-Amin," 21 March 2000.

26. Council on American-Islamic Relations, "CAIR Official Visits Imam Jamil Al-Amin, Urges Support at Rally," 1 August 2000; Southern California Association of Muslim Activists, "A Telephone Fund-Raising Script for the Jamil Al-Amin Legal Defense Fund," 5 April 2000; Support Committee for Imam Jamil, flyer dated 27 April 2001.

27. International Committee to Support Imam Jamil Abdullah Al-Amin, 2001 statement.

28. Council on American-Islamic Relations, "Imam Jamil Al-Amin Legal Defense Fund," 5 April 2000.

29. *Atlanta Journal-Constitution*, 18 and 19 May 2000.

30. Community of Masjid Al-Islam, "URGENT: Emergency Fundraiser for Imam Jamil Al-Amin!," 31 March 2000.

31. Council on American-Islamic Relations, "Muslim Graduate Student Wrongly Convicted," 1 January 2001.

32. Islamic Association for Palestine backing indicated in *Muslim World Monitor*, 21 November 1997.

33. Interview with Abdurahman Alamoudi of the American Muslim Council on *Middle East TV*, 26 March 1996.

23. Conclusion: Who Is the Enemy?

1. "President Says Terrorists Won't Change American Way of Life," 23 October 2001, at www.whitehouse.gov/news/releases/2001/10/20011 023-33.html.
2. "President Rallies Troops at Travis Air Force Base," 17 October 2001, at www.whitehouse.gov/news/releases/2001/10/20011017-20.html.
3. "President Bush and Russian President Putin Discuss Progress," 21 October 2001, at www.whitehouse.gov/news/releases/2001/10/20011021-3.html.
4. "President Calls for Economic Stimulus," 31 October 2001, at www.whitehouse.gov/news/releases/2001/10/20011031-1.html.
5. "President Unveils 'Most Wanted' Terrorists," 10 October 2001, at www.whitehouse.gov/news/releases/2001/10/20011010-3.html.
6. "President Unveils Back to Work Plan," 4 October 2001, at www.whitehouse.gov/news/releases/2001/10/20011004-8.html.
7. "President Asks American Children to Help Afghan Children," 12 October 2001, at www.whitehouse.gov/news/releases/2001/10/20011012-4.html.
8. *Inside the Pentagon* (Arlington, VA), 27 September 2001. Rumsfeld spoke on 24 September.
9. Robert Kagan, "On to Phase II," *The Washington Post*, 27 November 2001.
10. ABC News, 12 October 2001, at http://abcnews.go.com/sections/us/DailyNews/strike_bush011011.html.
11. *The Washington Post*, 7 February 1995.
12. *Suddeutsche Zeitung* (Munich), 2 February 1995.
13. *Die Financieel-Ekonomische Tijd* (Antwerp), 8 February 1995.
14. *Financial Times*, 20 February 1995.
15. Specifically, Olivier Roy in *L'Echec de l'Islam politique*, trans. Carol Volk, and *The Failure of Political Islam* (Cambridge, MA: Harvard University Press, 1994).
16. *The New York Times*, 13 November 2001.
17. Published in *Pour Rushdie: Cent intellectuels arabes et musulmans pour la liberté d'expression* (Paris: La Découverte, 1993).
18. *Der Spiegel*, 27 February 1989.
19. *Albuquerque Tribune*, 22 September 2001, at www.abqtrib.com/archives/news01/092201-news-berthold.shtml.
20. Under this definition, Yasir Arafat and Saddam Husayn are moderates.
21. *The New York Times*, October 19, 2001.
22. Ibid.
23. Reuters, 1 December 2001.
24. I discuss these measures in chapter 13.

25. Associated Press, 29 October 2001.
26. *Salon.com*, 7 November 2001.
27. *Time*, 8 November 2001, at www.time.com/time/columnist/printout/0,8816,183734,00.html.
28. *Variety*, 19 November 2001.
29. *The Washington Post*, 15 November 2001.
30. *Newsweek*, 26 November 2001.
31. *Los Angeles Times*, 19 November 2001.

ACKNOWLEDGMENTS

Most of the chapters in this book have seen light in other forms and formats, as listed below. The texts that appear here are the preferred version. They have systematized terminology and spelling and have been edited to eliminate duplications. In addition, the text has been updated to reflect recent events.

The author gratefully acknowledges the publishers for permission to draw on the following published materials:

"Islam and Islamism—Faith and Ideology." *National Interest* (Spring 2000).

"The Muslims Are Coming! The Muslims Are Coming!" *National Review*, 19 November 1990.

"Islam: Option turque." *Politique Internationale* (Summer 1995).

"There Are No Moderates." *National Interest* (Fall 1995).

"Does Poverty Cause Islamism?" *National Interest* (Winter 2002).

"Planning an Islamist State." *Middle East Quarterly* (September 1997).

"The Western Mind of Radical Islam." *First Things* (December 1995).

"Same Difference." *National Review*, 7 November 1994, pp. 61–65.

"The United States Government: Patron of Islam?" (with Mimi Stillman). *Middle East Quarterly* (Winter 2002).

Review of John L. Esposito, ed., *The Oxford Encyclopedia of the Modern Islamic World*, 4 vols. *Middle East Quarterly* (September 1995).

"The Danger Within: Militant Islam in America." *Commentary* (November 2001).

"America's Muslims Against America's Jews." *Commentary* (May 1999).

" 'How Dare You Defame Islam.' " *Commentary* (November 1999).

"In Muslim America: A Presence and a Challenge." *National Review*, 21 February 2000.

"Enslaved Muslims in the Americas." *Middle East Quarterly* (December 2000).

"How Elijah Muhammad Won." *Commentary* (June 2000).

"Are Muslim Americans Victimized?" *Commentary* (November 2000).

"Fighting Militant Islam, Without Bias." *City Journal* (Winter 2002).

"Lessons from the Prophet Muhammad's Diplomacy." *Middle East Quarterly* (September 1999).

"The Hezbollah in America: An Alarming Network." *National Review*, 28 August 2000.

"The Curious Case of Jamil Al-Amin." *American Spectator* (November–December 2001).

"Who Is the Enemy?" *Commentary* (January 2002).

INDEX

ABOUT THE AUTHOR

DANIEL PIPES is director of the Middle East Forum and a columnist for the *New York Post* and *The Jerusalem Post*.

Mr. Pipes was one of the few analysts who understood the threat of militant Islam ("Unnoticed by most Westerners," he wrote in 1995, "war has called unilaterally declared on Europe and the United States"). *The Wall Street Journal* has called him "an authoritative commentator on the Middle East," while MSNBC describes him as one of the best-known "Mideast policy luminaries."

He received his A.B. (1971) and Ph.D. (1978) from Harvard University, both in history. He spent six years studying abroad, including three years in Egypt. He has taught at the University of Chicago, Harvard University, and the U.S. Naval War College. He has served in the Departments of State and Defense. As vice chairman of the presidentially appointed Fulbright Board of Foreign Scholarships in 1992–95, Mr. Pipes oversaw U.S. government international exchange programs. He was director of the Foreign Policy Research Institute in 1986–93.

Mr. Pipes frequently discusses current issues on television, appearing on such programs as ABC *World News*, CBS *Reports*, *Crossfire*, *Good Morning*

America, *NewsHour with Jim Lehrer*, *Nightline*, *The O'Reilly Factor*, and *Today*. He has lectured in twenty-five countries. He has consulted on Middle Eastern topics for prominent financial, manufacturing, and service companies, law firms, bar associations, trade groups, agencies of the U.S. government, and law courts in the United States and Canada.

Mr. Pipes has published in such magazines as *The Atlantic Monthly*, *Commentary*, *Foreign Affairs*, *Harper's*, *National Review*, *New Republic*, and *The Weekly Standard*. Many newspapers carry his articles, including the *Los Angeles Times*, *The New York Times*, *The Wall Street Journal*, *The Washington Post*, another seventy dailies, plus hundreds of Web sites. His writings have been translated into seventeen languages.

Mr. Pipes has written ten books. Three of them deal with Islam, three with Syria, and three deal with miscellaneous Middle Eastern topics. *Conspiracy: How the Paranoid Style Flourishes, and Where It Comes From* (1997) establishes the importance of conspiracy theories in modern European and American politics. In addition, Mr. Pipes has edited two collections of essays and is also the joint author of eight books.

Mr. Pipes serves on the "Special Task Force on Terrorism Technology" at the Department of Defense. He sits on three editorial boards, has testified before many congressional committees, and worked on four presidential campaigns. He is or has been listed in *Who's Who in the East*, *Who's Who in Entertainment*, *Who's Who in America*, and *Who's Who in the World*. He has one honorary degree.

His Web site, www.DanielPipes.org, offers an archive of his newspaper columns and other writings, as well as a sign-up list to receive his new articles as they appear.